The Complete

CREDIT REPAIR

Kit

GET STARTED NOW with Every Form You Need on CD-ROM

2ND EDITION

The Complete
CREDIT REPAIR
Kit

GET STARTED NOW with Every Form You Need on CD-ROM

2ND EDITION

BRETTE MCWHORTER SEMBER | **ATTORNEY AT LAW**

SPHINX® PUBLISHING
AN IMPRINT OF SOURCEBOOKS, INC.®
NAPERVILLE, ILLINOIS
www.SphinxLegal.com

Second Edition: 2008

Published by: **Sphinx® Publishing, An Imprint of Sourcebooks, Inc.®**
Naperville Office
P.O. Box 4410
Naperville, Illinois 60567-4410
(630) 961-3900
Fax: 630-961-2168
www.sourcebooks.com
www.SphinxLegal.com

This publication is designed to provide accurate and authoritative information in regard to the subject matter covered. It is sold with the understanding that the publisher is not engaged in rendering legal, accounting, or other professional service. If legal advice or other expert assistance is required, the services of a competent professional person should be sought.

From a Declaration of Principles Jointly Adopted by a Committee of the American Bar Association and a Committee of Publishers and Associations

This product is not a substitute for legal advice.

Disclaimer required by Texas statutes.

Cataloguing-in-Publication Data

Sember, Brette McWhorter
  The complete credit repair kit (with CD-ROM) / by Brette McWhorter Sember.
~ 2nd ed.
    p. cm.
  Includes index.
  ISBN 978-1-57248-681-2 (pbk. : alk. paper) 1. Consumer credit~United States. 2. Credit ratings~United States. 3. Consumer credit~Law and legislation~United States-Popular works. I. Title.
  HG3756.U54S463 2008
  332.7'43~dc22
                                    2008024381

Printed and bound in the United State of America.

CHG – 10 9 8 7 6 5 4 3 2 1

CONTENTS

How to Use the CD-ROM

Thank you for purchasing *The Complete Credit Repair Kit, Second Edition*. In this book, I have worked hard to compile exactly what you need to fix your credit. To make this material even more useful, I have included every worksheet, letter, and form in the book on the CD-ROM, which is attached to the inside back cover of the book.

You can use these forms just as you would the forms in the book. Print them out, fill them in, and use them however you need. You can also fill in the forms directly on your computer. Just identify the form you need, open it, click on the space where the information should go, and input your information. Customize each form for your particular needs. Use them over and over again.

The CD-ROM is compatible with both PC and Mac operating systems. (While it should work with either operating system, we cannot guarantee that it will work with your particular system and we cannot provide technical assistance.) To use the forms on your computer, you will need to use Adobe Reader. The CD-ROM does not contain this program. You can download this program from Adobe's website at **www.adobe.com**. Click on the "Get Adobe Reader" icon to begin the download process and follow the instructions.

Once you have Adobe Reader installed, insert the CD-ROM into your computer. Double-click on the icon representing the disc on your desktop or go through your hard drive to identify the drive that contains the disc and click on it.

Once opened, you will see the files contained on the CD-ROM listed as "Form #: [Form Title]." Open the file you need through Adobe Reader. You may print the form to fill it out manually at this point, or you can use the "Hand Tool" and click on the appropriate line to fill it in using your computer.

Any time you see bracketed information, "[ ]," on the form, you can click on it and delete the bracketed information from your final form. This information is only a reference guide to assist you in filling in the forms and should be removed from your final version. Once all your information is filled in, you can print your filled-in form.

Note: *Adobe Reader does not allow you to save the PDF with the boxes filled in.*

• • • • •

Purchasers of this book are granted a license to use the forms contained in it for their own personal use. By purchasing this book, you have also purchased a limited license to use all forms on the accompanying CD-ROM. The license limits you to personal use only and all other copyright laws must be adhered. No claim of copyright is made in any government form reproduced in the book or on the CD-ROM. You are free to modify the forms and tailor them to your specific situation.

The author and publisher have attempted to provide the most current and up-to-date information available. However, the courts, Congress, and your state's legislatures review, modify, and change laws on an ongoing basis, as well as create new laws from time to time. By the very nature of the information and due to the continual changes in our legal system, to be sure that you have the current and best information for your situation, you should consult a local attorney or research the current laws yourself.

• • • • •

Using Self-Help Law Books

Before using a self-help law book, you should realize the advantages and disadvantages of doing your own legal work and understand the challenges and diligence that this requires.

The Growing Trend

Rest assured that you will not be the first or only person handling your own legal matter. For example, in some states, more than 75% of the people in divorces and other cases represent themselves. Because of the high cost of legal services, this is a major trend, and many courts are struggling to make it easier for people to represent themselves. However, some courts are not happy with people who do not use attorneys and refuse to help them in any way. For some, the attitude is, "Go to the law library and figure it out for yourself."

We write and publish self-help law books to give people an alternative to the often complicated and confusing legal books found in most law libraries. We have made the explanations of the law as simple and easy to understand as possible. Of course, unlike an attorney advising an individual client, we cannot cover every conceivable possibility.

Cost/Value Analysis

Whenever you shop for a product or service, you are faced with various levels of quality and price. In deciding what product or service to buy, you make a cost/value analysis on the basis of your willingness to pay and the quality you desire.

When buying a car, you decide whether you want transportation, comfort, status, or sex appeal. Accordingly, you decide among choices such as a Neon, a Lincoln, a Rolls Royce, or a Porsche. Before making a decision, you usually weigh the merits of each option against the cost.

When you get a headache, you can take a pain reliever (such as aspirin) or visit a medical specialist for a neurological examination. Given this choice, most people, of course, take a pain reliever, since it costs only pennies, whereas a medical examination costs hundreds of dollars and takes a lot of time. This is usually a logical choice because it is rare to need anything more than a pain reliever for a headache. But in some cases, a headache may indicate a brain tumor, and failing to see a specialist right away can result in complications. Should everyone with a headache go to a specialist? Of course not, but people treating their own illnesses must realize that they are betting, on the basis of their cost/value analysis of the situation, that they are taking the most logical option.

The same cost/value analysis must be made when deciding to do one's own legal work. Many legal situations are very straightforward, requiring a simple form and no complicated analysis. Anyone with a little intelligence and a book of instructions can handle the matter without outside help.

But there is always the chance that complications are involved that only an attorney would notice. To simplify the law into a book like this, several legal cases often must be condensed into a single sentence or paragraph. Otherwise, the book would be several hundred pages long and too complicated for most people. However, this simplification necessarily leaves out many details and nuances that would apply to special or unusual situations. Also, there are many ways to interpret most legal questions. Your case may come before a judge who disagrees with the analysis of our authors.

Therefore, in deciding to use a self-help law book and to do your own legal work, you must realize that you are making a cost/value analysis. You have decided that the money you will save in doing it yourself outweighs the chance that your case will not turn out to your satisfaction. Most people handling their own simple legal matters never have a problem, but occasionally people find that it ended up costing them more to have an attorney straighten out the situation than it would have if they had hired an attorney in the beginning. Keep this in mind while handling your case, and be sure to consult an attorney if you feel you might need further guidance.

Local Rules

The next thing to remember is that a book that covers the law for the entire nation, or even for an entire state, cannot possibly include every procedural difference of every jurisdiction. Whenever possible, we provide the exact form needed; however, in some areas, each county, or even each judge, may require unique forms and procedures. In our state books, our forms usually cover the majority of counties in the state or provide examples of the type of form that will be required. In our national books, our forms are sometimes even more general in nature but are designed to give a good idea of the type of form that will be needed in most locations. Nonetheless, keep in mind that your state, county, or judge may have a requirement or use a form that is not included in this book.

You should not necessarily expect to be able to get all the information and resources you need solely from within the pages of this book. This book will serve as your guide, giving you specific information whenever possible and helping you to find out what else you will need to know. This is just like if you decided to build your own backyard deck. You might purchase a book on how to build decks. However, such a book would not include the building codes and permit requirements of every city, town, county, and township in the nation, nor would it include the lumber, nails, saws, hammers, and other materials and tools you would need to actually build the deck. You would use the book as your guide, and then do some work and research involving such matters as whether you need a permit of some kind, what type and grade of wood is available in your area, whether to use hand tools or power tools, and how to use those tools.

Before using the forms in a book like this, you should check with your court clerk to see if there are any local rules of which you should be aware or local forms you will need to use. Often, such forms will require the same information as the forms in the book but are merely laid out differently or use slightly different language. They will sometimes require additional information.

Changes in the Law

Besides being subject to local rules and practices, the law is subject to change at any time. The courts and the legislatures of all fifty states are constantly revising the laws. It is possible that while you are reading this book, some aspect of the law is being changed.

In most cases, the change will be of minimal significance. A form will be redesigned, additional information will be required, or a waiting period will be extended. As a result, you might need to revise a form, file an extra form, or wait out a longer time period. These types of changes will not usually affect the outcome of your case. On the other hand, sometimes a major part of the law is changed, the entire law in a particular area is rewritten, or a case that was the basis of a central legal point is overruled. In such instances, your entire ability to pursue your case may be impaired.

Again, you should weigh the value of your case against the cost of an attorney and make a decision as to what you believe is in your best interest.

INTRODUCTION

Most people have credit cards and debts. But very few people understand how to deal with both effectively. This book helps answer your questions, shows you your options, and helps you make good choices. This book and the forms it contains are designed to help you understand your credit report, understand your debt load, help you clean up your credit report, develop a workable budget, avoid scams, and ease your debt situation. The book is also designed to be a resource to you as you learn how to use credit wisely and protect yourself from identity theft.

You might be in the middle of a debt emergency, with no cash on hand to pay bills. You might feel as though your credit card debt is just getting bigger and bigger and you have decided now is the time to take action. Or perhaps you just feel like you want to improve your credit rating and become a better manager of your credit cards. In any of these situations, this book is your road map.

Chapter 1 helps you take a look at your financial situation, understand it, and deal with any pressing financial problems. Chapter 2 talks about making better choices as a consumer. Chapters 3 and 4 guide you through obtaining and understanding your credit report and credit score, which is the information used by all creditors when deciding whether or not to lend you money. Chapter 5 walks you through ways to correct errors on your credit report as well as ideas for improving and adding positive items to your credit report. Chapter 6 helps you find ways to cut back and reduce your debt, your expenses, and your spending habits.

If you need further help with your financial situation, Chapter 7 tells you where to find it, with an extensive list of resources. Marriage and divorce are always deeply intertwined with debt, and Chapter 8 helps you understand all the ramifications of debt in those situations. Chapter 9 explains identity theft and shows how you can best protect yourself from this frightening problem. You are given practical advice about steps you can take to make certain your future credit reports will be positive in Chapter 10.

When you are facing any kind of financial difficulties, budgeting is a tool you need to learn about and incorporate into your daily life. Chapter 11 shows you how to do this. Finally, Chapter 12 talks about how to go forward with your life and face the future, while putting your financial worries behind you.

To accomplish your goals, you will need to take certain steps with any number of creditors or organizations. To assist you with this, three separate appendixes are included. Appendix A looks at state-by-state resources so you can get state-specific information. Appendix B provides parts of important federal statutes affecting you as a consumer. Appendix C contains all the blank forms and letters that you need to deal with creditors. If you are using the forms printed in the book, it is recommended that you make copies of the forms before writing on them. You may also wish to copy the words from the forms onto your own paper or stationery so that it is not obvious you are using a form from a book. Always keep copies of everything you send, whether it is from this book or something you write yourself. (All the forms and letters in Appendix C are contained on the CD-ROM for your convenience. See "How to Use the CD-ROM" on page xi.)

You have probably seen ads for companies that promise to erase your bad credit or give you new good credit for a fee. Don't bother! This book tells you every legal method available for repairing your credit on your own, with no fees. Everything you need to know is contained in this book. Many consumers find that they use credit cards and end up with more debt than they can handle. This book is your guide to learning how to use your credit wisely.

This book also helps you get a handle on your debt and discusses how you can actually reduce it. You have probably also seen ads for attorneys or other professionals who advertise that they can reduce your debt and get creditors to stop bothering you. Of course, there is a fee involved for these services. Forget it! You can reduce your debt and negotiate with creditors yourself for no fee if you follow the instructions in this book. You will also save yourself lots of money.

All the information contained in this book is accurate as of the time it was written, but laws are constantly changing. You can obtain updated information about current laws at libraries and online. For personal legal advice, you should consult an attorney. Note also that all the links to websites contained in the book worked at the time the book was published, but websites change frequently. If a link does not work, try going to the main page of the site listed and looking for a link to the information you need. If the site no longer exists, try finding similar information using a search engine such as **www.google.com**. This book is not a substitute for legal advice. To get current legal advice as it applies to your situation, you should consult with an attorney.

With this book, you are on the pathway to a new approach to your finances. Good luck on your journey!

ASSESSING YOUR SITUATION | 1

You have already decided that your financial situation either needs help right now or soon will. Buying this book was an important first step in getting a handle on and solving your financial worries. The first thing to do is remember not to panic. No matter how bad things are, there are steps you can take to improve your situation.

To really know how to solve your problems, you must first understand the details about your situation. Knowing that you do not have enough money to pay all your bills, that your credit report is unfavorable, or that you were denied credit is not enough information. You must sit down with all your financial records and all your bills and get a clear picture of what you have, what you owe, and what you can do about the rest. This can be very hard to do if you are certain you're not going to like what you will see. However, you have to bite the bullet and face reality. It is also important that you understand how the law applies to the different kinds of bills you have. Taking some time to understand the details about your finances will enable you to take steps to fix your problems and avoid problems in the future.

Debt—The American Way

Debt is a huge problem in our society. Even our government is deep into debt. We have developed a culture of debt. It is completely acceptable in the United States to have large amounts of debt. In fact, you are expected to. You are not really an adult until you have a car payment, a mortgage, and several credit cards. And no one seems to realize that you should pay off your entire credit card balance each month and not let that balance continue to add up. While some debt can be useful and even important, having too much can simply overwhelm you and your finances. It is time to stop thinking about debt as something acceptable and common, and instead come to grips with the fact that it may not be healthy for you, and find ways to control it. Use debt when it makes sense, but never let it control you.

IT'S A FACT

The average U.S. household carries $8,000 in debt on their credit cards and has 12.71 credit cards. There are 1.3 billion credit cards in use in the United States at this time. Forty-three percent of U.S. households spend more than they earn each year. And the dramatic increase in personal bankruptcies is a red flag that Americans have too much, take on too much debt, and fail to pay off their debt.

Debt is too easy to get—as evidenced by the home foreclosure crisis—and too hard to pay off for most people. Until we as a culture change the way we think about and manage debt, it will continue to plague many people.

Debt is a problem faced by every age group in the country. Children are affected by debt when it affects their parents. Young adults are at high risk for debt problems because very little is done to educate teens about how to manage money and debt. Students go to college and find themselves on their own for the first time, often with a credit card available for use, with no experience in using it wisely. College students also take out student loans and find themselves unable to make payments when they first enter the workforce. Young married couples and new parents find that mortgages, car payments, and credit card bills can soon become overwhelming. Middle-aged people often take out home equity loans, finance little luxuries, and face debt overload. Even the elderly are not exempt as they face high medical expenses, low set incomes, and rising costs. Debt has permeated every aspect of our society.

Just because everyone else is getting in over their heads with debt does not mean you should do it too. If you ignore your debts or avoid coping with them, the consequences can be tremendous— tremendously awful. First, you will find that you will be denied credit. You will not be able to get a car loan or a mortgage because you are carrying too much debt. Second, you will max out your current credit and be unable to use your credit cards. You will eventually find that your utilities are turned off, your car is repossessed, and your checks are bouncing. If you are a renter, you can be evicted. If you apply for a new apartment, the landlord can check your credit report and reject you based on poor credit. If you are a homeowner, your home can be foreclosed, leaving you with no place to live. Potential employers may get your credit report and choose not to hire you based on what it says. So, if you lose your job, you may not be able to get another one. Your creditors can obtain judgments against you, which will give them the right to seize your assets and take part of your paycheck. It is easy to quickly get in over your head with debt. The best plan is to fix things before they get this bad. It is easier to deal with your debt before these consequences begin happening. This scenario is frightening, but it does not have to happen to you.

Dealing with Debt Emergencies

If you are experiencing a debt emergency, you need to handle it immediately. An *emergency* is an eviction, foreclosure, vehicle repossession, or other matter that will directly and immediately impact your housing, health, or transportation situation. If you are in an emergency, you have to cope with it first, before using the rest of this book to solve your other debt problems.

If you are facing one of these emergencies, contact that creditor immediately and tell him or her you would like to work out a payment plan. Explain that you are having financial troubles and want to make sure that creditor is paid, but that you need to work something out for the short-term. Get the best plan you can and agree to it. (See Chapter 6 for more discussion of payment plans.) This will give you at least a few months to try to make some permanent changes to your overall situation.

The following are emergency measures you can take to get cash fast to bail yourself out of a bad situation.

- Consider asking a friend or family member for money to get the lights back on, keep your car from being repossessed, or prevent an eviction.

- If you have credit left, you may be able to cash advance some money or use your credit card to make a payment to the creditor. Keep in mind, though, that this is not a solution and is just a temporary fix, since you will still need to find a way to pay off the credit card.

- If you have a retirement plan or pension, you may be able to take a loan against it. If you do not pay the loan back, though, you will have to pay a 10% penalty.

- If you have personal items of value, you can consider selling them.

If the creditor is unwilling to work any payment plan out and you are going to lose your home or vehicle and cannot make any other arrangements for yourself, consider filing for *bankruptcy*. (Bankruptcy is discussed more fully in Chapter 7.) When you file for bankruptcy, at the moment your petition is filed, all creditors must stop any and all collection efforts. All foreclosures and evictions must also stop. Talk to an attorney who specializes in bankruptcies. When you call for an appointment, explain that you have an emergency and need to file as soon as possible. Do not put off this phone call.

If you are having difficulty paying all your debts and are in a difficult situation, one tactic you can use is asking your creditors to provide you with documentation of the debt. Under the *Fair Debt Collection Practices Act* (FDCPA), you have the right to request this of any creditor. It often takes several weeks for a creditor to provide the documentation, giving you a little extra time to try to pull some money or a plan together. (FDCPA, Section (Sec.) 809.)

Other tactics some people use include moving with no forwarding address and not registering to vote in the new location, or closing bank accounts and opening new ones at a different bank. These tactics are just delay strategies that make it hard for the creditor to locate you, and in no way will reduce your debt. In fact, they will increase your debt because interest will continue to build. When it all catches up to you, it is going to be worse than it is right now.

To delay having your credit cards reported as past due, make the minimum payments. This will keep the account current and keep your credit report clean. Interest will continue to accrue on your balance, though, so this is only a temporary solution. You need to find a permanent solution.

If you are facing eviction or foreclosure, you need legal help. If bankruptcy is not a choice, you need an attorney to help with the eviction or foreclosure. (See Chapter 7 for information about finding low- or no-cost legal help.)

Remember that though your situation may feel out of control, there is a way out. It means taking the reins, facing the facts, and developing a plan to help keep a roof over your head and food on the table. Avoiding the bad news will not help. Stop and develop a plan that includes working with your creditors.

REAL LIFE CREDIT

Tim graduated from college and was working part-time at a bar to make some money, but he had not yet found a job in his career path. His roommate moved out, leaving him to pay all the rent on the apartment. Tim didn't want to take a job that wasn't in his field and was keeping his days open for interviews. His cash supply was quite low though, and with his student loans coming up for payment, he was in a debt emergency. He didn't know whether to pay his rent, utilities, or loans.

Tim sat down and thought about the situation. If he didn't pay his utilities, they were going to be turned off. He needed water and electricity to get ready for interviews, so he decided those were priorities. Rent was next on his list. He knew that if he was late with the rent, the landlord could not immediately evict him, so waiting a few weeks would not be the end of the world. Student loans were another problem. He knew that if he did not pay them, fees and interest would pile up. Tim applied for an economic hardship forbearance for his student loans and received it, which let him put his student loans on hold. Within a few weeks he found a job in his field and was able to catch up on his rent and begin paying his student loans.

Strategies for Dealing with a Debt Emergency

☐ Continue to make the minimum payments for as long as you can.

☐ Request a **VALIDATION OF DEBT** under the *Fair Debt Collection Practices Act*. (see form 1, p.346.)

☐ Work out a payment plan with the creditor.

☐ Seek legal advice.

☐ Borrow money from family or friends to stay afloat in the short-term.

☐ Consider cash advances on credit or loans against retirement accounts.

☐ File for bankruptcy. (The automatic stay will put a stop to debt collecting.)

☐ Take control of your situation and develop a plan.

Get a Clear Picture of Your Finances

Assemble all your bills, including mortgage or rent, home equity loans, bank and store credit cards, medical bills, car loans, insurance bills, utility bills, student loans, back taxes, and all other bills and debts. Make sure you have the most current statement from each creditor. If you cannot locate the most current bill, call and request one from the creditor.

Next, get together all records of money or assets you have— checking and savings accounts, CDs, retirement accounts, bonds, investments, credit unions accounts, current pay stubs, information on property you own, as well as any vehicles or anything else of value.

Now that you have assembled all of this information, you need to organize it in a way that will make it easy to work with. Start by filling out the **DEBT ASSESSMENT** worksheet. (see form 2, p.347.)

Use these tips when completing the **DEBT ASSESSMENT** worksheet.

- List each creditor separately.

- Place your account number, the total amount owed, and monthly payment in the correct columns for each creditor.

- Be sure to get up-to-date balances, even if it means calling the creditor to check.

- Total the monthly payment amounts and the total amounts owed at the bottom of the page.

Sample Debt Assessment Worksheet

Fill in the blanks to list all your monthly debts. Total the items at the bottom to get the number for your total monthly debts.

Name of Creditor	Account Number	Total Due	Monthly Payment
Sunshine Auto	9-988-7766	$8,736	$400
Joe's Apartments		$950	$950
University Accounting	123-45-6789	$11,409	$210
First National Bank	123987456	$4,961	$575

(cont.)

Com Ed	98765	$120	$120
Visa	44332211	$3,000	$25
Cable	999999999	$80	$80
Cell Phone	88888888	$100	$100
		Total Amount Due: $29,356	Total Monthly Payment Due: $2,460

Next look at your pile of information concerning your assets and complete the ASSET ASSESSMENT worksheet. (see form 3, p.348.)

Use these tips to help you complete the ASSET ASSESSMENT worksheet.

- Fill in your monthly salary amounts and the yearly amounts earned.

- Include all other money coming into your household, such as child support, alimony, disability payments, interest, etc. Also include money you can earn or receive from things like eBay sales, garage sales, gifts from family, gambling, money from odd jobs, and so on.

- Total all monthly amounts and yearly amounts. Write those amounts on the respective lines.

- List each account or item separately and give its current value.

- Total all asset values at the bottom of the form.

Sample Asset Assessment

Salary:

Monthly amount earned:	$2,000
Yearly amount earned:	$24,000

Other income (such as child support, alimony, etc.):

Monthly amount:	$400
Yearly amount:	$4,800

Other income (include interest, unreported income, etc.):

Monthly amount:	$100
Yearly amount:	$1,200

Total Income:

Monthly:	$2,500
Yearly:	$30,000

Other Assets: List name of item, account number if applicable, and value.

Name/Description	Account Number	Value
Snowmobile		$6,000
Savings Account	12-3456-78	$467
Antique Lamp		$150
Total value of other assets:		$6,617

Finally, compare your assets and debts on the TOTAL ASSESSMENT worksheet. (see form 4, p.349.) Follow these steps.

- Transfer the totals you reached on the ASSET ASSESSMENT and DEBT ASSESSMENT worksheets to the monthly income and monthly debts lines and the total assets and total debts lines. Your total debt will almost definitely be larger than your total assets. (Don't panic. This even happens to people who are not experiencing credit problems.)

- Compare your monthly income to your monthly minimum debt payments by subtracting your debts from your assets. Write this amount on the respective line.

Total Assessment

Monthly:

Total monthly income:	$2,500
Total monthly debts:	$2,460

Subtract debts from assets and you get this: $40

Note: *If this is a negative number, you know you need to make some changes. If this is a positive number but is not enough to pay your other nonitemized expenses, such as food and gas, you need to make some changes.*

Total assets:	$6,617
Total debts:	$29,356

Compare your total assets to your total debts. If your assets are significantly larger than your debts, you are in good shape. If your debts are larger than your assets, then this is something you need to work on. If they are pretty close, you are moving in the right direction but need to make sure you continue an upward trend.

Look at your total monthly income and determine how much of that you would realistically like to have available and not tied up in monthly payments. This is the goal you are going to work toward. After paying for housing, utilities, vehicles, and miscellaneous expenses, how much do you want to have left over?

Understanding Debt

People often ask how much debt is okay to have. There is no good answer to that question. There are some generally accepted rules of thumb people like to use—your debt payments should be no more than 20% of your disposable income and your total debt should be no more than one-third of your total yearly income. These rules of thumb do not work for everyone, however. You should only have debt that is necessary—such as a mortgage—and that you can manage and pay off without incurring a lot of unnecessary interest. There is no magic number or magic percentage. If you have so much debt that you find yourself worrying about it, then you have too much debt. If you struggle to make more than the minimum payments, you have too much debt.

Practical Point

It is important to save money so that you can plan for retirement, save for emergencies, and handle big expenses like college tuition. Financial experts suggest you develop a cushion equal to six months of your income. For many people, this is difficult to do. However, if you can commit to saving some amount each month, you will be on your way there.

In general, debt is bad because, in effect, it increases the cost of the things you buy on it. Instead of paying $29.99 for a sweater, you are paying $29.99 *plus* the interest charges. Debt is dangerous because it allows you to spend beyond your means. It gives you a false sense of security and allows you to spend money without directly relating your purchase to the funds you have at your disposal at that moment.

However, debt allows you to buy a home and car when, like most people, you are not able to pay cash for them. Debt for these large items is often the only way to afford them. Taking on these kinds of debt can be very good if you only take on as much debt as you can handle, and you budget for it. Debt can also be a way to save money. Let's say you go to TVs-R-Us to buy a new flat screen television. The salesperson tells you if you open an account with the store, you can save 20% on your purchase. This can be a nice way to save some money—but only if you pay the charge off immediately without incurring interest and then close the account. Your overall goal should be to reduce your debt to a manageable level, and eventually to eliminate all but home and car loans.

Before you take any steps to clear your credit rating and get yourself out of debt, you have to look closely at the debts you have and understand what type of debts they are. Different kinds of creditors are treated differently.

Secured Loans

Secured loans are loans in which you borrow money or buy a certain item and give the creditor a *security interest* or collateral in the item. An example of this is a car loan. When you take out a car loan, you give the creditor the right to take the car back if you do not pay the loan. Should this happen, you are responsible for the difference between the value of the car (what it can be sold for at auction) and the balance on the loan as well as fees and costs of the repossession. So, allowing a car to be repossessed does not wipe out that debt entirely and may leave you owing money even after your car is sold.

Unsecured Loans

Unsecured loans occur when a creditor lends you money and does not have a security interest in anything you own. Credit cards are unsecured loans, unless you have a card that is secured through your bank account (i.e., the creditor can seize your bank account if you do not pay the amount owed). Personal loans are also usually unsecured.

IT'S A FACT

One in every three consumer purchases in the United States is made with a credit card.

Student Loans

Student loans are unsecured loans that are usually offered through a bank or loan agency and backed by the government. Student loans cannot be discharged in bankruptcy and are often a source of credit problems. Student loans can be *consolidated* (rolled together into one loan), which is one way to manage this type of debt. Student loans can be dangerous because they are gradually added to each semester, and then suddenly after graduation, and possibly before you have a job, you're responsible for paying them back.

Mortgage

A *mortgage* occurs when you buy a home and borrow money from a bank. The bank loans you the money to pay for the house, but maintains a type of security interest in the home. You cannot sell the home without paying the mortgage, and if you fail to make payments, the bank can foreclose on the home and sell it to pay for the loan (and just like with a car, if the home is foreclosed, you will likely still owe the bank money for the difference between the sale at auction and the balance, as well as fees). A home equity loan is a type of mortgage.

Taxes

Taxes are an amount owed to the state or federal government. Taxes cannot be discharged in bankruptcy and swiftly pile up fees and penalties for nonpayment.

Dealing with Your Emotions

It is likely that your credit situation or financial problems are causing you a lot of stress. You are worried about how to handle the debt you have or how to clean up your credit history so that you are not always being turned down for loans, credit cards, or mortgages. It is hard to act rationally if you are panicked. You need to take a deep breath and focus on the facts of the situation and not on your emotional reaction to it. Remind yourself that you are going to resolve the situation. There are solutions to your problems. Read this book and follow the suggestions. If you take action, you will feel more in control of your situation.

Practical Point

If you find that the stress is too much for you to handle, talk to a friend, clergy member, or mental health professional.

A common reaction to credit and debt problems is avoidance. People avoid understanding or even thinking about their situation. They often reason that if they do not think about it, it cannot be all that bad—but ignoring your problems will not make them go away. Looking the other way just makes things worse because your debt continues to mount. You need to get a handle on your credit and debt problems by taking action today.

The sooner you face your money problems, the sooner they can be resolved. Many people avoid dealing with their situation out of embarrassment. They feel too embarrassed to contact a creditor to make payment arrangements or to ask a family member for financial assistance. Just remember that creditors deal with these problems on a daily basis, and you are not alone. If you are in a situation where you must turn to family for help, remind yourself that this is what family is for.

You must put your feelings aside and deal with this problem as if it were someone else's problem that you are handling for him or her. Look at the facts and focus on what concrete things you can do to change the situation. Do not get caught up in your emotions. Take a problem-solving approach.

Your Rights

You have many specific rights provided by the federal government with regard to your debts and credit report. Different states provide for different rights as well. Check your state's laws at your local library or online at **www.findlaw.com**. Chapter 7 lists organizations that can help you understand and exercise your rights.

There are two important federal laws that you need to know about to protect yourself and exercise your rights—the federal *Fair Debt Collection Practices Act* and the federal *Fair Credit Reporting Act*.

Fair Debt Collection Practices Act

The *Fair Debt Collection Practices Act* (FDCPA) sets out specifics about how a collection agency may behave toward others. Understand that the FDCPA applies not just to actual collection agencies, but to people acting as debt collectors as well.

Contact with You

Debt collectors may not contact you at unusual or inconvenient times—which includes before 8 a.m. and after 9 p.m.—or at work if you are not permitted to accept such calls there. They may not call you repeatedly or call you without identifying themselves. They may not call you collect or cause you to be responsible for any costs of the phone call. They may not identify themselves as part of law enforcement or as attorneys. They may not harass, oppress, or abuse you. They may not use or threaten to use violence or harm toward you or anyone else and they may not threaten to damage anyone's reputation. They cannot threaten to garnish your wages or sue you unless they actually intend to do so. They cannot threaten you with arrest or jail. If you have an attorney, they must speak with your attorney and not to you directly unless you give permission. (FDCPA, Secs. 1692(c) and (d).)

Obscene language is not permitted. Your name cannot be published on a deadbeat list. If you are contacted by a debt collector, you can instruct him or her not to call you again. Debt collectors must abide by this request and can only notify you by mail of the status of your account, such as when it is being forwarded to an attorney for a lawsuit. (FDCPA, Secs. 1692(c) through (f).)

Whenever you speak to a debt collector, get his or her name, the name of the agency, business address, and phone number. Document all contact, including dates, times, and the gist of the conversations. If you believe you are being treated in a way that violates the law or if your request for no contact is being ignored, write to the agency and complain (and keep a copy of the letter, also sending it with a signature necessary for delivery). Contact your state attorney general about the problem.

Collectors cannot lie about the amount you owe nor can they threaten to take action against you that they do not intend to take. No unfair or outrageous attempts to collect the money are permitted. This includes adding interest or fees that are not part of the original debt, asking for a postdated check by threatening you with criminal action, or accepting a check that is more than five days postdated unless they notify you three to ten days before cashing it. They may not deposit a postdated check before the date on it. (FDCPA, Sec. 1692(f).)

Practical Point

If you tell a collection agency not to contact you again, it must comply, unless it is giving you notice of plans to sue or to stop collection attempts.

Correspondence with You

When you receive correspondence from a debt collector, it must not appear to resemble court documents or correspondence from a government agency. It may not appear as if it is from an attorney. The envelope containing the correspondence must be a plain envelope and may not indicate anywhere on it that it is in reference to the collection of a debt or that it is from a collection agency. (FDCPA, Sec. 1692(e).)

Contact with Others

Debt collectors must give their names when contacting other people and state that they are confirming or correcting residence or employment information about you. If asked, they can give the name of the agency they work for. They may not talk about you owing a debt at all and may not call anyone more than once unless they received incorrect or incomplete information the first time. (FDCPA, Sec. 1692(b).)

Your Remedy

If a creditor violates any provision of this law, you can take action against him or her. Make sure that you keep detailed records and keep all evidence of the violation. If possible, you should have a witness as well, i.e., someone who saw or heard the improper act. Be aware that in some states, you can record phone conversations without permission; however, in many states you must have permission from the person you are recording.

Send a letter to the original creditor and your state's attorney general detailing the violation. You should also send a letter to the *Federal Trade Commission* at your regional office listed in the phone book, or online at **www.ftc.gov**. Use the LETTER COMPLAINING OF UNFAIR DEBT COLLECTION PRACTICES. (see form 7, p.353.) You may be able to get the entire debt canceled because of this. If you have been harassed, you could also bring a case in small claims court in your local area for damages for your pain and suffering as well as *punitive damages* of up to $1,000 to punish the collection agency for its actions. (FDCPA, Sec. 1692(k).)

Dealing with Collection Agencies

Collection agencies are businesses that earn money by collecting debts. Your debt can end up in collection in one of two ways. Either the creditor forwards your debt to the collection agency and agrees to pay the agency a percentage of the amount collected, or the creditor sells the right to collect on your debt to the agency and the agency gets to keep whatever it collects from you. The individual collection agents who work for the agency do so on commission. They are paid a percentage of what they collect from you, so they are highly motivated to get you to pay. Collection agencies have a bad reputation and some people see them as sharks that bother people at home and at work and collect money any way they can. In reality, as previously discussed, the law is quite clear about what collection agencies can and cannot do. The people who work there do not have a personal vendetta against you—they are people trying to do their job and earn a living. You may of course disagree with their tactics and with their choice of line of work.

When you decide to talk to a collection agency, you must remember that you are dealing with a professional debt collector. Do not let yourself be talked into paying more than you are able. Know what your *bottom line* is (the most you can agree to pay monthly) before talking with the agency. Realize that the agent may act friendly and seem as if he or she is on your side and wants to help you. Never believe this. Collections is a big business and you are the only one who can safeguard your financial situation. The agents are very skilled at talking people into paying as much as possible. The more they collect, the more they earn. They are persistent and persuasive. Remember, you can always tell them not to call you anymore.

Tips for Dealing with Collection Agencies

☐ No matter how friendly and understanding the person on the phone sounds, remember that he or she is doing a job and just wants to get money from you.

☐ If you work out a settlement with the collection agency, get everything in writing before paying.

☐ Do not share your other phone numbers or other ways a collection agency can reach you.

☐ Treat the call as a business call. Do not get emotional or caught up in the situation.

☐ Direct collection agents not to call you anymore if you do not wish to receive these calls.

☐ If you choose to take the calls, keep a journal of all the calls.

☐ Negotiate a settlement (see Chapter 6 for information about settlements).

Fair Credit Reporting Act

The *Fair Credit Reporting Act* (FCRA) deals with credit reports and credit reporting agencies. Consumers can now obtain a free copy of their credit report once a year, but if you need to obtain additional copies, the FCRA provides the fee structure for credit reports. (See Chapter 4 for more information about this.)

A report must be requested within sixty days of the receipt of the denial of credit or employment. The FCRA also provides that if you find an error or incorrect information on your report, you can inform the reporting agency, and it must reinvestigate the matter at no charge to you. You must receive a response from the agency within thirty days. The information must be corrected or deleted if it is wrong. (FCRA, Sec. 1681(i).)

Practical Point

In addition to a free annual credit report, consumers can obtain free reports if they have been denied credit.

Credit reporting agencies are required to include a record of all inquiries about you received in the last six months on your credit report. They must also include a listing of all people who have purchased your report within the last two years for employment purposes and within the last year for other reasons. (FCRA, Sec. 1681(g).)

Credit reporting agencies are not required to disclose your credit scores or credit risk rating. This is an internal evaluation the reporting agency makes about your creditworthiness. It is like a grade for your credit history, and is furnished to employers and creditors. Many credit reporting agencies do release this information, but they are not required to do so by law. (FCRA, Sec. 1681(g).)

If you would like to read the complete FCRA, you can find it online at **www.ftc.gov/os/statutes/031224fcra.pdf**.

Creditor Tactics

While creditors must follow the law in how they deal with you, there are many different tactics creditors can legally use to collect the money you owe. In this section, we will explore these.

Wage Attachments

Often, creditors will look to your wages for payment and seek a way to have your employer make payments directly to the creditor. There are two ways a creditor can attach your wages. A *wage garnishment* occurs when a court enters a judgment against you and the creditor is then allowed to have a certain portion taken out of your salary (consult your state's laws to understand how much is permitted) and paid directly to the creditor. You must be served with court papers and a court must hear the case before a wage garnishment can be ordered. However, if you ignore court papers, a court can go ahead and order it without your knowledge.

There are state and federal restrictions on garnishments. The *Federal Wage Garnishment Law*—which is part of the *Consumer Credit Protection Act* (CCPA)—limits wage garnishment to:

1. 25% of disposable earnings for that week; or,

2. the amount by which disposable earnings for that week exceed thirty times the federal minimum hourly wage prescribed by Section 206(a)(1) of Title 29 in effect at the time the earnings are payable, whichever is less.

The law allows tax debt to be garnished up to 15% of weekly disposable income. Ten percent of your disposable income can be garnished to pay back a defaulted student loan.

This law also prevents an employer from firing you because your wages are being garnished. The laws about child support garnishment are different, so don't get them confused. You can read the entire text of the law online at **www4.law.cornell.edu/uscode/ uscode15/usc_sup_01_15_10_41_20_II.html**.

A *wage assignment* occurs when a debtor agrees to have part of his or her pay sent directly to a creditor. Never agree to this! Do not let a creditor talk you into this, no matter what. It is vital that you know and understand this before you read further. It will come up early on in your dealings with creditors. You want to have complete control over your income at all times. A wage assignment can never happen without your knowledge and consent.

Repossession

Repossession occurs when a creditor has a *security interest* in an item you purchased. This means the creditor has the right to take back the item if you do not make payments on the loan. The most common example is with an automobile. When you purchase the car and take out the loan, you will be given papers indicating the security interest the creditor retains. Repossession is just a way of saying the creditor takes the car away from you for failure to pay. If you take out a loan from an appliance or furniture store, you may be giving the store a security interest in the items you buy.

You can best prevent repossession by making your car payments. If you are going to miss a payment, call the creditor and explain in advance. If you have a continuing problem making payments, you need to speak to the creditor and try to work out a payment plan that will work for you. This may include several months of reduced payments or an extension of the life of the loan to give you a longer period of time to make the payments. (Note that this will end up costing you more since you will have to pay more interest.) If you are still unable to make the payments, it is likely the car will be repossessed. Some people avoid this by keeping the car someplace where the creditor cannot find it. This means you will not be able to use it, though, since your creditor knows where you live and work.

If your car is repossessed, you should contact the creditor immediately and try to work out an arrangement for you to make some payments in order to have the car returned to you. You have to understand, though, that once the car is repossessed, the creditor does not have much incentive to return it to you. If you decide to just give up and allow the car to be repossessed, you need to know that this is not as simple as it sounds. If your car is repossessed, the creditor can (and usually will) charge you additional fees. (If you have no choice but to have the car repossessed, you may be able to keep down the fees involved by agreeing to voluntarily surrender the car so the creditor does not pay to have it towed.) You will also still owe the remaining loan amount minus the current value or amount the car has been sold for.

Practical Point

If you find you can no longer make car payments, it is better to turn the car over to the creditor. This will cost you less than repossession. Note that if you are able to sell the car quickly yourself, you can likely get more for it than the creditor can at auction. However, you need to make the sale very quickly before repossession happens.

Foreclosure

Foreclosure occurs when a bank takes possession of *real property* (such as your home) that you have failed to make mortgage payments on. Foreclosure is a long process and banks usually prefer to help you find a way to make your payment rather than go through the foreclosure process. Just as with repossession, there are costs and fees associated with the process for which you will be responsible. Additionally, repossessed homes are usually sold at auction for a fraction of their value. You will be responsible for the difference between the sale price and the amount of the mortgage, as well as costs and fees.

The best way to deal with a foreclosure is to prevent it from happening. Try to work with your lender. Some solutions include the following:

- having a missed payment incorporated back into the loan;

- extending your loan period;

- changing the terms of your loan (e.g., a lower interest rate); or,

- spreading out the missing payments throughout the rest of the loan.

Note that any solution is going to involve you paying what you owe at some point, in some way. Another thing to consider is selling the house yourself and moving someplace less expensive, or going back to being a renter.

Once a foreclosure is under way (i.e., the *Notice of Default* has been filed), you still have some options. One is what is called a *short sale*, where you get the lender to agree to let you sell the property and close the loan with the proceeds of the sale (which will usually be less than the loan is worth). Another option is a *deed in lieu of foreclosure*, where you essentially turn the house back over to the bank without the expenses of a true foreclosure. However, in terms of your credit report, this is still reported as a foreclosure.

Becoming a Wise Consumer

The best thing you can do to protect your credit and your finances is to be a wise consumer. The best way to achieve financial health is to avoid problems and be prepared to handle problems that do come up. Learning how to use your credit cards and be a smart shopper will go a long way toward helping you create a good record for yourself.

Credit Card Usage

Credit cards are one area where people are often confused about their rights and how best to use their credit. The following sections will help clear up some of the most common things consumers want to know.

Payments

You should have an idea as to when each of your bills will arrive each month. If you do not get a bill, call the company. The bill could have been lost in the mail, and if you do not pay it you will be charged late fees. It is a good idea to create an online account for each of your credit cards. This way you can log on and check your balance and make online payments. Online payments are the safest way to make sure your bill is paid on time. If you drop a check in the mail, it can take a long time for it to arrive. An online payment is credited on the day you choose.

Change of Address

It is your responsibility to notify creditors when you move. Most credit cards have a form you can fill out for a change of address, or you can change it by calling your card's customer service number. If your credit card does not offer this form, use the NEW ADDRESS LETTER to let your credit card company know of your move. (see form 5, p.350.) Do not rely on the forwarding order you gave the post office to get your mail to you in time to pay your bill before it is due. If the bill gets to you late, resulting in you making a late payment, you are responsible for late fees.

Opening Cards for Discounts

Many stores offer special discounts if you open a credit account with them, with savings up to 20% of your purchase that day. These offers can be a great deal; however, opening too many can cause problems. First, having too many cards is just a license to spend and is not a good idea. In general, it is a good idea to have only three or four credit cards.

Second, every time you open a new card, a credit inquiry is placed on your credit report. Every inquiry made causes your credit score to drop up to five points. Too many inquiries in a short time can significantly lower your credit score.

REAL LIFE CREDIT

Kyra loved a good bargain. Whenever a store offered a discount for opening a credit account, she jumped on it. In fact, she had been known to close an existing account with a store just to turn around and open a new one to get the latest discount or deal. She didn't think that this would be any problem in terms of her credit report since she paid off all the balances every time and was never late with a payment. She was shocked when one day she went to open a new account and was denied. She got her credit report and was surprised at how long it was, with all the accounts she had opened. She never realized that credit reporting agencies penalize you for having too many accounts open and for having so many inquiries on your account.

Kyra decided to change her ways. Twenty percent off was not a good reason to do more damage to her credit account. First, she closed some of the accounts she had opened because she had too many listed. Then, she focused on using only the credit she had and making sure her payments continued to be on time. Within a year, her credit had improved and her credit score went up. She could then get more credit should she need it. She decided she didn't need any more credit, though, and began to concentrate on saving money for a down payment on a house.

Card Incentives

It can be hard to choose which credit card to open when so many different incentives are offered—cash back, mileage points, and so on. When considering mileage points, remember that they mean nothing unless you will actually use them. It can be quite difficult to use airline miles that have blackout periods. Rewards cards tend to have higher interest rates, so putting large balances on them is not smart. Always find out if there are annual fees—try to get a no-fee card if possible. Some rewards cards cap the number of points you can earn, so be sure to ask about restrictions before signing up for any card. If you have to carry a balance, do it on a low-interest card, not a high-interest rewards card.

Balances

If you have a large balance on a card that maxes it out, consider transferring some of the balance to other cards. Having a card maxed out looks like you are having credit trouble. However, if one card has a great low interest rate, the benefits of paying less interest will likely outweigh the detriments to your credit history.

Late Payments

If you know you are going to have to make a late payment, always call the company and tell them. Ask them to waive the late fee if you have been on time up until now. They usually have discretion to waive one late fee. To avoid a late fee, you can pay online or by phone the day the bill is due. You may also be able to pay at a store or bank location, so ask if you are not sure if that is an option. If you must pay by mail, pay the bill the same day it arrives, so that you do not forget about it and are certain it will arrive in time.

If you must make a late payment, you will likely be charged a late payment fee. You should also be aware that your cardholder may immediately increase the interest rate on your card.

Balance Transfers

Balance transfers are a great way to take advantage of low interest rate offers. Moving your debt around from various cards is not detrimental to your credit rating. Make sure you verify that the interest rate will not change after a certain period of time and learn what other restrictions are applicable. Once you have transferred a balance to a low-rate card, do not use that card for anything else. Anything you charge to the card is automatically charged interest (instead of the usual situation where you have a month to pay it).

Credit Line Increases

If an increase is made to your credit line, it is not detrimental to accept it. If you continue your same rate of spending, it can actually help you, by showing a low rate of credit usage. An increase in your credit line might be harmful, though, if you are trying to get a mortgage—it may mean you have too much available credit.

Travel

If you plan to travel outside your normal area, it is a good idea to call your credit card companies and let them know. If you do not call them ahead of time, they may automatically place a stop on your account if they see charges from a location far from home.

IT'S A FACT

The first widely accepted and used plastic credit card was issued by American Express in 1958.

Shopping in Stores

When you shop in a store, always be sure to check the price of an item and make sure that it is the price that rings up at the register. Most states have consumer protection laws that require stores to have accurate registers that ring up the price listed on the item. In many states, if an error is made, you can get a refund of the difference as well as an additional amount, such as 10%. Always bring a sale ad with you when you shop. If you are not charged the correct price, show the clerk the ad and ask that you be given that price. Many states have laws about sale ads, so contact your state attorney general if there is a problem. Check your receipt for errors before you leave the store. Keep your receipts for all purchases. Write on the back of them what they are for, so that you can easily find them if you need them.

When paying with a credit card in a store, be sure your card is returned to you and that it is not left in plain sight while you are paying so anyone can copy the numbers. This may seem like common sense, but it is incredibly easy to let this happen while your mind is on something else.

Some stores will accept competitors' coupons or match their prices, so be sure to ask about this as a way to save some additional money. Always ask about the refund and return policy before you buy. Some stores may only offer store credit on returns, even with a receipt. If a refund is made to your credit card, it must appear within one billing cycle.

Unfortunately, there will be times when you purchase a product that is defective or broken. Your first step should be to return the item to the store at which you purchased it. If you do not receive the type of response you want, use the LETTER TO MERCHANT to request closer consideration of your problem. (see form 6, p.351.) If you still do not receive the service you want and you paid with a credit card, you should contact your credit card company and dispute the charge. You can also contact the *Federal Trade Commission* (FTC) at **www.ftc.gov** or call 877-FTC-HELP. It is important that throughout this process you keep careful records of all phone calls and copies of all correspondence.

Rebates

If you are using a rebate, keep copies of your receipt, UPC symbol, and the rebate form itself. If you do not receive your rebate within the promised time, contact the company and provide copies of all your documentation. You can also file a complaint with the FTC (**www.ftc.gov**). It is a good idea to keep a file in which you save all rebate information. Go through it once a month to check if your rebates have been paid. Throw out your copies when your check arrives. It can sometimes be tempting to buy something you normally would not because it has a rebate. Ask yourself whether the product is worth the price after rebate and whether it is something you really need.

Dispute Resolution Programs

Many consumers and businesses use *dispute resolution programs*— mediation and arbitration—as an alternative to going to court. Some businesses require consumers to arbitrate their disputes and waive their right to go to court. Check your contract or product packaging for details. *Mediation* involves a neutral third party—a *mediator*—who helps you and the other party try to resolve the problem. However, it is up to you and the other party to reach an agreement.

Arbitration is less formal than court, though you and the other party may appear at hearings, present evidence, call witnesses, and question each other's witnesses. Unlike mediation, an arbitrator or panel makes a decision once you have presented your case. The decision may be legally binding.

The following organizations can help you find a program near you.

- Your state attorney general or local consumer protection agency

- Small claims courts and court systems

- Nonprofit dispute resolution organizations

- Bar associations and law school clinics

- Better Business Bureaus

- Association for Conflict Resolution at:

    5151 Wisconsin Ave., NW Suite 500,
    Washington, DC 20016
    202-464-9720
    www.acrnet.org

Some programs are free. Others charge a flat fee or a rate based on your ability to pay.

Shopping from Catalogs or Online

When you shop online or in a catalog, you are protected by the *Mail or Telephone Merchandise Order Rule*. By law, a merchant should ship your order within the time stated in its ads or over the phone. If the merchant does not promise a time, you can expect it to ship your order within thirty days.

The shipment clock begins when the merchant receives a properly completed order, which includes your name, address, and payment (check, money order, or authorization to charge an existing credit account—whether the account is debited at that time or not).

If the merchant is unable to ship your order within the promised time, it must notify you by mail, telephone, or email, give a revised shipping date, and give you the chance to cancel for a full refund or accept the new shipping date. The merchant must allow you to cancel the order without cost, by supplying a prepaid reply card or staffing a toll-free telephone number. If you ignore the option notice, and the delay is thirty days or less, it is assumed that you accept the delay and are willing to wait for the merchandise. If you do not respond and the delay is more than thirty days, the order must be canceled by the thirtieth day of the delay period and a full refund must be issued promptly.

If the merchant cannot meet the revised shipping date, it must notify you again by mail, email, or telephone and give you a new shipping date or cancel your order and give you a refund. The order will be canceled and a refund will be issued promptly unless you indicate by the revised shipping date that you are willing to wait. If you do not respond at all to the second notice, it is assumed that you are not willing to wait, and a full refund must be issued promptly.

When shopping online or by catalog, be sure to keep a copy of your receipt or at least your confirmation number. If you received a confirmation email, make sure you save it.

Refunds

When you purchase something at a store, make sure you understand its refund policy. Many stores will not give a cash refund for something that was purchased by check. Some stores have a strict thirty-day refund policy. If you return the item after the thirty-day period, you will only be eligible for store credit.

Tips for Shopping by Phone, by Mail, or Online

- Consider your experience with the company or its general reputation before you order. If you have never heard of the seller, check on its actual location and find out about its reputation with the local Better Business Bureau or the state attorney general's office. If ordering from a website, make sure it is a secure site for ordering purposes.

- Ask about the company's refund and return policies, the product's availability, and the total cost of your order before you place your order.

- Get a shipment date and write it down so you can remember it.

- Keep records of your order, such as the ad or catalog from which you ordered; the company's name, address, and phone number; any shipment representation the company made to you and when it made it; the date of your order; a copy of the order form you sent to the company or, if you are ordering by phone, a list of the items and their stock codes and the order confirmation code or your confirming email; your canceled check or the charge or debit statement showing the charge for your order; and, any communications to or from the company.

- Track the shipment. Many websites allow you to log into their site and view your item's status. Keep an eye on when an item is due to be shipped. If you do not receive your order in a timely way, follow up. Many sites provide you with a shipping tracking number so that you can log onto **www.FedEx.com** or **www.UPS.com** to see exactly when your item will be delivered.

Gift Cards

Gift cards are growing in popularity. If you receive a gift card, make sure you find out if there are any restrictions on the card. Some gift cards begin to lose their value after a certain period of time. If your gift card is to a store that does not exist in your area or is something you do not want, you can sell or trade the card online at sites such as **www.plasticjungle.com** or **www.cardavenue.com**. Another concern with gift cards is that the store in question could go out of business before you can use it. This is usually a concern with smaller local stores.

Resolving Problems with Telephone or Online Merchants

If you have other problems with your purchase, try to resolve your dispute with the company using the LETTER TO MERCHANT. (see form 6, p.351.) If that does not work, the following resources may be helpful.

- State and local consumer protection offices—contact the offices in your home state and where the company is located.

- The Direct Marketing Association (DMA) at:

  DMA Mail Order Action Line
  1120 Avenue of the Americas
  New York, NY 10036
  212-768-7277

- Postal inspectors—call your local post office and ask for the inspector in charge.

- The FTC at **www.ftc.gov** or 877-FTC-HELP.

IT'S A FACT

The most popular type of credit card is Visa, followed by MasterCard, American Express, and Discover.

Merchandise You Never Received

If you ordered something, never received it, and were billed for it, your first course of action should be to report this to your credit card company, since many companies prohibit merchants from charging a card until merchandise has been shipped. Follow the procedure previously described for reporting the error to your credit card company in writing.

If the merchandise has been delayed, tell the credit card company you were not told of this at the time of order and did not know you would be charged in advance. Tell the company the date of estimated delivery, so that your time to dispute the charge can begin on that date, not on the date of the actual charge to your account.

The rules for debit cards are different (and are covered by the *Electronic Fund Transfer Act*) and do not offer the same protections as when you use a credit card. You should check with your debit card issuer to find out what protections it offers you.

If you financed your purchase through the merchant, you may still have some protections. Check your credit contract for the following language.

Note: *Any holder of this consumer credit contract is subject to all claims and defenses that the debtor could assert against the seller of goods or services obtained with the proceeds hereof.*

This language means that you may be able to claim that the seller failed to deliver the goods as stated in your credit contract.

Merchandise You Did Not Order

If you receive merchandise that you did not order, you have several options. You can simply refuse to accept the package, by marking it "Refused" and returning it to the mail carrier, or by refusing to accept delivery from the private service delivery person.

You can open the package and return it for a refund. If you do this, you will likely have to pay return postage, at least until you can get that amount refunded to you by the seller, which it must do if it sent you something you did not order. If the merchandise was sent to you as part of a club (where you receive certain items each month), make sure that you have your membership canceled.

eBay Purchases

When you bid on an item through eBay or another online auction site, you are entering into a contract for a sale. You cannot change your mind and decide not to buy the item should you win the auction. Before making any online auction bid, you should do the following.

- Check the seller's rating and comments to make sure he or she is a reputable seller.

- Verify the shipping charges.

- Read the website's return policy so you understand what your options are should the item arrive damaged or not as described.

- Remember that if you bid on several items, there is a chance you could end up winning all of them and having to pay for all of them.

For more information on being a wise consumer, see:

- The Federal Citizen Information Center at **www.pueblo. gsa.gov**

- The Consumer Federation of America at **www.consumer fed.org**

- Consumers' Union at **www.consumersunion.org**

- The National Consumers League at **www.natlconsumers league.org**

- Call for Action (an international nonprofit network of consumer hotlines) at **www.callforaction.org**

- The Better Business Bureau at **www.bbb.org**

CREDIT SCORES   3

Your credit score is a number that rates your overall credit. There is a lot of confusion and misinformation about credit scores, but because they are crucially important, it is essential that you understand what they are and how they work.

How a Credit Score is Calculated

Your *credit score* or *rating* is a number between about 300 and 850 that summarizes your credit worthiness. This score is often referred to as a *FICO score*, because *Fair Isaac and Company* developed it. Other names for it are a *Beacon score*, *Plus score*, *Score Power*, or an *Empirica score*. Credit scores came into being in the 1990s as a mortgage underwriting tool. They are now used by creditors across the board.

The current average U.S. credit score is 692. A score over 720 is considered to be very good and qualifies you for the best interest rate. Each credit report from the three major credit reporting agencies (see the next chapter for information) will have a credit score attached to it based on the information that is in the report. It is possible to have different scores for the different reports, because the information contained in them may be different.

Your score is based on all the information in your credit report and is a quick rating to sum up your overall credit health. The score is calculated by looking at:

- your payment history;

- amounts currently payable;

- how long you have had a credit history;

- the type of credit accounts you have;

- how many open accounts you have;

- how many inquiries there are on your account; and,

- how new your accounts are.

In general, about 35% of the score is based on your payment history, 30% is based on outstanding debt, 15% has to do with how long you have had credit, 10% is related to the number of *inquiries* (requests by potential creditors for information about your credit report), and 10% has to do with the types of credit you currently have. Fair Isaac does not consider whether you have attended credit counseling in calculating your score. However, creditors who create their own scores can do so.

Note that while the number of inquiries on your account does impact your score, a number of inquiries within a thirty-day period from similar lenders will not hurt your score. So if you are shopping for a car and apply for three different car loans to be able to compare, this will not hurt your credit score. Fair Isaac counts all of these inquiries as one.

Credit scores may not consider or be based on your race, color, religion, national origin, sex, or marital status, or whether you receive public assistance or exercise any consumer right under the federal *Equal Credit Opportunity Act* or the *Fair Credit Reporting Act*.

In order for your score to be calculated, you must have at least one account that has been open for a minimum of six months and at least one account that has been updated in the last six months. If you do not meet this requirement, you may not have a credit score yet. A good credit score starts around 680, but the higher, the better. Only about 11% of the population has a score over 800.

Note that individual lenders sometimes calculate a credit score for you themselves, using their own model. That score is used only by that lender and is not available to other lenders or to the three major credit reporting agencies.

VantageScore

In 2006, the three major credit reporting agencies worked together to create a new credit scoring system called *VantageScore*. It was designed to be a more uniform system; scores range from 501 to 990, with anything over 900 being considered the highest level. The score is then translated into a letter grade (A, B, C, and so on). Currently VantageScore is not the industry standard—FICO is. However, should that change, it is important to understand this new system. Whenever you get your credit score, be sure to ask what system the score was created with.

Why Your Credit Score is Important

Your credit score is important because it is the first thing a potential creditor is going to look at when considering your application for credit. Your credit score directly impacts loans and credit you apply for in the future. You may not qualify for a loan if your score is not high enough. Or, you may be charged a higher interest rate because of your credit score. The better your credit score, the easier it will be for you to obtain credit and the more likely it is that the terms of the credit offered to you will be good. A good credit score may also decrease the deposit required by utilities and make it easier to be approved to rent an apartment.

REAL LIFE CREDIT

Ryan had a credit score of 620 and applied for a thirty-year $150,000 mortgage. He qualified for an interest rate of 7.15% because of his credit rating. His monthly payment would be $1,013. However, if his credit score was 760, he would have qualified for a rate of 5.55% and paid only $856 a month. As Ryan's case demonstrates, the higher your score, the better the interest rate and the lower the payments you have to make. You can use the FICO calculator to calculate rates for scores under 620 at **www.myfico.com/ myfico/CreditCentral/LoanRates.asp**.

How to Get Your Credit Score

If a credit score is so important, it seems kind of ridiculous that you do not automatically get it when you get your free credit report (see Chapter 4 for information about obtaining credit reports). If you want to get your credit score, you will have to pay a fee—the federal Fair Credit Reporting Act says it has to be a "reasonable fee"—when ordering your credit report because it is not included in the free annual report. You will want to get your score from each of the three credit reporting agencies, as they each calculate them somewhat differently and can come up with different credit scores for you. It is possible to order just your credit score from companies such as FICO (**www.myfico.com**). *FICO* offers several packages that allow you to track your credit score throughout a year. It also offers an interesting simulator that lets you see how certain actions can potentially affect your credit score. All of this costs money, though, and in general, it is sufficient to see your credit score once a year when you order your credit reports.

If you have recently applied for credit, you can find out what your score is for free by asking the lender. When applying for a mortgage or home equity loan, the lender must give you a copy of the credit report and credit score it received, so you will be able to see it there.

Some credit card companies now offer a free monthly score along with your monthly statement. If you are very concerned about your credit score, this might be something to consider.

To make things confusing, you are entitled to receive two types of credit scores free, but neither of these is exactly what your creditors will see. You can get an *educational score*, which is designed to show you how scoring works, and get some information about how you rate as a credit risk. You are also entitled to get your mortgage score for free.

How to Improve Your Credit Score

There are many things you can do to improve your credit score. Many of these things are the same things you need to do to improve your credit report, because the two are dependent on each other. Consider the following tips.

☐ Try to get your debt-to-credit ratio to about 50%. You want creditors to see that you do not use all your existing credit. You are a much better risk if you do not appear to have all your credit maxed out. This means that if you have credit limits of $10,000 total, you do not want to have balances totaling more than $5,000. However, you should be careful in achieving this debt-to-credit ratio. Even with a 50% debt-to-credit ratio, if you have too much available credit, it can have a negative effect on your credit score, since there is the risk that you could go out tomorrow and charge to your credit limit and then be in way over your head.

☐ Keep old accounts open when possible. The older your accounts are, the better your score will be because you show your reliability over time.

☐ Review your credit report and correct any errors. Incorrect, negative information on your credit report will bring your score down.

☐ Pay your bills on time every single month. Late and missed payments affect your score. Use automatic payments if necessary. A missed payment can take fifty to one hundred points off your score.

☐ Do not open too many new accounts all at once. A flurry of activity with new accounts will damage your score.

☐ If you are denied credit because of your low credit score, you will receive disclosure as to why your score was so low. Read this carefully and take steps to correct or turn around the problems cited.

☐ Pay off debt instead of transferring balances between cards.

☐ Open new accounts only when you really need them.

Unlike with credit reports (see Chapter 4), you have no rights to dispute or change your credit score. To influence your credit score, you have to work on your credit report.

UNDERSTANDING YOUR CREDIT REPORT

4

When people talk about having *bad credit*, what they mean is that they have an unfavorable credit rating or unfavorable items on their credit report that makes it difficult to get new credit. When you find yourself falling behind on payments or you are rejected for credit that you apply for, you should review your credit report. It is also wise as a general policy to review your credit report at least every year. There are many things you can do to improve your credit rating, but you cannot do any of them unless you have your credit report. Your credit report is like your report card in school. It sums up who you are in the eyes of the bureaucracy. To improve your situation, you have to have all the information that is available about you financially. You cannot fix it if you do not know what is broken.

IT'S A FACT

Only 35% of people polled say they regularly check their credit report.

When you get your report, you are going to want to update accounts that have been paid in full or closed and get as many existing accounts listed with a positive rating as is possible. You ideally want to eliminate all negative ratings. You also want to try to upgrade neutral ratings to positive if possible and keep as many positive ratings as you can. (Chapter 5 discusses what you need to change in your report in more detail, as well as how to go about doing it.)

Credit Reporting Agencies

Credit reporting agencies are large corporations that make money by compiling financial information about consumers and selling it to potential lenders and employers. Anyone who has ever applied for a loan or credit of any kind will have a credit file with each of the major credit reporting agencies. People who pay cash for everything may not have anything in their credit report. A credit report lists personal data, employment, credit cards, and debts in a person's name.

How did these people get all this information about you? The information is taken from credit applications you have completed as well as from reports your creditors make about how well you meet your obligations to them.

There are many small credit reporting agencies that are often hired to examine and investigate credit histories by banks or loan agencies. However, they all obtain their information from the same sources—the big three credit reporting agencies:

Equifax
www.equifax.com
To order your report, call: 800-685-1111
To report fraud, call: 888-766-0008
and write:
P.O. Box 740241
Atlanta, GA 30374

Experian
www.experian.com
To order your report, call: 888-EXPERIAN (397-3742)
To report fraud, call: 888-EXPERIAN (397-3742)
and write:
P.O. Box 2104
Allen, TX 75013

TransUnion
www.transunion.com
To order your report, call: 877-322-8228
To report fraud, call: 800-680-7289
and write:
P.O. Box 105281
Atlanta, GA 30348

Additional Services

While your credit report offers valuable information, it is important to realize that credit reporting companies are in the business of making money. In recent years, they have realized that consumers are a big market for them. Thus, you will see that on their websites, they offer a variety of products. (See the next section for information about obtaining free credit reports and scores.) Some agencies offer special services, such as alerting you to changes to your report or credit score. These services are useful for some people, but do not automatically assume you need them. You should consider these services if:

- you have recently been a victim of identity theft;

- you need to improve your report or score very quickly and need to know when changes happen; or,

- you are in a situation where it is worth the expense in order to get frequent updates.

Your Credit Report

Your credit report shows your entire financial life on paper. It lists your Social Security number, current and past addresses, employment, loans, credit cards, mortgages, and all other debts. It shows which accounts are paid in full, which are late, and which are in collection, as well as any liens against you and any bankruptcies you may have filed. Whenever you apply for a loan or a credit card, your credit report is examined by the potential creditor. The report rates your financial status, and the creditor uses it to decide how likely it is you will pay back the money you want to borrow. If your credit report shows many delinquent (late) accounts, a bankruptcy, or more loans than you are capable of paying, you are a bad credit risk. Employers, insurance companies, and child support agencies can obtain your credit report. Since you are judged almost solely on the basis of your credit report, you need to make sure that it is accurate and as positive as possible.

Obtaining Your Credit Report

You can now obtain a free credit report once a year. To obtain it, call 877-322-8228, go online to **www.annualcreditreport.com**, or send a written request to:

Annual Credit Report Request Service
P.O. Box 105283
Atlanta, GA 30348

Note that you must obtain your free report through the government mechanism set up for this. Do not go to the individual credit reporting companies. They do not provide the free report directly. The easiest way to access your report is online. If you do access it this way, be sure to print out the entire report so that you have a hard copy to work with. The site is secure, so you do not need to worry about your information being misused. However, if you do go to the website, make sure you type in the address accurately since someone else could own websites with misspellings that are very similar.

You can obtain one free report from each of the three main reporting agencies every twelve months. Note that if you are married, you and your spouse are each entitled to three free reports per year. If most of your accounts are joint, this means you can actually check the status more frequently. You are not authorized to obtain your spouse's report. If either of you are experiencing credit problems, you should obtain reports for both of you so that you can correct all errors. The free report contains the same information as the purchased reports, but it does *not* contain your credit score.

It may make sense to space out your requests for the reports from the three different companies. For example, get the Experian report now and order the Equifax one in three or four months, so that you can monitor your credit report in an ongoing way. Note that when you order your free credit report, you must enter your Social Security number. The site is secure and your information is protected.

You can obtain additional paid reports from the credit reporting agencies by phone, mail, or online. Use the LETTER REQUESTING CREDIT REPORT to order one by mail. (see form 8, p.354.) You may need to do this if you have already obtained your free report from all three companies and now suspect fraud or an error on your account and need another report immediately.

If you have been denied credit, employment, rental housing, or insurance based on your credit report, you can obtain a free report from each agency within sixty days of the denial.

What Your Credit Report Contains

Your credit report contains personal information about you, including your Social Security number, your past and current addresses and employers, your past and present mortgages, loans, credit cards, installment agreements, and public records about you, such as bankruptcies and liens. The report will list if your accounts are current or thirty, sixty, or ninety days past due. It will also indicate if you have moved without notifying a creditor.

The items listed can be positive, negative, or neutral. Items that are negative, such as an overdue account, can only remain on your credit report for seven years. Bankruptcies may remain on your report for no more than ten years. However, if you apply for a job that pays over $75,000, for credit of $150,000 or more, or life insurance for $150,000 or more, then these previously mentioned negative items will appear on the report without regard to how old the items are. (FCRA, Sec. 1681(c).)

The report also shows what creditors have requested information about you from that credit reporting agency.

Reading and Understanding Your Report

The three credit reporting agencies present credit information in different ways on their reports. If you request your report from all three companies, you will probably find that none of them contain exactly the same information in the same way. Often certain debts are included in one company's report, but left out of another's. To completely review your credit history, you will need to obtain all three reports.

Look at the sample reports reproduced in this chapter starting on page 63. Read the following descriptions to help you interpret them. All three agencies must accept phone calls from consumers with questions about information in a report. Customer service employees are available to help you if there is something you do not understand in your report.

Reading Your Credit Report

Note: *At the time this book was written, the following descriptions were accurate based on the way the agencies were reporting information at the time. However, companies are constantly updating their forms and websites, so the forms used by the agencies may change at any time.*

The forms always contain the same basic information, and if changes are made, they are usually done to make the forms easier to read and understand. These descriptions are based on the online versions of the forms. Forms requested by mail may be organized slightly differently.

Equifax

The Equifax report is the longest of the three. When you view your report online, each section will be on a separate page and you will need to click on links to go to each separate page.

- **Personal Identification Information.** This section gives your basic information, previous addresses, and employment history. It also contains any alerts that have been added to your file about identity theft and an alert if you are on active duty in the military. This section includes a written statement you have provided (if any) explaining your situation (see page 88 for more information about this).

- **Credit Account Information.** This section is a summary of all the following information.

- **Mortgage Accounts.** This section lists mortgages in your name (including home equity loans) and shows the balance, status, and credit limit amounts.

- **Installment Accounts.** This section lists installment loans, such as car loans, and offers balances, dates, status, and credit limits.

- **Revolving Accounts.** These are accounts such as credit cards, and this page shows balances, dates, and status.

- **Other Accounts.** These are accounts that do not fall under any of the previous descriptions.

- **Open Accounts.** This shows accounts that are currently open and active.

- **Closed Accounts.** These are accounts that you have closed and no longer use.

- **Accounts in Good Standing.** This information is repetitive and shows accounts listed elsewhere that are currently not overdue.

- **Accounts Currently Past Due.** These are the accounts that you have missed payments on.

- **Negative Account History.** These are accounts with ongoing payment problems.

- **Inquiries within the Last 12 Months.** These are inquiries made by companies you gave permission to in order to check your credit, such as when you applied for a loan.

- **Account Information Summary.** This lists all the accounts described on previous pages, all together in one place.

- **Inquiries.** These are companies that requested information about you. It separates inquiries that affect your credit rating from those that do not. (For more information about the number of inquiries affecting your rating, see page 46.)

- **Collection Agency Information.** These are accounts that are currently being handled by collection agencies. This offers a very detailed look at the account and provides contact information for the bill collector.

- **Public Record Information.** This section shows bankruptcies, judgments, and liens against you. Detailed information about each listing is provided.

- **Dispute File Information.** This describes the steps to take to dispute information in your report and gives you an important confirmation number you must use when corresponding with Equifax about your report.

(The following information (pages 63–64) is a blank credit report from Equifax.)

EQUIFAX

SAMPLE CREDIT FILE

CREDIT FILE : October 1, 2007

Confirmation # 5556677722

Please address all future correspondence to:

www.investigate.equifax.com
Equifax Information Services LLC
P.O. Box 740256, Atlanta, GA 30348
Phone (800)685-1111 M-F 9:00am to 5:00pm in your time zone

In order to speak with a Customer Service Representative regarding the specific information in this credit file, you must call **WITHIN 60 DAYS** of the date of this credit file **AND** have a copy of this credit file along with the confirmation number.

Personal Identification Information: This section includes your name, current and previous addresses, and any other identifying information reported by your creditors.

Name On File: Mark Allen Customer
Social Security #: 123 - 45 - 6789   Date of Birth: November 8, 1964
Current Address: 123 Main St., Metaire, LA 70005
Previous Address(es): RR 4 Box 27, Sulphur Springs, LA 70726
Last Reported Employment: Owner: Ace Garden Supply

Public Record Information - This section includes public records obtained from local, state and federal courts.

Bankruptcy filed 06/2006: Eastern district of LA: Case or I.D. # 0015458: Type - Personal; Filer - Individual: Current Disposition - Discharged CH-7

Collection Agency Information - This section includes accounts that credit grantors have placed for collection with a collection agency.

Blue Tiger Collection Agency Inc. (555) 703-0020: Collection Reported: Assigned 07/2007 Client -First Bank Colo. Amount $1,831: Status as of 07/2007-In Bankruptcy: Balance: as of 07/2007 -$0:
Individual Account: Account # - 98105444; ADDITIONAL INFORMATION - Bankruptcy Chapter 7

Credit Account Information

*For your security, the last 4 digits of account number(s) have been replaced by an *. This section includes open and closed accounts reported by credit grantors.*

Department Store

Account Number	Date Opened	High Credit	Credit Limit	Terms Duration	Terms Frequency	Months Rev'd	Activity Description	Creditor Classification	
529107200678*	10/1997	$795			Monthly	76			
Items as of / Date Reported	Amount Past Due	Balance	Date of Last Payment	Actual Payment Amount	Scheduled Payment Amount	Date of Last Activity	Date Maj. Del. 1st Rptd.	Charge Off Amount	Deferred Pay Start Date	Balloon Pay Amount	Date Closed
09/2007	$774	08/2007				09/2007			

Current Status - Pays As Agreed; Type of Loan - Credit Card; Whose Account - Individual Account

Finance Company   Phone: (800)555-9200

Account Number	Date Opened	High Credit	Credit Limit	Terms Duration	Terms Frequency	Months Rev'd	Activity Description	Creditor Classification	
2483*	02/1995	$36,381		47 Months	Monthly	78			
Items as of / Date Reported	Amount Past Due	Balance	Date of Last Payment	Actual Payment Amount	Scheduled Payment Amount	Date of Last Activity	Date Maj. Del. 1st Rptd.	Charge Off Amount	Deferred Pay Start Date	Balloon Pay Amount	Date Closed
01/2007	$0			$23		01/2007			07/2003

Current Status - Pays As Agreed; Type of Account - Installment; Whose Account - Individual Account: ADDITIONAL INFORMATION - Account Paid/Zero Balance; Auto

Account History 10/2004 09/2004 08/2004 07/2004 06/2004 05/2004 04/2004 03/2004 02/2004 01/2004 12/2003 11/2003 09/2005 07/2003
with Status Codes 2 2 3 4 3 2 2 1 2 2 2 2

Inquiries that display to companies (may impact your credit score). This section lists companies that requested your credit file. Credit grantors may view these requests when evaluating your credit worthiness. Employment inquiries do not impact your credit score.

Company Information	Inquiry Date(s)
Auto Finance	11/2006
Car Dealer	11/2006

Inquiries that do not display to companies (do not impact your credit score). This section includes inquiries which display only to you and are not considered when evaluating your credit worthiness. Examples of this inquiry type include a pre-approved offer of credit, insurance, or periodic account review by an existing creditor.

Company Information - Prefix Descriptions:

PRM - Inquiries with this prefix indicate that only your name and address were given to a credit grantor so they can provide you a firm offer of credit or insurance. (PRM inquiries remain for twelve months.)
AM or AR - Inquiries with these prefixes indicate a periodic review of your credit history by one of your creditors.
Equifax or EFX - Inquiries with these prefixes indicate Equifax's activity in response to your contact with us for a copy of your credit file or a research request.
ND - Inquiries with this prefix are general inquiries that do not display to credit grantors. (ND inquiries remain for twelve months.)

Company Information	Inquiry Date(s)	
Equifax	03/2007	02/2007
PRM-Financial	03/2007	11/2006
AR-Credit	12/2006	11/2006	07/2006	05/2006

Account Column Title Descriptions

1. The account number reported by credit grantor
2. The date that the credit grantor opened the account
3. The highest amount charged
4. The highest amount permitted
5. The number of installments or payments
6. The scheduled time between payments
7. The number of months reviewed
8. The most recent account activity
9. The type of company reporting the account
10. The month and year of the last account update
11. The total amount owed as of the date reported
12. The amount past due as of the date reported
13. The date of last payment
14. The actual amount of last payment
15. The requested amount of last payment
16. The date of the last account activity
17. The date the 1st major delinquency was reported
18. The amount charged off by creditor
19. The 1st payment due date for deferred loans
20. The amount of final balloon payment
21. The date of final balloon payment
22. The date the account was closed

Account Status Code Descriptions

1. 30-59 days past due
2. 60-89 days past due
3. 90-119 days past due
4. 120-149 days past due
5. 150-179 days past due
6. 180 or more days past due
G. Collection Account
H. Foreclosure
J. Voluntary Surrender
K. Repossession
L. Charge Off

Commonly Asked Questions About Credit Files

Q. How can I correct a mistake in my credit file ?
A. Complete the Research Request form and give details of the information you believe is incorrect. We will then check with the credit grantor, collection agency or public record source to see if any error has been reported. Information that cannot be verified will be removed from your file. If you and a credit grantor disagree on any information, you will need to resolve the dispute directly with the credit grantor who is the source of the information in question.

Q. Why doesn't my credit information from Equifax match that of Experian and TransUnion ?
A. Credit information providers do not share your credit data with each other. As a result, updates made to your Equifax credit file may not be reflected on reports from Experian and TransUnion. You will need to contact the other credit reporting agencies directly to correct any inaccurate information. Contact information is provided below:

TransUnion, PO Box 1000, Chester, PA 19022 Phone: (800) 888-4213

Experian, P.O. Box 9530 Allen, TX 75013 Phone: (888) 397-3742

Q. If I do have credit problems, is there someplace where I can get advice and assistance ?
A. Yes, there are a number of organizations that offer assistance. For example, the Consumer Credit Counseling Service (CCCS) is a non-profit organization that offers free or low-cost financial counseling to help people solve their financial problems. CCCS can help you analyze your situation and work with you to develop solutions. There are more than 600 CCCS offices throughout the country. Call 1 (800) 388-2227 for the telephone number of the office nearest you.

Q. Once the fraud alert is added to my credit file, who will contact me to verify if an application is legitimate ?
A. When the credit grantor accesses your credit file, they should contact you as a part of their credit application approval process.

Facts You Should Know

• Payment history on your credit file is supplied by credit grantors with whom you have credit. This includes both open accounts and accounts that have already been closed. Payment in full does not remove your payment history. The length of time information remains in your credit file is shown below:
　Collection Accounts: Remain for 7 years.
　Credit Accounts:Accounts paid as agreed remain for up to 10 years. Accounts not paid as agreed remain for 7 years.
　(The time periods listed above are measured from the date in your credit file shown in the "date of last activity" field accompanying the particular credit or collection account.)
　Public Records: Remain for 7 years from the date filed, except:
　　• Bankruptcy-Chapters 7 and 11 remain 10 years from the date filed.
　　• Bankruptcy-Chapter 13 dismissed or no disposition rendered remain 10 years from the date filed.
　　• Unpaid tax liens remain indefinitely.
　　• Paid tax liens remain for up to 7 years from the date released.

　New York State Residents Only: Satisfied judgments remain 5 years from the date filed; paid collections remain 5 years from the "date of last activity".
　California State Residents Only: Unpaid tax liens remain 10 years from the date filed.

• Many companies market consumer products and services by mail. Millions of people take advantage of these direct marketing opportunities because it is a convenient way to shop. If you prefer to reduce the number of direct marketing mailings, you can write to: Direct Marketing Association, Mail Preference Service, P.O. Box 9008, Farmingdale, NY 11735-9008. To request that your name be removed from Direct Marketing Association member lists, include your complete name, full address and signature.

• Name, address, and Social Security number information may be provided to businesses that have a legitimate need to locate or identify a consumer.

• To protect your information from misuse, you should monitor any change in mail receipt patterns. Ensure that documents containing personal data or account numbers are destroyed or made illegible before disposing of them. Do not preprint checks or other documents with unique identifiers such as your driver's license or Social Security number. Never give out your account number or identifying information on phone calls in which you did not initiate the contact.

• To have a fraud alert removed from your credit file, identification information, such as, a copy of your driver's license or utility bill reflecting your current address along with a copy of your Social Security card must be provided.

Notice: Dispute Review Process and Your Rights:

Upon receipt of your dispute, we first review and consider the relevant information you have submitted regarding the nature of your dispute. If that review does not resolve your dispute and further investigation is required, notification of your dispute, including the relevant information you submitted, is provided to the source that furnished the disputed information. The source reviews the information provided, conducts an investigation with respect to the disputed information, and reports the results back to us. The credit reporting agency then makes deletions or changes to your credit file as appropriate based on the results of the reinvestigation. The name and address and, if reasonably available, the phone number of the furnisher(s) of information contacted while processing your dispute(s) is shown under the Results of Your Investigation section on the cover letter that accompanies the copy of your revised credit file.

If you still disagree with an item after it has been verified, you may send to us a brief statement, not to exceed 100 words (200 words for Maine residents) explaining the nature of your disagreement. Your statement will become part of your credit file and will be disclosed each time your credit file is accessed.

If the reinvestigation results in a change to or deletion of the information you are concerned about, or you submit a statement in accordance with the preceding paragraph, you have the right to request that we send your revised credit file to any company that received your credit file in the past 6 months for any purpose (12 months for California, Colorado, Maryland, New Jersey and New York residents) or in the past two years for employment purposes.

The FBI has named identity theft as the fastest growing crime in America.
Protect yourself with Equifax Credit Watch TM , a service that monitors your credit file every business day and notifies you within 24 hours of any activity. To order, go to: *www.creditwatch.equifax.com*

EQUIFAX

Experian

The following Experian sample report has notes on the side to help you interpret it.

- **Header.** The report begins with personal information and provides a report number you need for further correspondence about the report.

- **Potentially Negative Items.** These are past-due accounts and judgments, bankruptcies, and liens. You can view the details of these accounts and records here.

- **Credit Items.** This is a listing of your creditor accounts, and it provides dates, status, and amounts.

- **Accounts in Good Standing.** These are accounts that are current and not overdue.

- **Requests for Your Credit History.** This section shows requests for information about you that affect your credit rating (those requests that you authorized) and requests that do not impact your rating.

- **Personal Information.** Your name, address, Social Security number, employers, and past addresses are listed here.

- **Your Personal Statement.** This is the space for a statement you can write explaining your report.

experian®

Online Personal Credit Report from Experian for

Experian credit report prepared for
JOHN Q CONSUMER
Your report number is
1562064065   **1**
Report date:
01/24/2005

Index:
- Potentially negative items
- Accounts in good standing
- Requests for your credit history
- Personal Information
- Important message from Experian   **2**
- Contact us

Experian collects and organizes information about you and your credit history from public records, your creditors and other reliable sources. Experian makes your credit history available to your current and prospective creditors, employers and others as allowed by law, which can expedite your ability to obtain credit and can make offers of credit available to you. We do not grant or deny credit; each credit grantor makes that decision based on its own guidelines.

Potentially Negative Items   **3**   Back to top

Public Records

Credit grantors may carefully review the items listed below when they check your credit history. Please note that the account information connected with some public records, such as bankruptcy, also may appear with your credit items listed later in this report.

MAIN COUNTY CLERK

Address:	Identification Number:	Plaintiff:
123 MAINTOWN S	1	ANY COMMISSIONER O.
BUFFALO , NY 10000		

Status:		Status Details:
Civil claim paid.		This item was verified and updated on 06-2001.

Date Filed:	Claim Amount:
10/15/2000	$200
Date Resolved:	Liability
01/04/2001	Amount:
	NA
Responsibility:	
INDIVIDUAL	

Credit Items

For your protection, the last few digits of your account numbers do not display.

ABCD BANKS

Address:	Account Number:
100 CENTER RD	1000000....
BUFFALO, NY 10000	
(000) 000-0000	
Status: Paid/Past due 60 days.	**4**

Date Opened:	Type:	Credit Limit/Original Amount:
10/1997	Installment	$523
Reported Since:	Terms:	High Balance:
11/1997	12 Months	NA
Date of Status:	Monthly	Recent Balance:
01/1999	Payment:	$0 as of 01/1999
	$0	Recent Payment:
Last Reported:	Responsibility:	$0
01/1999	Individual	

Account History:
60 days as of 12-1998
30 days as of 11-1998

Report number:

You will need your report number to contact Experian online, by phone or by mail.

Index:

Navigate through the sections of your credit report using these links.

Potentially negative items:

Items that creditors may view less favorably. It includes the creditor's name and address, your account number (shortened for security), account status, type and terms of the account and any other information reported to Experian by the creditor. Also includes any bankruptcy, lien and judgment information obtained directly from the courts.

Status:

Indicates the current status of the account.

If you believe information in your report is inaccurate, you can dispute that item quickly, effectively and cost free by using Experian's online dispute service located at:

www.experian.com/disputes

Disputing online is the fastest way to address any concern you may have about the information in your credit report.

MAIN COLL AGENCIES

Address:	Account Number:	Original Creditor:
PO BOX 123	0123456789	TELEVISE CABLE COMM
ANYTOWN, PA 10000		
(555) 555 5555		

Status: Collection account. $95 past due as of 4 2000.

Date Opened:	Type:	Credit Limit/Original Amount:
01/2000	Installment	$95
Reported Since:	Terms:	High Balance:
04/2000	NA	NA
Date of Status:	Monthly	Recent Balance:
04/2000	Payment:	$95 as of 04/2000
	$0	Recent Payment:
Last Reported:	Responsibility:	$0
04/2000	Individual	

Your statement: ITEM DISPUTED BY CONSUMER

Account History:
Collection as of 4-2000

Accounts in Good Standing   **5**   back to top

AUTOMOBILE AUTO FINANCE

Address:	Account Number:
100 MAIN ST F	12345678998
SMALLTOWN, MD xxxxx	
(xxx) xxx-xxxx	

Status: Open/Never late

Date Opened:	Type:	**6**	Credit Limit/Original Amount:
01/2000	Installment		$10,355
Reported Since:	Terms:		High Balance:
01/2000	65 Months		NA
Date of Status:	Monthly		Recent Balance:
08/2001	Payment:		$7,984 as of 08/2001
	$210		Recent Payment:
Last Reported:	Responsibility:		$0
08/2001	Individual		

MAIN

Address:	Account Number:
PO BOX 1234	123456/8998/6
FORT LAUDERDALE, FL 10009	

Status: Closed/Never late.

Date Opened:	Type:	Credit Limit/Original Amount:
03/1991	Revolving	NA
Reported Since:	Terms:	High Balance:
03/1991	1 Months	$3,228
Date of Status:	Monthly	Recent Balance:
08/2000	Payment:	$0 /paid as of 08/2000
	$0	Recent Payment:
Last Reported:	Responsibility:	$0
08/2000	Individual	

Your statement:
Account closed at consumer's request

Accounts in good standing:

Lists accounts that have a positive status and may be viewed favorably by creditors. Some creditors do not report to us, so some of your accounts may not be listed.

Type:

Account type indicates whether your account is a revolving or an installment account.

Requests for Your Credit History   `7`   back to top

Requests Viewed By Others

We make your credit history available to your current and prospective creditors and employers as allowed by law. Personal data about you may be made available to companies whose products and services may interest you.

The section below lists all who have requested in the recent past to review your credit history as a result of actions involving you, such as the completion of a credit application or the transfer of an account to a collection agency, mortgage or loan application, etc. Creditors may view these requests when evaluating your creditworthiness.

HOMESALE REALTY CO

Address: Date of Request:
2000 S MAINROAD BLVD STE   07/16/2001
ANYTOWN CA 11111
(555) 555-5555
Comments:
Real estate loan on behalf of 1000 CORPORATE COMPANY. This inquiry is scheduled to continue on record until 8-2003.

ABC BANK

Address: Date of Request:
PO BOX 100   02/23/2001
BUFFALO NY 10000
(555) 555-5555
Comments:
Permissible purpose. This inquiry is scheduled to continue on record until 3-2003.

ANYTOWN FUNDING INC

Address: Date of Request:
100 W MAIN AVE STE 100   07/25/2000
INTOWN CA 10000
(555) 555-5555
Comments:
Permissible purpose. This inquiry is scheduled to continue on record until 8-2002.

Requests Viewed Only By You

The section below lists all who have a permissible purpose by law and have requested in the recent past to review your information. You may not have initiated these requests, so you may not recognize each source. We offer information about you to those with a permissible purpose, for example, to

- other creditors who want to offer you preapproved credit;
- an employer who wishes to extend an offer of employment;
- a potential investor in assessing the risk of a current obligation;
- Experian or other credit reporting agencies to process a report for you;
- your existing creditors to monitor your credit activity (date listed may reflect only the most recent request)

We report these requests only to you as a record of activities. We do not provide this information to other creditors who evaluate your creditworthiness.

MAIN BANK USA

Address: Date of Request:
1 MAIN CTR AA 11   08/10/2001
BUFFALO NY 10000

MAINTOWN BANK

Address: Date of Request:
PO BOX 100   08/05/2001
MAINTOWN UL 10000
(555) 555-5555

ANYTOWN DATA CORPS

Address: Date of Request:
2000 S MAINTOWN BLVD STE   07/16/2001
INTOWN CO 11111
(555) 555-5555

Requests for your credit history:

Also called "inquiries", requests for your credit history are logged on your report whenever anyone reviews your credit information. There are two types of inquiries.

Requests viewed by others

Inquiries resulting from a transaction initiated by you. These include inquiries from your applications for credit, housing or other loans. They also include transfer of an account to a collection agency. Creditors may view these items when evaluating your creditworthiness.

Requests viewed only by you

Inquiries resulting from transactions you may not have initiated but that are allowed under the FCRA. These include preapproved offers, as well as for employment, investment review, account monitoring by existing creditors, and requests by you for your own report. These items are shown only to you and have no impact on your creditworthiness or risk scores.

Sample Credit Report   Page 4 of 4

Personal Information   [8]

The following information is reported to us by you, your creditors and other sources. Each source may report your personal information differently, which may result in variations of your name, address, Social Security number, etc. As part of our fraud-prevention program, a notice with additional information may appear. As a security precaution, the Social Security number that you used to obtain this report is not displayed. The Geographical Code shown with each address identifies the state, county, census tract, block group and Metropolitan Statistical Area associated with each address.

Personal information associated with your history that has been reported to Experian by you, your creditors and other sources.

Names:
JOHN Q CONSUMLR
JONATHON Q CONSUMER
J Q CONSUMER

Social Security number variations:
999999999

Year of birth:
1954

Employers:
ARDDF ENGINEERING CORP

Telephone numbers:
(555) 595 5555 Residential

Address: 120 MAIN STREET
ANYTOWN, MD 90001-9999
Type of Residence: Multifamily
Geographical Code: 0-15b510-31-8840   [9]

Address: 555 SIMPLE PLACE
ANYTOWN, MD 90002-7777
Type of Residence: Single family
Geographical Code: 0-176510-33-8840

Address: 999 HIGH DRIVE APT 15B
ANYTOWN, MD 90000-5555
Type of Residence: Apartment complex
Geographical Code: 0-15b510-31-8840

May include name and Social Security number variations, employers, telephone numbers, etc. Experian lists all variations so you know what is being reported to us as belonging to you.

Address information:

Your current address and previous address(es)

Your Personal Statement   [10]

No general personal statements appear on your report.

Personal statement:

Any personal statement that you added to your report appears here.

Important Message From Experian   back to top

By law, we cannot disclose certain medical information (relating to physical, mental, or behavioral health or condition). Although we do not generally collect such information, it could appear in the name of a data furnisher (i.e., "Cancer Center") that reports your payment history to us. If so, those names display in your report, but in reports to others they display only as MEDICAL PAYMENT DATA. Consumer statements included on your report at your request that contain medical information are disclosed to others.

Note - statements remain as part of the report for 2 years and display to anyone who has permission to review your report.

Contacting Us   back to top

Contact address and phone number for your area will display here.

TransUnion

The following TransUnion report is similar to the Experian report, but it is visually more friendly with buttons illustrating past due dates.

- **Personal Information.** Your address, Social Security number, and employment information is included here.

- **Public Records.** Bankruptcies, liens, and judgments appear in this section.

- **Adverse Accounts.** These are accounts that are past due or negative. Note the key above this that shows the meaning of the buttons.

- **Satisfactory Accounts.** These are your accounts that are not past due or negative.

- **Regular Inquiries.** These are inquiries into your credit standing that affect your credit rating.

- **Inquiry Analysis.** These are requests for your report by people who provided information about you when inquiring.

- **Promotional Inquiries.** These are inquiries that do not affect your credit rating.

- **Account Review Inquiries.** These are companies that reviewed your account when you requested it or in order to do a transaction with you (such as paying off an account balance).

- **Consumer Statement.** This is the space for the statement you can provide that explains your report.

- **Special Messages.** Alerts about identity fraud would appear here.

Credit Reports
May 5, 2007

PERSONAL INFORMATION

CREDIT REPORTING AGENCY:	TransUnion.	experian	EQUIFAX
NAME: ALSO KNOWN AS:	JANE SMITH	JANE SMITH	JANE SMITH
DATE OF BIRTH:	01/1956	01/1956	01/1956
CURRENT ADDRESS:	12345 MAIN ST ANY TOWN, CA 12345 06/01/2005	12345 MAIN ST ANY TOWN, CA 12345 06/01/2005	12345 MAIN ST ANY TOWN, CA 12345 06/01/2005
PREVIOUS ADDRESS:	54321 1ST STREET ANY TOWN, CA 12345 05/10/2004	54321 1ST STREET ANY TOWN, CA 12345 05/10/2004	54321 1ST STREET ANY TOWN, CA 12345 05/10/2004
	123 SOUTH MAIN ST HOLLYWOOD, FL 54321 06/05/2001	123 SOUTH MAIN ST HOLLYWOOD, FL 54321 08/1998	123 SOUTH MAIN ST HOLLYWOOD, FL 54321 06/2001
EMPLOYER:	TRANSUNION 06/01/2004		

CONSUMER STATEMENT

NONE REPORTED

SUMMARY

	TransUnion	Experian	Equifax
TOTAL ACCOUNTS:	9	9	9
OPEN ACCOUNTS:	5	5	5
CLOSED ACCOUNTS:	4	4	4
DELINQUENT:	0	0	0
DEROGATORY:	0	0	0
BALANCES:	11,123	11,123	11,123
PAYMENTS:	56	56	56
PUBLIC RECORDS:	0	0	0
INQUIRIES:	1	1	1

CREDITOR CONTACTS

Creditor Name	Address	Phone Number
CAPITAL 1 BNK	11013 W BROAD ST GLEN ALLEN , VA 23060	
CHASE	BANK ONE CARD SERV 800 BROOKSEDGE BLV WESTERVILLE , OH 43081	(800) 955 - 9900
HOUSEHOLD BNK		(800) 921-1234
DIRECT LOAN SVC SYSTEM	501 BLEEKER STREET UTICA , NY 13502	
COLLEGE LOAN CORP	C/O ACS 501 B UTICA , NY 13501	
CITI CARDS CBSDNA	POB 6241 SIOUX FALLS , SD 57117	(800) 843 - 0777

ACCOUNT HISTORY

At-a-glance viewing of your payment history

	OK	30	60	90	120	150	PP	RF	CO
Not Applicable	Unknown	Current	30 days late	60 days late	90 days late	120 days late	150+ days late	Payment plan	Repossession Foreclosure	Collection Chargeoff

Real Estate Accounts: Primary and secondary mortgages on your home
None Reported

Revolving Accounts: Accounts with an open-end term

CAPITAL 1 BK   More about this

	TransUnion	Experian	Equifax
Account No.:	12345678****	12345678****	12345678****
Condition:	Closed	Closed	Open (Paid)
Balance:	$0	$0	$0
Types:	Credit Card	Credit Card	Credit Card
Pay Status:	Current	Current	Current

Two Year Payment History:

TransUnion	OK OK OK OK OK OK OK OK OK OK OK OK OK OK OK OK OK OK OK OK OK OK OK OK
Experian	OK OK OK OK OK OK OK OK OK OK OK OK OK OK OK OK OK OK OK OK OK OK OK
Equifax	OK OK OK OK OK OK OK OK OK OK OK OK OK OK OK OK OK OK OK OK OK OK

CHASE

More about this

	TransUnion	Experian	Equifax
Account No.:	12345678****	12345678****	12345678****
Condition:	Closed	Closed	Open (Paid)
Balance:	$0	$0	$0
Types:	Credit Card	Credit Card	Credit Card
Pay Status:	Current	Current	Current

Two Year Payment History:

TransUnion	OK OK OK OK OK OK OK OK OK OK OK OK OK OK OK OK OK OK OK OK OK OK OK OK
Experian	OK OK OK OK OK OK OK OK OK OK OK OK OK OK 90 OK OK OK OK OK OK OK OK OK
Equifax	OK OK OK OK OK OK OK OK OK OK OK OK OK OK OK OK OK OK OK OK OK OK

Other Accounts: Accounts in which the exact category is unknown
None Reported

Collection Accounts: Accounts seriously past due
None Reported

PUBLIC INFORMATION

None Reported

INQUIRIES

Creditor Name	Date of Inquiry	Credit Bureau
CAPITAL 1 BNK	05/31/2005	TRANSUNION
CHASE	02/12/2005	EQUIFAX
HOUSEHOLD BNK	02/17/2005	TRANSUNION

Your Spouse and Your Report

If you are still unclear about anything on your own credit report, do not hesitate to call the company that prepared it. Credit reporting agencies are not your creditors, and they will not harass you for money if you call them. Call and ask for an explanation of whatever you do not understand.

You and your spouse are considered to be two separate entities in terms of your credit. However, you have the right to have each other's credit information appear on each other's reports. This may be a good idea if one of you has poor credit and the other has terrific credit. Use the LETTER REQUESTING MERGER OF SPOUSE'S REPORT to request that an agency do this. (see form 9, p.355.) You also have the right to have each other's negative reports removed from each other's files. If your spouse has terrible credit and it shows up on your report, you need to request that it be removed from yours. Then you can use your good credit to apply for loans and credit cards that can benefit you both. Use the LETTER REQUESTING INDIVIDUALIZATION OF CREDIT REPORT. (see form 10, p.356.)

What Makes a Good Credit Report

In general, the following factors make for a good credit report:

- no more than eleven accounts, open or closed, on the report;

- no more than one change of address on the report;

- steady employment;

- regular payments;

- no overdue payments, no defaults, no foreclosure, no late fees;

- low balances; and,

- a credit score of at least 680.

Some people think that they will have a better credit report if they have no balances due on anything. In fact, you are a more attractive customer if you have successfully carried balances and made regular payments without any delinquencies.

The following things make financial sense, but in fact can look bad on a credit report.

- Opening accounts to get special offers (for example, 15% off your purchases with a new account) and then closing them after paying the balance. While this is a deal, it increases the number of accounts on your credit report and in fact looks bad for the consumer. It is okay to do this if you have good credit, but if your credit is questionable, it will only make it worse.

- Applying for credit you probably do not need and will not use, just so you can have it as an emergency line of credit. This simply adds to your available credit and may make it difficult for you to get other credit you genuinely need.

- Using a credit card for a lot of purchases to take advantage of convenience and the thirty-day grace period and then paying off the balance each month. While this offers convenience and does not cost you any interest, future creditors who get your report will only see the current balance on the account and will not realize you pay it off each month. This will appear as a large balance.

- Consolidating student loans. While this may get you a better interest rate and offer the convenience of one payment per month, it increases the number of accounts on your report. The more accounts you have, the lower your credit score.

Note: *Taking special offers, paying your balance in full every month, and consolidating loans have advantages that more often outweigh the disadvantages. However, you should be aware of the effect they have on your credit report and make the decision that is best for your personal situation.*

CHANGING YOUR CREDIT REPORT

5

Now that you have learned what a credit report contains and how to obtain yours, you need to look over yours very closely. Organize all the debt information that you used to complete the **DEBT ASSESSMENT** worksheet in Chapter 1. (see form 2, p.347.) Compare this information to the information on your three separate credit reports. Check everything, from account numbers to high balances to payment dates. To compare some of this information, you are going to have to sort through some of your old records. If the items on the report are favorable, do not worry too much about cross-checking them (unless they are accounts that you know are closed, but are not listed as closed on the report). If they are negative, you should examine them very closely for errors.

IT'S A FACT!

Studies have shown that 70% of credit reports contain serious errors.

Disputing Bills

While this chapter is primarily about how to change your credit report, it is important to understand how to deal with incorrect charges on credit cards and other bills. Resolving these problems *before* they affect your credit report is the simplest and best way to maintain good credit. Remember, as a consumer, it is your right to insist that the bills you receive are accurate. You are not asking for a favor or stepping outside your bounds. It is the creditor's responsibility to ensure that your bills are correct.

Credit Cards

If you find an error on a current credit card bill—not a credit report, but an actual bill from one of your credit cards—you need to:

- contact your credit card company immediately—remember, credit reporting agencies do not handle these disputes, so you have to contact the credit card company; and,

- send a LETTER TO CREDITOR REGARDING BILLING ERROR. (see form 11, p.357.)

A phone call is not the way to handle this. It is fine to make an initial call to see if the bill can be corrected easily; however, you need to put your concern in writing for the *Fair Credit Billing Act* to cover you on this situation. You must send the letter within *sixty days of the date of the bill* and send it certified mail, return receipt requested. The creditor has thirty days to acknowledge receipt of your letter. Make sure you keep a copy of the letter and that you keep the postage receipt. Make notes of any phone calls you have made to try to resolve the issue as well.

You may withhold payment for a disputed item on the credit card bill (not the whole credit card bill—just the item you are disputing) if:

- the charge is over $50; and,

- the store is within one hundred miles of your residence or is in your state.

Before you do so, you must:

- first attempt to resolve the billing dispute with the store the item is from; and,

- inform the credit card company in writing about the dispute.

The credit card company cannot report your account as delinquent while the dispute is being handled, and it must resolve the dispute within two billing cycles (or ninety days).

Practical Point

Remember to send all correspondence to the address for customer service and not to the address for making payments—call and ask for the address if you cannot find it on your bill.

Other Bills

You should always check other bills for errors as well. Make sure you are being charged for services or goods you used or purchased. If you find an error on a bill, it is okay to call about it, but always follow up a phone call with a letter to document the problem and your telephone call that reported it.

Types of errors you might find include:

- a misreading of your gas or electric meter, leading to an excessively large charge;

- failure to credit a payment you made to an account; or,

- charges for services you did not receive (such as premium cable channels or phone services like call waiting).

Bank Statements

Bank statements are another item you might receive that could contain errors. The errors could include:

- incorrect deposit amounts;

- incorrect withdrawal amounts; or,

- checks cashed against the account in the wrong amount.

If you find a mistake on a bank statement, call the bank. If the call does not resolve your problem, then follow it up with a letter including documentation of the problem. If the problem is not resolved to your satisfaction, follow up with your state banking authority.

Dealing with a Collection Agency

Often a disputed bill will be sent to collection. The first thing you can try is a letter to the collection agency telling it to cease and desist contacting you and that you will only deal with the original creditor. This usually does not work, however. If you are disputing the bill, the next step is to send a request for validation of the debt. You can use a COLLECTION AGENCY VALIDATION LETTER to make this request. (see form 12, p.358.) This forces the agency to prove that it is authorized to collect this debt. If you still believe the agency is trying to collect on something that is incorrect, you should gather documentation of this error and send it to the agency via certified mail. If it continues to try to collect the debt, you need to contact the *Federal Trade Commission* (FTC) or your state attorney general. *Do not* ignore the problem because you know you are right. You may be right, but if the collection agency pursues action against you, you could still end up with a judgment against you if you do nothing.

Correcting Your Credit Report

After obtaining a copy of your credit report, you need to check it carefully for errors, out-of-date information, and items that are misleading. Errors are not at all uncommon on credit reports, so do not assume that yours is correct without completely checking it over.

If you have identified any items on your credit report that you believe are out of date or wrong, you have the right to dispute them under the Fair Credit Reporting Act. You are permitted to dispute any items you reasonably believe to be wrong or incomplete.

To dispute an item, you need to send a letter to the credit agency via certified mail.

Often, credit reporting agencies enclose a form called a *Request for Reinvestigation* or *Request for Dispute Resolution* with your mailed credit report, which you should use since it will be easier for them to process.

Note: *This is not how to submit a personal statement (also called a 100 Word Statement). See page 88 for information about this.*

Practical Point

Keep a log of all correspondence and phone calls. (see form 23, p.374).

You can use the form provided by the credit reporting agencies to list the items you are disputing, or if one has not been enclosed, you can send a letter such as the Letter to Creditor Disputing Credit Report. (see form 13, p.361.) It is best to not dispute more than three items in one letter. If you wish to dispute more then three items, use separate letters for each group of three. A long list of disputes can indicate to the agency that you are not serious and are disputing everything just to make trouble. Include copies of any documents that support your position, such as letters or statements confirming that an account has been paid off or closed.

Generally, the agency has thirty days to contact you after receiving your letter. There is no cost to you to dispute your credit report. This is your legal right, so do not be afraid to exercise it! Disputing an item does not damage your credit rating in any way.

If you do not hear back from the agency within thirty days, send a SECOND REQUEST FOR REINVESTIGATION. (see form 14, p.363.) Once the agency receives your request, it has thirty days to reinvestigate the items you are disputing. If you provide the agency with additional information about the item, then the agency has fifteen extra days to investigate, for a total of forty-five days. If the agency does not respond to your requests, contact the FTC to file a complaint. You can file a complaint using the FTC's online form at:

www.ftccomplaintassistant.gov

The agency is required to consider information and documentation from you as well as contact the creditor whose item you are disputing. Once all the facts have been reviewed, the agency must:

- give you the results of the reinvestigation within five days of its completion;

- remove the item you are disputing if you are correct or if it is unverifiable (most creditors destroy records after twenty-five months, so it is very possible that the item you are disputing can no longer be verified);

- ensure that an item that was corrected does not incorrectly reappear on your report; and,

- provide you with a copy of your corrected report.

If the agency determines that the item you are disputing is correct and that you are wrong, then it will remain on the report.

If your report is corrected, the agency must send a copy of the corrected report to any creditor who has requested your report in the last year and to any employer who has requested it in the last two years.

Wait a few months after your credit report has been corrected, and then request a copy of it—you will need to pay for a copy this time. Verify that the error was corrected and has not reappeared. If it has reappeared—and this does happen—send a letter indicating this to the credit reporting agency and detail the history of the matter. Use the LETTER REQUESTING CORRECTION OF REAPPEARING INCORRECT ITEM. (see form 15, p.364.)

Steps to Take When Dealing with Credit Report Errors

1. Request credit report.

2. Review credit report.

3. Note errors in credit report, and compile evidence you have that proves your position.

4. Send LETTER TO CREDITOR DISPUTING CREDIT REPORT (form 13, p.361).

5. Begin log of correspondence.

6. Wait thirty days.

7. If no response, send SECOND REQUEST FOR REINVESTI-
GATION (form 14, p.363).

8. Wait thirty days (or forty-five days if you provide additional information).

9. If no response, contact the FTC.

10. Once the error has supposedly been corrected, request a
new copy of your credit report to verify correction has
been made.

Disputing after Reinvestigation

If the credit agency determines that it believes an item you are
disputing is in fact correct, it will not remove the item. If you still
believe that the item is wrong, there are further steps you can take
to attempt to have it removed.

First, contact the creditor the item is from. Do so in writing, using
the LETTER TO CREDITOR REGARDING INCORRECT CREDIT REPORT.
(see form 16, p.366.) Send this letter to the customer service department. You can also send this letter to the director of marketing and
to the president or CEO of the company if you wish. Send a copy
of the letter to the credit reporting agency as well. As always, keep
copies of your correspondence and the certified mail receipt.

Follow up your letter with phone calls or in-person visits to the
customer service office.

You are not asking a favor of the creditor; you are insisting that it follow the *Fair Credit Reporting Act* (FCRA), which requires it to provide credit reporting agencies with correct information when it is brought to its attention that it has reported incorrect information. Insist that the law be followed. (FCRA, Secs. 1681(c) and (n).)

Get any correction from the creditor in writing and send it yourself to the credit reporting agency. Do not rely on the creditor to send this information in. Send it with the LETTER SHOWING CREDITOR ERROR. (see form 17, p.367.)

If the creditor is not willing to discuss or deal with your problem, then you should contact a credit reporting agency and ask that it handle this dispute. Agencies have a customer service department that is paid to assist consumers in resolving disputes. If you still get nowhere, you need to hire an attorney to bring a lawsuit. You can also contact your state attorney general's office.

If you are disputing a listing on your credit report of a judgment against you that you have paid in full, you will need to obtain a discharge of the judgment from the creditor who sued you. Use the LETTER REQUESTING DISCHARGE, and mail it to the creditor. (see form 18, p.368.) Once you receive the discharge, file it with the court your case was decided in and also send a copy of it to each of the credit reporting agencies and request that they remove the judgment from your report.

REAL LIFE CREDIT

Michael got his credit report and discovered that his last car loan through his credit union was listed as having several late payments. He had paid the loan off last year when he bought a new car and knew that he had made every payment on time. He sent a letter to the credit reporting agency disputing this listing. The agency replied that this information was the information they had received from the creditor and was correct according to its records. Michael called the credit union. It gave him the dates of the late payments. Michael went through his records and found canceled checks and statements from the credit union showing he had paid and that there was no indication anywhere of a late payment. The credit union agreed to correct the mistake. It sent a letter to the credit reporting agency and also sent a letter to Michael making it clear there were no late payments.

Adding Accounts to Your Credit Report

When you reviewed your credit reports, you may have found that you have accounts that were not listed on the report. If you are trying to build a positive credit report, you may wish to ask the credit reporting agencies to include these accounts on your report. To do so, send the LETTER REQUESTING INCLUSION OF ACCOUNTS to the credit reporting agency along with copies of recent statements of the accounts you want included. (see form 19, p.369.) You can be charged a fee for this, and nothing requires the agencies to honor your request to include the accounts. You may also wish to contact the creditor directly and ask that it report the information to the credit reporting agencies. Note that some creditors simply will not do so. They report only to one or two agencies and will not change their standard business practice.

If your credit report is missing personal information about you, you should send the LETTER REQUESTING ADDITION OF INFORMATION. (see form 20, p.370.) You may wish to ask that updated information about your employment, past and present residences, phone number, date of birth, Social Security number, bank accounts, and investments be included. This type of information can show stability and improve your credit rating. The agencies are not required to add any of this information, but often they will do so at your request. You should enclose something to verify the information you are giving, such as a copy of your driver's license or Social Security card.

Removing Inquiries

If there are inquiries on your credit report that you did not authorize but that appear in the authorized column, you should contact the companies that made them and request that they remove them. You can use the LETTER REQUESTING REMOVAL OF INQUIRY to do this. (see form 21, p.371.) If they do not comply, contact the credit reporting agency that lists the inquiries and notify it that these inquiries were not authorized.

Adding a Statement to Your Credit Report

You have the right to add a *100 word statement* to your credit report to explain something in your report or to point out an error the credit agency will not correct. These statements can be very useful, and add a human explanation for something that is just portrayed in numbers on your credit report.

Understand that although the agency must accept such a statement from you, it is not required to include the entire thing on your credit report and may include only a summary of what you have written. It is important to understand that creditors will often ignore this type of statement and that the statement may end up remaining in your file even after the item you are explaining or disputing is removed. This means that even if the bad credit you are writing about ages off your report, your statement defending it could still remain, which would alert creditors that there was a problem in the past, whereas otherwise they would have no way of knowing about it.

This kind of statement can be useful if you have had temporary financial problems due to losing your job, being in the military, dealing with medical bills, or being unable to work due to illness or caring for an ill family member. Make it short and sweet, and be sure to include good news—that your financial situation has improved because you found a job, recovered, or are no longer caring for the ill family member. Use the LETTER WITH 100 WORD STATEMENT to submit this type of statement to the agency. (see form 22, p.372.) Be sure you only send it to the agency that is reporting the item you wish to explain or dispute since not every credit reporting agency reports about every single one of your creditors.

Sample 100 Word Statement

On May 5 of this year, I was called up to active duty in the

National Guard and shipped to Iraq. This service to our country has significantly reduced my income and ability to make credit card payments and caused me great financial hardship while I fulfill my duty to my country. As soon as I am released from active duty and return to the United States and can return to my job, it is my intention to pay all my debts in full.

Suing a Credit Agency

Sometimes you may request reinvestigation of an incorrect item and the credit agency fails to reinvestigate or leaves the incorrect item on your report despite a reinvestigation that showed it to be incorrect. If you are seriously harmed because of it—for example, you were denied a mortgage or were not hired for a job because of it—the FCRA gives you the right to sue the credit agency.

You have two years after you are harmed by a credit agency's willful or negligent failure to comply with the law to file a lawsuit against it. Your lawsuit can ask for expenses you have incurred because of the error, such as lost wages, attorneys' fees, and court costs, as well as emotional distress you have suffered. You can also sue for punitive damages for malicious acts by the agency against you.

You may also sue a credit reporting agency that refuses to disclose your credit information to you or that gives false information about you. Another possible lawsuit can be based on a credit reporting agency breaking the rules about who they may give your credit report to. You may also sue a creditor who fails to correct billing errors. (FCRA, Sec. 1681(n).)

The laws discussed here are federal laws. Many states have their own laws about creditors and credit reporting agencies. You can also bring a lawsuit under your state law if you meet the requirements set forth in the law.

You will need to consult an attorney who is experienced in this area of law. Contact your local county, city, or state bar association for the name of an attorney experienced in these matters in your area. Many attorneys will handle these types of cases with little or no cash up front and will take a percentage of what you win (called a *contingency*).

To find an attorney who specializes in this area of law, contact the *National Association of Consumer Advocates* at **www.naca.net** or 202-452-1989.

Organizing Your Correspondence

It is important to keep copies of all your correspondence and notes of all phone calls. Get an expandable, divided file folder and keep a section for each creditor, credit agency, or collection agency you deal with. Place a copy of all correspondence you send and all correspondence you receive in the folder. Send all mailed items by certified mail, return receipt requested.

You also need to keep a CORRESPONDENCE LOG (form 23, p.374). Fill out a section of this log each time you receive or send correspondence or have a phone call with a creditor, collection agency, credit reporting agency, attorney, etc. Recording this information makes it easy to determine the status of something and helps you follow up with creditors and credit reporting agencies.

Reducing Your Debt and Improving Cash Flow | 6

If you find yourself with more debt than you can handle, the simplest solution is to reduce the amount of debt you are facing. This is easier said than done because you do not have enough money to pay your bills. However, there are steps you can take to reduce your debt load of which you may not be aware. Reducing your debt will not only get you out of financial trouble, but will also improve your credit report, particularly if it means you will be able to make payments on time for all or most of your obligations.

Prioritizing Your Debts

The first thing you need to do is get out your DEBT ASSESSMENT (form 2, p.347) and look closely at the obligations listed there. Fill out the DEBT PRIORITIZATION form. (see form 24, p.375.) You need to list your debts in order of importance on this form. *Importance* is not determined by who is bothering you the most with calls or letters (however, if this is a problem, read the section in Chapter 1 about your rights as a debtor). Importance is determined by what debt will most negatively impact your life the fastest. You need to think about what effect nonpayment will have on you and your family. You also have to consider how easy it is for the creditor to stop its service or take back the property.

For example, if you are three months behind on your electric bill, it is likely that the electric company will soon turn off your power unless you get it some money. If you cannot make your car payments, your car will be repossessed, but it will not happen immediately. If you are two months behind on your mortgage, the bank's computers will not be happy with you, but because foreclosure is an expensive process, the bank is probably not ready to foreclose yet. If you do not pay your doctor, he or she will eventually refuse to see you and eventually may sue you or send the debt to collection, but you can find another doctor if necessary. Your credit cards are probably at the bottom of your list based on importance. Credit card companies make a lot of noise when they are not paid, but the only thing they can do to you is obtain a judgment in court. This is a process that takes time and is a hassle for them.

IT'S A FACT!

According to the 2007 Consumer Action survey, the average credit card interest rate is 14.53%.

Dealing with Your Creditors

When you are dealing with creditors, you will need to keep very good records. Create a log and write in dates, times, and contact people for phone calls, as well as the status and any details. Include any written correspondence in the log with the same information recorded. (see form 23, p.392.) This way you will have a record of what is going on and can easily find when your last contact was and what the result of it was.

Prioritize

Start at the top of your list of priorities on your DEBT PRIORITIZATION (form 24, p.375) and list how much you have to pay the creditor to keep yourself out of immediate hot water. The electric company may be happy if you pay one month's bill. The bank may be willing to accept 60% of your monthly mortgage payment for a few months. You may not know how much is necessary until you begin to negotiate with the creditor.

Be Aggressive

Many people just want to run and hide from creditors and send in money when they can, hoping it will take care of the problem. The best solution is to be aggressive. If you are not going to be able to make a payment, call *before* it is due. If you are already past due, still call. Call the creditor and tell the representative that you are having money problems. Give the real reason, such as you were laid off from work or are getting a divorce. You should not give them the real reason if it is something like you went on a spending spree or you decided to just take the summer off. You want to appear as a reliable person who has fallen on hard times. Creditors are often sympathetic to consumers with real problems, and you may be pleasantly surprised by the reaction you receive.

Arrange a Payment Plan

When you call, be polite, calm, and firm. Explain that you want to make a payment arrangement. Tell them what you can afford to pay this month and what you can afford to pay next month. Be clear that you intend to make payment in full eventually, even if this is not the case. You can also consider extending your payment plan with smaller payments or arranging to defer payment for one month. Get all payment plans in writing. Use the LETTER REQUESTING PAYMENT PLAN to request a payment plan in writing. (see form 25, p.376.)

Don't Take a Payment Vacation!

From time to time you might receive a letter from a creditor offering you a payment vacation—the ability to skip a payment with no penalties. The fine print on these offers is that the payment you skip is added back into your loan, extending the length and amount of the loan. This is no vacation—it is a costly trick used by creditors. As tempting as it might seem, do not take them up on this offer unless you are in a dire financial situation and this allows you to miss a payment you would have anyhow.

Set Your Bottom Line

Before you call a creditor, you need to keep in mind exactly how much you can afford to pay. Do not agree to pay more than this amount no matter what. It may take you several phone calls to get the creditor to agree to a reduced payment. If you are told no, keep calling until you get a different answer. Ask to speak to a supervisor if you cannot make headway with the representative. Explain that you want to arrange a payment plan in exchange for the creditor removing negative references on your credit report. One such plan would be that you agree to a certain amount, and if you make the payments for three months, the creditor will change the account status to a neutral status and then if you continue to pay for another three months, the creditor will change it to a positive status.

Most creditors are going to agree to accept partial payments from you. Some money is better than no money in their eyes. But you have to be willing to go to them, ask for this type of arrangement, and stand your ground. Most creditors will find this type of arrangement easier and cheaper than repossessing the item or obtaining a judgment against you.

Dealing with Specific Types of Debt

Here are some specific negotiation strategies to use with certain types of debt.

Rent

Negotiate with your landlord to miss a payment and make it up at the end of the lease. Consider asking for a reduction in your rent amount. Try offering to do repairs or improvements to the unit in exchange for a rent reduction or for missing one month's payment. Consider taking on a roommate—you will need your landlord's permission for this—who will pay a portion of the rent. You could also consider subletting the unit and living in a less expensive one.

Remember that eviction is a lengthy process, so you probably have some time to work out a payment plan with your landlord. Landlords would much rather get partial payment from you than have to go through the time-consuming process of evicting you.

Mortgage

Explain that you will be paying late and ask to have late fees waived. Ask the lender about working out a *financial hardship plan*. There are programs in place to do this with federal *Fannie Mae* (202-752-7000) and *Freddie Mac* (800-FREDDIE) loans. One common plan is to pay interest only for a period of time. Realize that it takes between six and eighteen months for a foreclosure to actually happen, so you have time to negotiate on this type of loan. You may wish to refinance your loan and obtain a lower interest rate with lower payments. You could also refinance and get a loan with a longer lifetime.

Selling your home and paying off the loan is another option. You get the lender to agree to a *short sale*—where you sell the home for its value, and the lender writes off the amount of the loan that is higher than what the home sold for. You could rent the home out for the amount of the mortgage, make the payments using the rent, and live somewhere cheaper yourself.

A last resort is to sign the home over to the bank with a *quit claim deed* so that you can avoid the costs of foreclosure. The debt is canceled and no negative remarks appear on your credit report. You could also get the bank to agree to a preforeclosure sale, where you sell the home yourself and give the bank the proceeds to cancel the mortgage.

Should your mortgage company threaten foreclosure, it is important to realize that foreclosure is a lengthy legal process that takes many months. When a foreclosure actually happens, the bank sells your home at auction. Your existing debt and the costs of the foreclosure sale are then subtracted from the proceeds. Usually there is nothing left over, or there is debt left over for which you will still be responsible.

Service Provider Bills

If you have outstanding bills from service providers such as lawyers, doctors, dentists, dry cleaners, and so on, you usually have three billing cycles to make payments before the debt will be sent to a collection agency. These types of providers may be very willing to work out a payment plan for you, particularly if it is a small office and you have a good relationship with them. Call and explain your situation and ask what they can work out with you. Often, offering to begin making small payments will be a sign of good faith.

Insurance Policies

If you are late making payment on an automobile (or other vehicle) insurance policy, health insurance policy, or home or renter's policy, your insurance company must provide you with a notice that it is going to cancel your policy for nonpayment with an indication of exactly when coverage will end and when it needs to receive payment to reinstate it. If you lose your auto insurance, you cannot drive your car until you get it reinstated or get a new policy from another company. If you have a mortgage, homeowner's insurance may be part of your agreement with the bank, and cancellation of the policy could mean the bank could demand payment on the mortgage. Insurance companies are not very open to negotiation, but it cannot hurt to call and ask what they can work out with you.

Utilities

Consider switching to a budget plan. Under this kind of plan, you pay a monthly average of your yearly charges, avoiding high payments in some months, or you could set up a partial payment plan. As long as you are making some type of payment, the utility company will be unlikely to cut off your service. Note that in many northern areas, it is illegal for a utility company to turn off a utility that provides heat during winter months.

Automobiles

If you cannot make your car payments, you could sell your car and purchase a less expensive, used one. Always notify the lender before you make a late payment. Cars can be quickly repossessed. Consider asking for an extension on the loan or permission to defer a payment. If you lease, terminate your lease early. Refuse to pay posttermination payments based on the *Consumer Leasing Act*. (United States Code (U.S.C.), Title 15, Section (Sec.) 1667-1667c.)

Taxes

Contrary to popular belief, the *Internal Revenue Service* (IRS) is willing to help taxpayers who are unable to pay their tax obligations. If you are in this situation, contact your local IRS office for information about payment plans with the *Collection Information Statement for Individuals* (IRS Form 433-A) and *Offers in Compromise* (IRS Form 656). Fill out Form 433-A as follows.

- Complete your personal information in Items 1, 2, 3, 4a, and 4b.

- Fill in your employment information in Section I.

- Give the information requested in Section II. (*Order of kin* is your children, then parents, then siblings. List your oldest child. If you do not have children, list one parent. If your parents are deceased, list your oldest sibling.)

- List all of your bank accounts, retirement accounts, CDs, etc., in number 13 in Section III.

- Credit cards and loan information should be filled in under number 14.

- List safe-deposit box information in number 15.

- List real estate you own under number 16.

- Fill in life insurance information under number 17. (*Face amount* means the death benefit the policy will pay. The *loan value* is how much you can borrow against it.)

- Number 18 is where you list stocks and bonds and mutual funds.

- Complete number 19 if any items listed apply to you.

- Fill in the chart in Section IV. List what each item is currently worth (*current market value*), how much you owe on each (*amount owed*), your equity in the asset, the amount of your last monthly payment, the name and address of the creditor, the date the loan was signed (*date pledged*), and the date the final payment will be made.

- Do not complete the box after Section IV as it is for IRS use only.

- Give information about your monthly income in Section V and detail your living expenses. Total each column.

- Sign the form and have your spouse sign it as well. You may add any other information in the box under the signature area and attach anything you would like.

Credit Cards

Remember that interest continues to accrue on credit cards. However, you can negotiate about future interest. Ask that it be reduced or eliminated for a certain period of time. If you have several credit cards, you can transfer the balances to a card with the lowest interest rate and save a lot of money in doing so. Credit card companies are often receptive to settlements where you pay 70% of the balance and they cancel the debt in return. Ask to have yearly fees waived.

Secured Goods

If you have purchased items for your home, such as furniture or appliances, in which the lender holds a security interest in the item, it is important to understand that the lender cannot enter your home to repossess the goods without a court order. Therefore, it takes time and money for the creditor to repossess them. This works in your favor because lenders like these are more likely to agree to a settlement than go to the expense of getting the item back.

Determine what the resale value of the item in dispute is. Offer the creditor a settlement fee. Use the LETTER OFFERING TO RETURN

SECURED PROPERTY. (see form 29, p.392.) If the creditor has to hire an attorney, go to court, repossess the item, and then sell it, the company will net less money than what you are offering and your offer may thus seem like a good one. Be sure to get the agreement in writing, and make sure that any negative entries on your credit report from this creditor will be removed as part of the agreement.

Student Loans

Student loans are one very complicated area of debt. It is important to understand that student loans are not dischargeable in bankruptcy, so you cannot plan to take out student loans and then get them eliminated in bankruptcy.

There are several types of student loans. *Stafford Loans* are federally subsidized loans made to you by the federal government. *Perkins Loans* are federally subsidized loans for financially needy students. The loans are made directly by your school. *Guaranteed Student Loans* (GSLs) are no longer available, but if you have older loans, you may have one of these. When you fall behind on payments for a loan, it becomes overdue. If you have not made payments for 270 days (if you make monthly payments) or 330 days (if your payments are less frequent) then your loan is in *default*, which authorizes the lender to begin collection procedures.

Once you are in default, it is reported to credit reporting agencies. You also become ineligible for other student loans while it is in default. If you have a loan in default, you should do the following.

• Contact the lender as soon as possible.

- Explain your situation in detail and discuss why you are unable to make payments right now.

- Tell them that you want to repay the loan, but need some help to do so.

- Ask them what options you have available to you.

If you have problems paying your student loans, there are a variety of options you can use to help you deal with it. To apply for any of these options, you must contact your lender and complete an application. It is important to keep a copy of the application and a log of all phone calls and correspondence with your lender. Use the STUDENT LOAN LOG to help you keep this information. (see form 26, p.378.)

Consider the following options when dealing with student loans.

Forbearance

Forbearance occurs when the lender allows you to postpone or make temporary reductions in payments due to financial hardship (by proving that you do not work full-time and your monthly income is not more than twice the federal minimum wage). Forbearance forms for direct Stafford loans are available online at **www.dl.ed. gov/borrower/ForebearanceFormList.do?cmd=initializeContext.**

Deferment

You can put your loan on hold, called *deferment*, while you are enrolled in school, if you cannot find a job, during a period of financial hardship, if you are raising preschool children, or if you become disabled. Interest still accrues—the federal government pays the interest if it is a subsidized Stafford loan—while the loan is in deferment. Deferment forms for direct Stafford loans are available online at **www.dl.ed.gov/borrower/DefermentFormList. do?cmd=initializeContext**.

Graduated Payments

Graduated payments allow you to make interest-only payments on a short-term basis while dealing with financial hardship. Your payments start low and go up every few years. This option works well for people who go into careers where they plan to have a lot of upward mobility. Payments are capped at 150% of the regular monthly payment amounts.

Rehabilitation

Once you are in default, you can make arrangements with your lender for a payment plan. You then have to make twelve consecutive on-time payments in accordance with the plan. At the end of the twelve months, the loan is then purchased by a new lender, and you must pay off the rest of the loan in nine years. This is necessary so that the loan becomes a completely new loan and the default status disappears. You will be responsible for all interest for the old and new loans.

Income-Sensitive Payments

This type of plan looks at your income each year and sets payments based on how much you make. This works well for those with low or variable incomes.

Cancellation or Discharge

If you become disabled, the school your loan is from has closed, you teach certain groups of children, the loan application was forged, or you die, your loan can be *canceled* or *discharged*, meaning you no longer have to pay.

Consolidation

Consolidation is an option that combines all your student loans into one large one. The monthly payments may be smaller initially and then escalate. The length of the loan may also be longer, meaning you will be paying more interest over time. Not all student loans are eligible for consolidation, so be sure to check with your consolidator about what is eligible. To qualify, you must be enrolled less than half-time and be in your grace period or repayment period. Your loan must be current—or if you are in default, you must have made three consecutive payments and have made arrangements with the lender to continue payments. If you are married, you and your spouse can consolidate all your loans together, but this is generally not a good idea since it makes you jointly and severally liable for the entire balance even if you divorce or one of you dies. For information about federal consolidation loans, see **www.loan consolidation.ed.gov**. Forms are available online at **www.dl.ed. gov/borrower/ConsolidationFormList.do?cmd=initializeContext**.

Note that you are able to pay off your student loans using a personal loan or home equity loan. Depending on the interest rate your student loan is at, rolling your balance into a home equity loan could make a lot of sense if the interest rate is low enough. If you have an old student loan that does not qualify for the student loan tax deduction, rolling it into a home equity makes the interest you are paying on that principal tax deductible.

Dealing with Student Loans

The first step to dealing with student loans is to find out exactly what you owe and to whom. If you do not know, go to the *National Student Clearinghouse* at **www.studentclearinghouse.org** and find out what loans you have outstanding.

Next, you need to look at activity on your account to be sure all payments have been credited. If you made a payment and it does not appear, you need to provide the canceled check. If you fall behind on your student loan payments, you can face several fees and charges. Collection agencies can charge fees up to 28% of the balance of the loan to collect the loan, and this does not include the interest. Your tax refund can be intercepted to pay for student loans, and 10% of your wages can be garnished to pay for them, as well.

Contact your lender, explain your problem, and ask what options are available to you. For help paying student loans, see the *Office of the Ombudsmen* website at: **www.fsahelp.ed.gov**. For more information on student loans, see:

Stafford Loans
www.staffordloan.com

National Student Loan Data System
www.nslds.ed.gov

General Negotiating Tips

It is important to remember that you will almost always obtain a better outcome when you negotiate directly with a creditor rather than with a collection agency. The collection agency is authorized to make only certain concessions to debtors. If you speak directly to the creditor, you may be able to work out a better deal.

If the creditor will not speak with you about your debt, ask how many payments you must make to the collection agency before it will agree to speak to you. Once you have demonstrated your willingness to pay, the creditor may be more willing to discuss the debt with you.

Some collection agencies buy debts from creditors, and your original creditor may be out of the picture completely. If this is the case, the collection agency can then negotiate with you. If you are not sure who owns the debt, ask the collection agent or call the original creditor. If you disagree with the amount of a debt, you will need to discuss this with the creditor. The collection agency will not have any records beyond the current amount owed and is not able to deal with adjustments for errors made by the creditor.

Eliminating Debts You Do Not Owe

You may have debts attributed to you that you are not really legally responsible for. You may have entered into a contract that is not legal, or you may have contracts you can dispute, such as a car you bought that is a *Lemon Law* car. You will need to consult an attorney or read up on contract law to determine this—but in general, look to see if there was any fraud involved or if the contract was grossly unfair.

Look closely at your debts and see if there are any that you truly do not owe. It is also possible to cancel some orders or contracts so that you will no longer be responsible for them, such as canceling a contract to have a new roof put on your house before the work is done.

Negotiating Settlements

Reducing monthly payments is at best a temporary measure in relieving debt and improving your credit. The interest on the debt is going to continue to pile up, especially when you are only making partial payments. To really reduce your debt, you need to work out settlements. A settlement is a legally binding agreement that ends your obligation to the creditor. The following are some examples of settlements you may wish to consider.

Example:

You owe $3,000 on your Visa card. The original amount charged was $1,900.

The rest of the amount is from accumulated interest. You have been behind on your payments for six months and have only been able to pay portions of the monthly amounts. The company is becoming more insistent that you pay the full monthly payment. You call the company and explain that your financial situation has become difficult since you became ill.

Solution: Agree to pay $2,000 as a settlement in full of the amount due. The company agrees to report your account as current to the credit reporting agency.

Example:

You lost your job and cannot make your mortgage payment. There is no job in sight and your wife is expecting a baby. You have not paid on your mortgage in four months. You contact the bank and explain your situation. There is simply no way you can get any money together to pay for the past or current mortgage payments. You know that if you fail to pay, the bank will eventually foreclose on the home. The bank will evict you, sell the home at auction, and accept a price less than it is really worth. The amount you owe, as well as all the costs of the sale and legal work, will be deducted from the sale price. Any money left over is yours. You should not expect to see anything unless you have a large amount of equity.

Solution: You tell the bank you would like to deed the house back to it as payment in full on the mortgage. You will be out, with no payments due and no costs of the sale or foreclosure. This method keeps your credit history clean and makes it possible for you to purchase a smaller, less expensive home when you get back on your feet.

When negotiating a payoff, your goal is to get the creditor to list the account as *paid as agreed* or *account closed—paid as agreed*. A listing of just *paid* is not positive. If you are working with a collection agency, you want to make sure it agrees to delete its listing entirely and change the listing for the original creditor to *paid as agreed* or *account closed—paid as agreed*. A creditor may tell you that it has an agreement with the credit agency not to change negative listings when there is a settlement.

Practical Point

When you make settlement payments, do not pay with a personal check, since this gives the creditor your bank account information. Always keep a copy of your money order or cashier's check.

However, even if this is the case, there is someone in the organization who has the authority to change negative listings after a settlement, and you simply have to keep asking until you get the right person.

If you cannot get your creditor to agree to a positive listing, then you may wish to ask for a listing of *settled*, which is not as negative as *paid—charge off* or even a listing like *repossession*. You should also avoid a listing of *paid—collection* or *paid—X days late*.

Make sure that part of the settlement is that the creditor agrees to report your account as paid in full with any negative indications removed from your credit report. Most creditors will require that you pay at least 70% of the debt before they will agree to remove negative references from your credit report. Whatever you get them to agree to do with regard to the credit reporting agencies, make sure it is included as a stipulation in the written agreement you will sign with them.

If you are negotiating a settlement with a collection agency, you also need to get the original creditor to sign off on the agreement—if you do not, you could still owe that company the balance of the debt. One caveat on settlements—if you negotiate a settlement that reduces your debt by more than $600, you could end up paying income tax on this debt reduction. Collection agencies do not have to report a settlement to the IRS if the reduction in debt is less than $600. If your reduction is under the $600 mark, make sure you get the agency to stipulate in your agreement that it will not report the reduction to the IRS.

When you negotiate a settlement, you get the creditor to agree to take less than you owe in exchange for your paying it immediately. Creditors are happier with cash in hand than with accounts they must continue to pursue for months or years. Keep this fact in mind as you negotiate.

Practical Point

If you need to skip a payment completely, use the LETTER REQUESTING NO PAYMENT. (see form 32, p.396.)

Finding the cash so you can live up to your settlement agreement is discussed in the next section. To create a settlement with a creditor, use the AGREEMENT TO SETTLE DEBT (form 31, p.395). Write *payment in full* on your money order or cashier's check and photocopy the check before you send it.

Finding Cash

To use some of the debt reduction strategies previously described, you need to find the money to make the settlement. Remember that there are ways to find large chunks of cash, but that it is also important to find ways to get together small amounts of cash or to save small amounts. If you can try a few of these strategies, the money you save will really add up. Follow some of these suggestions for raising or conserving cash.

Finances and Credit Cards

- Sell your investments.

- Sell other assets, such as a boat, coin collection, second car, jewelry, etc.

- Seek a reduction in your child support obligations.

- Use your tax refund or alimony payment.

- Transfer your credit card balances to a card with a low interest rate.

- Ask your credit card companies to waive your annual fee. Most are willing to do this.

- Get a second mortgage or home equity loan. Use the money to pay for your settlements and pay the loan back over time. Just be certain that you will be able to handle the monthly payments.

- Borrow money from family or friends. (Be aware that an outstanding loan can drastically change a relationship.)

- Get rid of overdraft protection on your bank accounts. This just gives you an excuse to overdraw your account.

- Shred any checks you are given by your credit card company. The interest rate on these will devastate you.

- Withdraw money from your bank accounts at the bank

and not at ATMs where you may be charged a fee.

- Cancel your credit cards so you cannot charge more than you can afford to spend.

- Increase the number of dependents you claim on your W-2 forms (but only if you can do so without owing taxes at the end of the year).

- Learn how to budget and stick to it (see Chapter 11).

- Find out if you qualify for assistance from a local food pantry or other charity.

- Keep your extra cash in a money market account where you can earn a few dollars on it in interest.

- Apply for public assistance if you are out of work or disabled. This money will not be enough to make even a medium-sized settlement, but it will keep food on your table.

- Withdraw money from a retirement account, but understand that you will have to pay associated fines.

- Use credit cards that offer incentives—such as money back—but only if you can control your credit card spending.

- Do not take cash advances on your credit cards. This is just a high-interest loan.

Utilities and Insurance

- Raise the deductible on your car insurance or reduce the amount of coverage you have.

- Cancel any insurance you have purchased from your credit card companies. It is overpriced.

- If you feel you must have some life insurance, shop around with local agents.

- Take out a loan against your life insurance or retirement accounts.

- Cancel any insurance against credit card theft or loss that you have purchased. You do not need this since you are only liable for the first $50 used on a card after you report it stolen or missing.

- Reduce the minutes on your cell phone plan and try not to use the phone as much. If you are consistently using more minutes than your plan allows, consider changing to a plan with more minutes to avoid high charges for out-of-plan minutes.

- Cancel your landline and just use your cell as your main phone.

- Block texting on your cell phone. Many people spend a lot of money on texting.

- Cancel your long-distance service.

- Turn off lights when you are not in the room.

- Lower the heat during the day when you are away at work and at night when you are asleep.

- Turn your thermostat down just one or two degrees when you are home.

- Turn down the thermostat on your water heater by one or two degrees.

- Do laundry with cold water instead of hot.

- Open the window instead of turning on the air conditioning.

- Cancel your cable service, or reduce the number of premium channels you pay for.

- Cancel your Internet account and sign up for a free service or a company that pays you to surf, or go to the library when you need to go online.

- Use a free email service, such as Gmail or Yahoo.

- Instead of turning all the lights on in a room, turn on just the one next to you. Turn it off when you leave the room.

- Turn off computers when you are not using them.

- Turn off the water while you are brushing your teeth.

Raise Cash

- Have a garage sale.

- Sell items to a pawn shop. Be aware that you will only receive about 50% of the value of the item this way.

- Sell items through a consignment shop.

- Turn a hobby into a money-making venture. Sell home-made pies to local restaurants, do website design, make birthday cakes for friends, sell birdhouses you make at a flea market, etc.

- Suggest that your teenage children get jobs and contribute to the household.

- Use free classifieds in local community newspapers to sell things.

- Sell things on eBay or through Craigslist.

- Get a part-time job. Even small jobs like baby-sitting or yard work can help you raise the money you need.

- Ask for a raise or for more hours at work.

- Return things you have purchased and do not need. Get cash back if you have the receipt. If you do not, you can get a store credit to purchase things you do need.

Reduce Expenses

- Barter. For example, fix your neighbor's car in exchange for haircuts.

- Cut coupons, shop sales, and use rebates.

- Sell your car and buy a less expensive used one or take public transportation until you can afford a new one.

- Do small home repairs yourself instead of paying someone.

- Sell your home and buy a smaller, less expensive one.

- Move in with family or friends for a short time to save on rent.

- Borrow books from the library instead of buying them.

- Rent videos and DVDs instead of going to movies, or borrow them from the library.

- Cook at home instead of getting takeout.

- Stop buying coffee or lunches out and bring your own instead.

- Find ways to reduce your grocery bill. Use leftovers, cook inexpensive meals such as soup, and create menus based on what is on sale.

- Do your own repairs, laundry, or other services.

- Reduce your children's allowances.

- Buy store brands instead of name brands.

- Do not gamble or buy lottery tickets.

- Plant a vegetable garden.

- Join a wholesale club and buy in bulk. Split large quantities with friends.

- Use a hose instead of the car wash.

- Carpool.

- Take the bus to work instead of driving.

- Reduce your number of meals at restaurants.

- Ride a bike or walk places if possible.

- Use birth control to avoid unplanned pregnancies.

- Buy nothing you do not need.

- Give up drinking or smoking.

- Put off giving to charity until you can afford to do so.

- Severely cut back on your gift-giving.

- Try making some gifts yourself instead of purchasing them.

- Cancel your newspaper and magazine subscriptions.

- Shop at secondhand stores.

- Accept hand-me-downs for your children.

- Save money in a special account or in an envelope instead of using layaway for which there are fees.

- Bake and cook items yourself that you normally purchase prepared.

- Cancel any trips you have planned or substitute less expensive vacations, such as camping.

- Send e-cards instead of buying and mailing cards.

REAL LIFE CREDIT

Lupe decided that it was time to get serious about her debt situation. She was tired of always being late with payments and never having enough money. She had a job and made decent money, but she simply had too much debt. She decided that she wanted to pay down her credit card debt and try to create a life for herself that did not involve huge credit card bills. She sat down and thought about how she could be smarter with her money. The first thing she did was transfer one of her credit cards to a lower-interest-rate card. This brought down the amount of interest she was paying.

Next she made a list of small ways she could save money, including turning down the thermostat, spending less on restaurants, carpooling to work, and cancelling her XM radio subscription. She made a concerted effort to spend only on necessities for a few months. The result was that she did not increase the balance on her card and she had more money to make payments with. After a year, she had the balance completely paid off.

Options to Avoid

When trying to find cash or decrease expenses, you may sometimes feel desperate and pressured. It is important to remember, though, that some of the choices you make today can have long-term effects on you and your finances. It is easy to grab at any available solution when you are feeling desperate, but it is essential that you make well-thought-out decisions that will protect your future, as well as helping you with your present problems.

Finance Company

It is rarely a good idea to borrow from a finance company when you are in financial trouble. The interest rates are likely to be very, very high and the penalties for missing payments will also be very expensive. Finance companies that lend money to people with poor credit ratings aggressively collect on their accounts. It might sound like a great idea to buy that new television with no payment and no interest for twelve months, but you should only make those kinds of purchases if you plan on making regular monthly payments so that you pay off the entire balance before the loan begins accruing interest.

Tax Refund Loans

If you believe you will get a large tax refund, it can be hard to wait for the money to come through and it can be tempting to take out a tax refund anticipation loan. However, these loans charge interest, so you are giving away part of the money that you are expecting to get back from the government. If you e-file and receive your refund by bank transfer, you can expect to receive it very quickly.

Payday Loans

Taking out a loan in anticipation of your paycheck is also a bad idea. The interest rates are phenomenal, and in most cases, waiting a few days to get paid by your employer is not going to have too great of a detrimental effect on your debt situation.

Pawn Shops

Pawn shops might seem like a quick way to make some money, but if there are items you want to sell, you can probably get more money selling them yourself on eBay, through a classified ad, or by putting up signs. Many people mistakenly believe that pawn shops are a good way to borrow money and then get their item back. In reality, though, a pawnbroker may sell your item quickly and will give you only a very small percentage of the item's actual value.

Debt Consolidation Loans

It might sound like a great idea—consolidate all your debts into one lower monthly payment—but in reality the interest rates are so high that you will end up paying far more in total. The only time debt consolidation works is when you work through a legitimate consumer credit counseling agency.

Home Equity Loans

Home equity loans allow you to borrow against the equity in your home. The problem is that you begin repayment immediately (unless you have an interest-only period on the loan). If you fail to repay the loan, you face foreclosure. Even if you manage to keep up with payments on the loan, it puts you in a tough position should you need to sell. You have to make sure you get enough from the sale to cover both the mortgage and home equity loan, and that may not leave you with any cash from the sale.

Dealing with Judgments and Liens

If you have been experiencing debt problems for some time, you may have a judgment against you. A *judgment* is a court order stating that you are ordered by the court to pay the amount owed. A judgment gives a creditor the right to garnish your wages or seize your assets. A *lien* is a court order that gives the creditor an interest in some piece of real property you own. Should you ever sell the property, the creditor must be paid out of the sale money. You have the right to a trial to contest a judgment that is being sought against you.

It is important to understand that once a lien has been placed against your property, the only way to get rid of it is to pay it or reach a settlement with the creditor for removing it. Even if a court proceeding has begun, there is still time to settle. Approach the creditor's attorney—if you have an attorney, he or she will do this for you—and offer to settle the case for a certain amount of money. Start with 40% of the total amount owed.

A settlement will save the creditor time and money in legal bills, which is why creditors are willing to consider it. If the case does not settle, the court can decide that you owe all or part of what the creditor is asking for. If that happens, a judgment or lien will be entered against you. Once a judgment is entered, the creditor can begin to collect the money from you. This can include *garnishing your wages* (taking a portion out of your paycheck) and seizing your assets and bank accounts.

Practical Point

If you cannot afford an attorney, contact your local *Legal Aid Society* for assistance. Many local bar associations have attorneys who provide legal help on a volunteer basis for people who cannot afford to pay for it. Call your local county or city bar association to inquire about this.

Once a judgment or lien is entered, you can still approach the creditor about a settlement. The creditor may agree because seizing assets, waiting on a lien, and garnishing wages can be expensive and time-consuming. Be sure if you do settle the judgment in this way that the creditor files papers with the court indicating that the judgment has been satisfied. (This is often called a *satisfaction of judgment* or *discharge*.)

It is important to note that some people are *judgment proof*. This means they have little or no assets, no income (other than government assistance), and have basically nothing a creditor can take. If you are judgment proof, you may not wish to make any attempt to settle your account. However, you must realize that if you rack up many judgments against you, it will be extremely difficult to obtain credit. Also, should your situation change in the future, you will have judgments and liens to pay off.

If you are judgment proof, you can use the LETTER EXPLAINING JUDGMENT PROOF STATUS to let your creditors know this. (see form 33, p.397.) This will discourage many from pursuing the debt, since they will not be able to collect anything. If you are planning to file for bankruptcy, you should let your creditors know this as well, as it will keep them from pursuing you. Use LETTER EXPLAINING PLAN TO GO BANKRUPT. (see form 34, p.398.)

Proof of Payment

Whether you settle with your creditor before, during, or after a court case or if you pay a judgment in full, you must make certain that you receive proof of payment. When reaching a settlement, you should not send any funds until you have a legal document in your hands that indicates the terms of the settlement. Keep a copy of it for yourself. Make the payment after you sign the document and request a receipt or proof of payment from the creditor. Keep these documents. Should you settle or pay a judgment, the creditor is responsible for filing a judgment discharge with the court, indicating that you have completely paid what you owe. If you do not receive a copy of this, request one. You may find it necessary to prod the creditor into filing this document since it often is not considered high priority.

If you owed taxes, the IRS may have filed a tax lien against you. Request a *Certificate of Release of Federal Tax Lien* from the IRS for each lien against you that you have paid in full. Have the credit reporting agencies contact the IRS to verify the release of the liens.

Closing Your Accounts

If you are deep in debt and many of your accounts are reporting you as delinquent to the credit reporting agencies, you may want to close all your credit card accounts. When you close an account, you still remain responsible for all the past charges and interest on the account, but you prevent yourself from adding more charges to the account and making your situation worse. Use the LETTER CLOSING ACCOUNT to notify the creditor with which you wish to close an account. (see form 35, p.399.)

Getting Help

There is nothing wrong with deciding you could use some assistance resolving your problems. When might you need help? You probably need help if you do not have enough money to pay even reduced payments on your accounts. You probably need some help if you just cannot work out a budget or if you can create a budget but cannot follow it no matter what you do. You need help if there are errors on your credit report and either you just cannot handle trying to get them fixed as discussed in Chapter 5, or if you have gone as far as you feel you can on your own in trying to get them fixed. If you are in danger of losing your home or your car and do not have enough money to survive on, you need to get some help.

Where to Turn

If you are in immediate danger of losing your home or face some other emergency situation, consider seeing an attorney to discuss bankruptcy (described later). If you are feeling deeply depressed or suicidal, you need to get help from a mental health professional. You should not feel embarrassed about these feelings. Considering the difficulties you have faced, they are a common reaction. If you are in a situation in which you have no money and cannot afford basic necessities, you need to get assistance from your local social services department. If you feel as if your bills are piling up and you don't know what to do, a credit counselor can be of help to you.

Agencies that Can Assist You

There are many different agencies that can provide various types of assistance, support, and information as you confront your debts.

Credit Counseling Agencies

Consumer Credit Counseling Service (CCCS, **www.cccsatl.org**) is the best known credit counseling agency. CCCS is a nonprofit corporation that is funded by creditors. CCCS can help you set up a payment plan to manage all your debt. There are many different consumer credit counseling services. You need to locate one in your area. You can check with the state attorney general's office or your local Better Business Bureau to ensure the agency you choose has no complaints against it.

Basically, CCCS negotiates with the creditors on your behalf to reduce interest or lower payments. Your debt is organized into one monthly payment that is less than the total of your normal monthly obligations (although it may not be by much). The agency also tries to provide clients with credit and finance education to help avoid future problems. You pay a small monthly fee to CCCS for the service. You do need to be aware that CCCS cannot reduce your total overall debt, and it requires that you pay all your debts in full. If you miss payments, collection actions can be pursued by your creditors. There may be a waiting list at CCCS, and the payment plan that is set up for you can last up to forty-two months.

IT'S A FACT!

Studies show that three out of four people drop out of credit counseling programs before completing them.

Your credit report will reflect the fact that you used credit counseling services, and some lenders may be hesitant to lend to you because of this, since it is a clear sign you are having trouble managing your payments. It is also important to realize that using this service will freeze your accounts. You will be able to make payments toward them but not use them. It is important to be careful when selecting a credit counseling agency. While CCCS is the best known, there are many others. Many charge a setup fee, as well as a monthly fee for their services, which consists mainly of consolidating a consumer's debt into one payment.

Selecting a Credit Counseling Agency

Make sure you choose an agency that:

- provides you with a written statement of your rights;

- sends you free information by mail if you request it;

- discloses all fees up front;

- makes payments to creditors on time;

- focuses on consumer education in addition to just working out how you will make payments; and,

- spends time with you—usually at least twenty minutes is recommended—before offering a debt management or consolidation plan that fits your needs.

Do not choose an agency that:

- asks for cash before speaking with you;

- promises to eliminate, reduce, or get rid of your debts;

- charges more than $100 for a setup or 25% for a monthly fee (although realize that if the agency provides extensive educational programs, you may have to pay for these);

- works for profit;

- uses employees who work on commission; and,

- promises free services (in credit counseling as elsewhere, there is no such thing as a free lunch).

Unfortunately, the quality of many agencies is decreasing, so it is important to shop around. Over nine million Americans seek help from credit counseling services each year, and this is often a last resort before bankruptcy for many people who are having debt problems. The *National Foundation for Credit Counseling* is the national nonprofit organization of consumer credit counseling agencies. The national office can direct you to a credit counseling office in your area and can also provide basic debt and budgeting information online. You can reach the National Foundation for Credit Counseling at 800-388-2227 or at **www.nfcc.org**. The *Association of Independent Consumer Credit Counseling Agencies* is a group of nonprofit agencies. You can search for an agency near you on its website at **www.aiccca.org**.

Debtors Anonymous

Debtors Anonymous offers a twelve-step program similar to Alcoholics Anonymous. The program helps people who have recurring debt problems face and overcome them. Contact the organization at 781-453-2743 or go to its website at **www.debtorsanonymous.org**.

Institute of Consumer Financial Education

Another organization to consider is the *Institute of Consumer Financial Education*. This is a nonprofit group that works with consumers to help them manage, invest, save, and spend money in an educated way. It has monthly newsletters and a packet about credit cards available.

Contact the institute at 619-239-1401 or at **www.icfe.info**. The institute also offers *credit card condoms*, which are sleeves that fit over credit cards. They are supposed to act as a deterrent to using them, or at least get the user to think for a moment before using them.

National Consumer Law Center

The *National Consumer Law Center* (NCLC) offers information for consumers about laws on credit and bankruptcy, as well as other topics. The NCLC has recently published a report called *Credit*

Counseling in Crisis: The Impact on Consumers of Funding Cuts, Higher Fees and Aggressive New Market Entrants. See this and other reports on its website at **www.nclc.org/issues/credit_counseling/archive.shtml**.

Better Business Bureau

The *Better Business Bureau* can assist you with complaints against any business, credit repair, or credit reporting agency that is a member. The national office address is:

4200 Wilson Boulevard
Suite 800
Arlington, VA 22203

You can find a local office using the search function on its website at **www.bbb.org**.

National Consumer League's Fraud Center

The *National Consumers League's Fraud Center* is a nonprofit organization designed to help consumers detect and avoid telemarketing and Internet fraud. You can call or email the organization with a report of suspicious activity or to get advice. For more information, visit its website at **www.fraud.org**.

Other Assistance

If you are looking to get some legal information beyond that which is offered in this book, go to **www.findlaw.com**. All federal and state statutes can be accessed there as well as many court decisions.

If you need legal assistance but cannot afford an attorney, you may qualify for a free attorney. Contact *Legal Services Corporation* (202-295-1500, **www.lsc.gov**) or *National Legal Aid & Defender Association* (202-452-0620, **www.nlada.org**).

Some websites that have a wealth of information about credit and debt include the following:

- **www.creditpage.com**—gives information on how to manage and protect your credit.

- **www.debtwizards.com/consolidate.html**—gives information about how to consolidate your debts.

- **www.freecreditanalyzer.com**—offers a free credit analysis.

- **www.quicken.com/shopping/parenting**—has a debt reduction planner and other calculating tools.

Other Credit Repair Agencies

There are many companies that advertise that they can help you reduce or eliminate your debt and quickly and easily repair your credit problems. Because many of these companies have proven to be less than honest, the *Credit Repair Organizations Act* (you can read it online at **www.ftc.gov/os/statutes/croa/croa.shtm**) was passed by Congress to try to control some of the problems that have happened with these types of companies. Under this act, it is illegal for such an agency to advise a consumer to alter identification—such as using a different name to get credit—or to hide accurate information in a credit report.

Credit repair agencies cannot accept any payment before performing work for a consumer and also must give each client a statement of their rights. You have the right to cancel any contract you agree to with a credit repair agency within three days of signing it. Should any agency request that you pay before they do any work for you, fail to give you a statement of your rights, or suggest you use a different name or identity to obtain credit, you need to refuse its services and report it to your local authorities. If you participate in any illegal activity with a credit repair agency, even if it is the agency's idea and it provides the paperwork, you can be criminally prosecuted and face jail time.

In general, you need to be wary of anyone who promises you quick and easy fixes for your credit problems. There is nothing that a credit repair agency can do for you that you cannot do yourself. There is no magic involved in credit repair, and there is nothing so highly technical that the average consumer cannot handle it. Do not let anyone pressure you into doing things you feel are dishonest or potentially illegal. If it sounds too good to be true, it probably is.

Government Agencies

Government agencies such as the *Federal Trade Commission* (FTC), or your state attorney general's office (in the government guide section of your phone book) can be of assistance to you if you need information about laws on credit or if you are experiencing difficulty dealing with a creditor or credit reporting agency. The FTC keeps records about credit reporting agencies and can prosecute them if they break the law. If you have a complaint against a credit reporting agency, you should always let the FTC know. It is unlikely the FTC will become involved in your particular situation, but the information you provide can assist it if it appears there is an ongoing pattern of problems with one agency. The FTC can be reached at:

Federal Trade Commission
600 Pennsylvania Avenue, NW
Washington, DC 20580
www.ftc.gov

The Federal Trade Commission will become involved in fraud issues and provides information designed to help consumers spot fraud in the marketplace. You can contact them at 877-FTCHELP (877-382-4357). Consumer Sentinel is run by the FTC and offers information on fraud and scams. You can find it online at **www. ftc.gov/sentinel.**

Practical Point

You can obtain information concerning handling credit problems from the federal government and learn about programs and services it offers at **www.pueblo.gsa.gov**.

State Banking Authorities

State banking authorities regulate and supervise state-chartered banks. Many also handle problems with other financial institutions. These agencies can answer questions about credit and also about banking. Contact your state agency to find out exactly what services it can provide. A list of state banking authorities can be found in Appendix A.

REAL LIFE CREDIT

Colin and Andrea had been through some hard times. Colin was deployed to Iraq, leaving Andrea to run their business. Andrea found out she was pregnant soon after he left and when their baby spent several months in the NICU, she had no time for the business. Once Colin returned, they attempted to get themselves back together financially, but their debts were huge and their income small. They went to credit counseling and consolidated their debt, which was somewhat helpful, but the fact that they simply did not have enough income to cover the debt made it impossible to get ahead. They took out a home equity loan to get some cash, but because they had to begin paying it back immediately it wasn't very helpful.

Colin sold some things they had that were of value, but it wasn't enough. Finally, they talked to an attorney and ended up filing for bankruptcy. What a relief it was not to have creditors calling and the fear of losing their house! They went through a Chapter 7 bankruptcy and removed most of their debt. Colin got a full-time job at a warehouse and Andrea stayed home with the baby, baby-sitting some neighbors' children for some extra cash. Eventually, it seemed that the financial crisis was behind them.

When to Get a Lawyer

Just because you are experiencing credit or debt problems, you do not automatically need a lawyer. You can negotiate arrangements with creditors yourself—without an attorney. You can get changes made to a credit report on your own. You have probably seen ads for attorneys who advertise that they can reduce your debt and help you avoid bankruptcy. Most of what they offer you can do yourself by following the procedures and suggestions in this book. There are times, however, when an attorney may be helpful. If you are dealing with credit reporting agencies about an incorrect entry on your report and you have sent letters and made phone calls for several months with little progress, it may be a good idea to get an attorney. This does not mean you must pay a retainer fee and then be billed by the hour. Start by hiring an attorney only to write a simple letter on your behalf to the credit agency. An attorney's letterhead will garner much more attention than yet another letter from you and may be just the thing to push things into motion. You can negotiate with the attorney about how much you will be charged should other services like phone calls or more correspondence be required.

If you have been served with court papers, you may wish to consult an attorney to at least have him or her look them over and help you understand them completely. If you are being sued for nonpayment of a debt you owe and have no defense, you will most likely be throwing good money after bad if you hire a lawyer to defend you in the case. If you are uncomfortable or unable to try to reach a settlement with the creditor's attorney yourself, you can hire an attorney for the specific purpose of working out a settlement.

If you believe that you need to at least consider bankruptcy, you should contact an attorney for a free consultation. To find a bankruptcy attorney, get in touch with attorneys you have had contact with in the past for a referral or call your state, county, or city bar association for a referral to an attorney in your area who practices bankruptcy law.

Bankruptcy

Bankruptcy is a procedure you can go through in a federal bankruptcy court that allows you to *discharge* (get rid of) all or a portion of your debt. One of the most important and beneficial things about bankruptcy is that the minute you file your petition with the court stating that you are asking to be declared bankrupt, all your creditors are stopped from any collection attempts. This is called an *automatic stay* and can do a lot to relieve the tension and mounting panic you feel. This means creditors cannot take your car, garnish your wages, foreclose on your home, call you about your debt, or try to collect in any way while the stay is in place. When a bankruptcy is filed, a *trustee* is appointed to handle the case. The trustee divides up your assets among your creditors.

There are two types of bankruptcies available to consumers— *Chapter 7* and *Chapter 13*. You must reside in a state for ninety days prior to filing for bankruptcy in that state. To file for bankruptcy, you will probably need an attorney who will require that you pay him or her. You must also pay a filing fee with the court. The attorney will complete a *Petition for Bankruptcy*, which is a very long document that lists your personal information as well as details of all your assets and your debts. If you do attempt to file bankruptcy without an attorney, bankruptcy forms are available online at **www.uslegalforms.com/findlaw/bankruptcy**.

When you go bankrupt, all your assets and debts come under the control of the court. It is important to understand that there are some assets that are called *exempt assets*. Things such as your clothing, food, books, personal belongings, furniture, some cash, and your wedding ring usually cannot be taken away from you. Other things such as your car and some real estate, especially your home, have additional protections. The law about what is considered exempt differs by state, but in general you are permitted to keep things you require for daily living.

Your *nonexempt assets* are those that the court can divide up among your creditors. These include investments, large amounts of cash, and valuable items you own. It is important to note that recently there has been an effort by bankruptcy judges to be harder on people who are going bankrupt since in the recent past there have been many abuses of the system. It is also important to know that if you believe you are going to go bankrupt, you should not go and max out all your credit cards right before you do so. The court will see this as an abuse and may not allow you to include those debts in your bankruptcy.

A new bankruptcy law went into effect in October 2005 that makes it more difficult to wipe out all your debt by filing for bankruptcy. In order to file, you must go for credit counseling and budget analysis in the 180 days before filing. To qualify for Chapter 7 bankruptcy, your income must be below the median income in your state for a family of your size, or you have to pass a *means test*—if you can pay $6,000 over five years of $100 a month toward your debt, you must file Chapter 13 only. You can find a *means test calculator* online at **www.legalconsumer.com**. Filing fees are currently $299 for Chapter 7 and $274 for Chapter 13.

Chapter 7

A *Chapter 7 bankruptcy* lets the debtor *discharge* (or wipe out) all his or her debts and is also called *liquidation bankruptcy*. This may sound like a pretty good deal, but it is not quite that simple. When a debtor goes into a Chapter 7 bankruptcy, the trustee takes legal possession of all the debtor's possessions that are not exempt under state or federal law. The trustee *liquidates,* or sells, all your nonexempt assets and uses the cash to pay your creditors. (Most creditors only get a small percentage, if that, of the total amount of the debt.) Debts are paid in order of priority. Debts are discharged, or forgiven, and completely wiped off the slate. Even if this sounds like a good deal, you must know that not all debts can be discharged in a bankruptcy. Those that cannot be include:

- taxes;

- child support;

- alimony;

- divorce property settlements (unless your ex agrees to discharge);

- student loans;

- criminal fines; and,

- fradulent debts (this includes huge debts run up right before filing).

You will be responsible for repaying these types of debt no matter what. You may only file for a Chapter 7 bankruptcy every six years, and you should be aware that bankruptcy courts in some areas are cracking down on what they see as consumer misuse of bankruptcy. Some Chapter 7 bankruptcies have been denied when it appears the debtor piled up debt without any plans to be able to pay it off. Chapter 7 bankruptcies appear on credit reports for ten years after the discharge.

A Chapter 7 bankruptcy can be a lifesaver for people who are overcome with debt and have no hope of reaching settlements or being able to make negotiated payments to creditors. It can also hurt your credit for a long time. Note that you will not necessarily lose everything in a Chapter 7. It is possible to *redeem* or *reaffirm* certain debts. This means you *redeem* the asset by paying the creditor the wholesale value of the asset (which you might do in order to keep your car) or *reaffirm the debt*, which means you agree to pay the debt after the case is over (which you might do to keep your home).

You are not eligible for a Chapter 7 bankruptcy if you have filed for bankruptcy in the last six years. If you filed for a Chapter 13 bankruptcy during that time period, you are only eligible for a Chapter 7 if you paid off 70% of your debt or more in the Chapter 13 case.

Chapter 13

Chapter 13 bankruptcies are also called *reorganizations*. A Chapter 13 bankruptcy allows the debtor to keep most assets and arranges for partial or full payment of the debts owed over three to five years. Creditors must be paid at least as much as they would have received in a Chapter 7 situation. The debtor must pay all *disposable* (not necessary for living essentials) income into the plan. Money is paid to the trustee who then pays the creditors. The major benefit of a Chapter 13 plan is that it allows the debtor to keep assets that would have to be liquidated in a Chapter 7 plan. However, a Chapter 13 bankruptcy can also stay on your credit report for ten years.

Other benefits of Chapter 13 plans are that they do include taxes into the plan and that the plan is like a consolidation loan. However, no interest is charged. Interest on your debts stops accumulating on the day you file for bankruptcy. The amount you owe does not continue to grow through accumulating interest.

If you are having problems making mortgage payments or some other similar situation, you would be better off working with your creditor independently and finding a way to catch up, so that the late or missed payments only haunt your credit report for seven years. Creditors are more afraid of bankruptcies on a credit report than they are of late payments. Creditors usually do not receive full payment in a bankruptcy, but if the debtor merely falls behind, a profit can still be made.

In general you are better off trying to make your own settlements or payment plans with your creditors than going into a Chapter 13 bankruptcy. Keep it as a last resort.

If you have already filed for bankruptcy before reading this book and feel you may have made a mistake in doing so, you may be able to withdraw your bankruptcy petition, depending on where your case is. You will need to consult with your attorney about this.

Reaffirmation Agreements

If you do file for bankruptcy, you will be surprised to find that as you literally walk out the courtroom door, you may be stopped by a representative from one of your creditors. This representative will offer you new credit if you agree to *reaffirm* your debt with the company—in other words, agree to owe them the money that your bankruptcy just wiped out. Many consumers have fallen into this trap and have found themselves deep in debt almost immediately after a bankruptcy. Note that this is a different situation than reaffirming a mortgage or some other secured debt. In that case, you get to keep your home or whatever piece of property is secured. In this case, all you are doing is promising to pay them something the court said you need not pay just so you can have credit.

Do not agree to anything right away. Take some time to reassess your financial situation. (Read Chapter 10 about how to reestablish credit.) Remember that reaffirming a debt you have just wiped out can be a foolish move. On the other hand, if it is a small amount, it might serve your purposes to agree to reaffirm it so that you can have immediate credit with that company.

There are many agencies and organizations available to assist you. Check Appendix A at the back of the book for listings of state banking authorities, consumer protection agencies, and state attorney general offices that can assist consumers with financial and debt problems and questions.

Coping with Bankruptcy

Many people feel embarrassed when bankruptcy becomes an option or a choice for them. It is important to remember that bankruptcy was invented to help people, and that it is okay to find yourself in a situation where you need help. Bankruptcy can relieve a lot of stress in a much more immediate way than most other options. Think for a minute about the many celebrities or famous people who have gone through bankruptcy—Larry King, Anna Nicole Smith, Kim Basinger, Burt Reynolds, Al Jolson, Cyndi Lauper, Henry Ford, Jerry Lee Lewis, and even presidents Ulysses S. Grant and Thomas Jefferson. Billionaire Donald Trump even filed for a business bankruptcy. Try to think of bankruptcy as a reorganization of your finances and as a way to get your debt (and stress) under control. Bankruptcy gives you a fresh start. Resolve to use that new start wisely. Do not let yourself fall into the same traps again after your bankruptcy. Above all, do not feel embarrassed or demeaned about going through bankruptcy.

COPING WITH MARRIAGE, DIVORCE, AND DEBT

8

Marriage has an impact on credit and debt, and it is important to be aware of the implications. It is also important to discuss divorce and debt together because many people who are experiencing debt or credit problems are either divorcing, recently divorced, or having marital difficulties and contemplating divorce. Because serious debt problems cause stress, and stress can lead to marital problems, this is not surprising. It can also work in the opposite direction as well—marital problems or divorce can be a direct cause of financial problems. Divorce can certainly complicate financial problems, but you should never stay in a marriage just to avoid dealing with these problems. Your problems can be worked out no matter how difficult they may seem. This chapter addresses these situations.

Your Credit Rights during Marriage

Women, and sometimes men, change their names when they marry. This happens when you take your spouse's last name, hyphenate the two names, or create a new surname to use together. When you do this, you risk losing your old credit history. If you change your name due to marriage, or for any other reason, be sure to have your accounts changed to your new name and ask that this change be reported on your credit report.

If joint accounts are opened during marriage, be sure that they are reported to both spouse's credit reports. If a woman changes her name due to marriage, she has the right to apply for and hold credit in her birth name, married name, or both. It is not so clear cut for men who change their names during marriage. The rules should apply to men as well, but our society does not take for granted that men may want to take on a marital name, and men may find there to be obstacles in the way.

There is no requirement to tell a creditor if you should be addressed as Miss, Ms., or Mrs. The *Equal Credit Opportunity Act* states that no one may be denied credit because of marital status. Creditors also may not ask about a person's desire to have children or his or her use of birth control. When a married person applies for credit, the creditor may not ask for information about the person's spouse unless his or her individual income is not high enough alone, he or she is in a community property state, or the spouse will be a joint holder or a user on the account. The most important thing to understand about marriage and credit is that what happens to one happens to both. If your spouse has a judgment against him or her, this will be noted on your report. You are both liable for debts incurred during the marriage on joint accounts, even if only one of you knew about them.

If you are in a situation where your credit has been impaired because of your spouse, you need to take steps to separate yourself from him or her and improve your credit rating. Obtain credit in your own name. Many women never do this and never develop an independent credit rating based on their own payment abilities. Upon divorce or the death of their spouse, they find themselves unable to get credit, even though the couple, as a marital unit, may have had a perfect credit rating.

Divorce is not a Debt Solution

Some people believe that if they could just get away from their spouse, they could get out of debt, or at least stop building up debt. While you are married, creditors can pursue you for your spouse's debts that were incurred without your knowledge on a joint account. If you live in a community property state, then you are both responsible for each other's individual debts incurred during marriage as well. Once you are divorced, a court rules who will be responsible for each debt, but until then, expect to hear from your spouse's creditors. If you are separated, you can simply tell them that you are divorcing and ask not to be contacted again.

Divorce usually makes financial troubles worse. When a couple is married, they have a certain combined income and pay for one residence and one set of furniture. They have one set of utility bills. After the divorce, they still have the same combined income, but must now pay for two residences, two sets of bills, and buy duplicate furnishings and household items. The expenses are doubled but the income stays the same. Divorce can cause tremendous debt problems for any couple. A divorce can also be expensive when you consider the attorney's fees and court costs involved in the process.

Marital Debt

When you are married, any debt either of you incurs during marriage is considered a marital debt. If your husband opens a credit card in his name only, racks up thousands of dollars in debt, and fails to pay it, the credit card company can come after you to pay it off, even if you did not know about it.

Debts incurred during marriage must be divided in the divorce. Debt incurred prior to marriage is separate debt and is not part of the divorce.

Dividing Debt

When you divorce, part of what happens is that the court takes a look at all your assets and debts and distributes them according to the laws of your state. You will need to consult an attorney or read a book to learn about the specific laws in your state that govern debt division. Once the judge divides these debts, you will only be responsible for the debts the judge assigns to you.

Before you divorce, you should try to work out a division of debts with your spouse, either on your own or with help from a mediator or attorney. If you are able to do this, you can divide your debts in a way that both of you can manage, rather than end up with a plan made by a judge who will not have the same insight into your situation. You will also save money since you will not have to pay your attorney *courtroom rates* (many attorneys charge more for time spent in court) to try these issues.

There are lots of ways to divide your marital debt, so it pays to be creative about it. You can even work out arrangements where one spouse agrees to take on added debt in order to get a certain asset—for example, your spouse agrees to pay off the Visa bill in exchange for being given a retirement account. When dividing debt, it is always important to look at the bottom line.

Mortgages

Often in a divorce, one spouse ends up keeping the house. Usually this means that the person who keeps the house assumes responsibility for the mortgage. What about the other spouse? When you bought the house, you did it together and you both signed the mortgage papers, making both of you responsible to the bank for the payments. When the judge awards the house to one spouse and makes that spouse responsible for the mortgage, the divorce decree often says that the other spouse is to be *held harmless* for the mortgage, meaning he or she is not to be responsible for the debt. This spouse sometimes thinks he or she is off the hook. However, the judge's ruling does not affect the bank at all. The judge's ruling means that the spouse keeping the house is supposed to make mortgage payments. If he or she does not and the bank comes after the other spouse, the spouse who is keeping the house can be sued by the other one. As far as the bank is concerned, though, you are both still responsible for the mortgage.

The only way to get around this is for the spouse who is keeping the house to refinance the mortgage, thereby removing the other spouse from the mortgage. It is sometimes possible to work with a bank and convince it to remove one person from the mortgage, though this is not a very common occurrence because the bank has little incentive to do so.

Practical Point

A divorce court judge has no authority over the bank holding a mortgage and cannot require the bank to take a name off the mortgage.

Joint Accounts

Most married couples have joint checking and savings accounts. This means that both people entirely own the total amount of money in the accounts. The wife can remove all the money and so can the husband. If you are divorcing and you have joint accounts, the best course of action is to divide them yourselves. If this is not possible, you can ask the court to freeze the account until it can be divided. If you empty out the accounts yourself once a divorce has been filed, you may be held liable to the other spouse for the amount you took, so do not do this without consulting an attorney or reaching an agreement with your spouse.

Most couples also have joint credit card accounts. You are both completely responsible for the total amount of the debt on these accounts. When it becomes clear that a divorce is imminent, it is best to close all joint credit cards and open individual accounts. You can pay off the balance on the joint account together if possible, or you can each transfer a portion of it to your own individual accounts. If you cannot agree, open individual accounts, cut up the joint cards, and each pay half of the monthly payment on the joint account until you can reach an agreement on how to divide it.

Child Support and Alimony

When you divorce, the court not only divides up your possessions, but must also make sure that every member of the family will be financially cared for after the divorce. This includes both spouses as well as the children. *Child support* is usually ordered by the judge in a divorce when there are children. Usually the *noncustodial parent* (the one who does not live with the children) pays a certain amount on a weekly or monthly basis to the other parent. The amount is determined using the noncustodial parent's income and a percentage based on the number of children. Child support is supposed to be used to pay for the children's expenses.

Alimony (also called *maintenance* or *spousal support* in some states) is an amount of money paid by one spouse to the other. It is often thought of as a way to help the nonmoneyed spouse get back on his or her feet financially after the divorce.

If you are the parent who is owed child support, it may make sense to ask that this be paid through your state child support enforcement agency. This agency will handle the collection of the payments and send you checks. This agency will also seek cost of living adjustments when permitted.

REAL LIFE CREDIT

Joy was getting a divorce from her husband. Before they got married, they each had a student loan. After they married, they bought a house, but the mortgage was only in her husband's name. They also had several credit card accounts and two car loans. Joy worked part-time at her daughter's school as an aide and her husband was a chemical engineer. Joy began to panic at the idea of dividing all the debt in half. When she thought about it, though, she realized the mortgage was in his name alone and so she assumed that was going to be his separate debt.

After Joy talked to an attorney, she realized that the mortgage was considered marital debt. The student loans were separate debt, however. Joy's attorney was able to work out a settlement with her husband's attorney. Under the agreement, Joy's husband was going to be responsible for all the credit card debt. Joy would take over the mortgage and keep the house. In addition, her husband paid child support and alimony, which made it possible for Joy to afford to remain in the home.

Divorce and Bankruptcy

Bankruptcy can be a solution to your financial problems. Be aware that you cannot discharge child support or alimony in bankruptcy. If your spouse or ex-spouse goes through a bankruptcy, he or she will get all the debt in his or her name discharged or forgiven. Be aware that if you still have joint debts and your spouse or ex-spouse includes them in the bankruptcy, you then end up being solely responsible for them.

Practical Point

After a divorce, a creditor may not inquire as to your marital status. If you apply for credit, all your income, including child support and alimony, must be considered. You can no longer include your spouse's income when applying for loans or credit.

The bankruptcy court may not always release a debtor from a property settlement agreement or a hold harmless agreement on a mortgage. If the court thinks that the debtor cannot meet basic living expenses, then these debts can be forgiven in bankruptcy. If your spouse files for bankruptcy and seeks to have these debts discharged, you need to hire an attorney and file an adversary proceeding with the bankruptcy court within sixty days of the creditors' meeting (you will be notified by the court of this date). (See Chapter 7 for more detailed information on bankruptcy.)

Death of a Spouse

If your spouse dies, creditors may not close or change the terms of joint accounts you held together. You would, however, be wise to open an account in your own name before notifying creditors of the death of your spouse so you have some credit should you have problems with the joint accounts. It is also important to understand that even if your spouse held debts in his or her name alone, the creditors can file claims against the deceased's estate to be paid. In essence, this will come out of your and your children's inheritance.

RECOGNIZING IDENTITY THEFT

9

Identity theft occurs when someone else uses your personal information, such as date of birth, name, or Social Security number, as his or her own. Identity thieves use this information to obtain new credit, or they use your existing credit and make purchases, leaving you responsible for them. They sometimes open new credit or phone accounts or take out loans using your name and Social Security number. Identity thieves sometimes completely change address forms to divert your mail to them. They also have been known to file for bankruptcy in your name to avoid creditors or eviction.

IT'S A FACT

According to the FTC, there are ten million cases of identity theft annually in the United States. Identity theft costs U.S. businesses $50 billion each year. It is a significant problem.

It can be hard to immediately recognize when identity theft is happening to you, so it is important to learn to spot the signals. Identity theft is a federal crime under the federal *Identity Theft and Assumption Deterrence Act* (which you can find online at **www.ftc. gov/os/statutes/itada/itadact.htm.**)

When identity theft happens, you may not be aware of it. Many people find out when they receive a call from a creditor about a charge or balance they did not create. You might also notice unknown charges on a credit card bill. Getting your credit report every year will help make sure no one is using your identity or accounts. If you spot things on your credit report that you know you were not responsible for, you need to take immediate action.

Preventing Identity Theft

To prevent identity theft, you need to pay attention to how you give out your personal information and how you dispose of garbage that contains your personal information. Before giving out any personal information, ask why it is needed and how it will be used.

Also ask how your personal information is kept at work and what safety measures are in place to protect it. Ask if you can request that your information be kept confidential and not shared in any way.

Keep your purse or wallet with you at all times and do not leave it in your desk at work or on a chair. If you are in the hospital as a patient, have a family member take it home and never leave it unattended in a hospital room or doctor's waiting room. Do not leave your purse in a shopping cart or in an unlocked car.

Social Security Number

Avoid giving out your Social Security number. There are times when it is necessary—when applying for a loan, opening a bank account, and so on. However, there is no reason to give out this information if you are making a purchase or filling out a background information form for a dentist. Your best line of defense is to keep this information to yourself except when it is absolutely necessary. Always ask why it is being requested and do not give it out unless there is a valid reason. Do not carry your Social Security card in your wallet or purse. You will hardly ever need it, so keep it in a safe place at home. Never give out your Social Security number over email. Some people make up a number if a dentist or doctor insists on having it for their files. They do not need this information to bill your insurance company, so there is no reason you should have to provide it.

Passwords and Account Numbers

Do not give your passwords, personal identification numbers (PINs), or account numbers to anyone. Use different passwords for different accounts. Choose passwords and PINs that are not easy to guess and use a combination of letters and numbers. Avoid using your birth date, anniversary, or middle name. Do not write your passwords down or carry them in your purse or wallet. If you find you need to keep a written record of them, keep it at home and do not label it clearly as such. Keep it in a hard-to-find place.

Credit and ATM Cards

Carry only those cards that you use on a regular basis. Leave the rest at home in a secure location. Close accounts that you do not use.

Before discarding credit card receipts, make sure you tear them up or shred them so the account number and expiration date are not readable. Cut up credit cards you are discarding.

Some credit cards offer you the option of including a small photo of yourself on the card. This can help reduce identity theft, or at least prevent that particular card from being used. Keep track of when your credit card bills are supposed to arrive in the mail. If they are more than two days late, call and ask if the statement has been sent and ask that another be sent to you. You can also monitor your account activity online, receive email notifications only when your online bill is ready, and pay your bills online as well.

Maintain a list of all your credit cards so that you know what you have, and if they are stolen you have an easy reference to use to report them. Use the CREDIT CARD LIST (form 36, p.400.)

Online Activities

When you make online purchases or apply for loans online, make sure the site you are dealing with is using a secure server. Never give out account numbers or Social Security numbers via email since the message could possibly be intercepted. If you must give an account number or Social Security number to a merchant who does not use a secure server, fax the information or call him or her and give the number over the phone

Be aware that one scam that identity thieves use is sending you email pretending to be from your Internet service provider or online banking system telling you that you need to update your account information or reverify your credit card information.

REAL LIFE CREDIT

Aaron left his wallet in the rental car he was using while on vacation in Florida. He parked it in a lot at the beach and left his wallet in the glove compartment. He came back to find that the car had been broken into and his wallet stolen. He called the police first and made a report. Next, he called his brother. Aaron and his brother exchanged lists of their credit cards each year in case of this kind of situation. His brother gave him the information he needed to call the companies and alert them of the theft. Because he called immediately, he was able to prevent attempted charges of $3,000 the thief tried to make within the next hour.

He alerted his bank that his ATM card was stolen, so it was stopped. Aaron notified all three credit reporting agencies about the theft and had a fraud alert placed on his account. He called his state motor vehicle department to report his license stolen. He did not carry his Social Security number in his wallet, and he did not keep any banking information there either, so he did not worry about that information being stolen.

Aaron checked his credit reports every few weeks for the next few months after the theft to be sure there was no further activity on his account related to the theft. The thief was never caught, but Aaron was able to prevent any huge financial loss.

Telephone Sales

Never give out your account numbers, Social Security information, or other personal information to a person over the phone. If someone contacts you by phone with a special offer or service for sale that you are interested in, ask for the information in writing.

If a bank or store calls you to verify information, always call them back—at the number you look up yourself and verify is correct.

Garbage Disposal

Be careful about how you dispose of garbage that contains account numbers or other personal information. Buy a shredder or rip things up before throwing them out. Cut up old credit cards before discarding them. Rip or shred credit card convenience checks before throwing them out. Shred account statements, deposit receipts, withdrawal receipts, and other documents with numbers on them that could be copied. If you do not have a shredder and do not want to buy one (they are inexpensive), some municipalities have recycling days when they will bring in an industrial-strength shredder to a public location for everyone to come use.

Home Security

Consider purchasing a small fireproof safe to keep at home. Some of these are the size of a shoebox and cost under $40. Keep birth certificates, Social Security cards, marriage licenses, bonds, and other valuable items in it. It is also a good idea to maintain a list of your credit cards, account numbers, and contact information at home so that if your purse or wallet is stolen, you can easily contact the credit card companies about the theft.

Protecting Your Mail

If your mailbox is a roadside box—or a box attached to the house and no one is home all day—make sure that you remove mail as soon as it is delivered. If you are unable to do so or are concerned about your mail sitting in the box all day, consider renting a post office box for all mail. Do not leave your outgoing mail sitting in a roadside box. Deposit it in a post office drop box. Mail that sits in boxes is easily stolen. Do not take your personal mail to work to be sent out with your employer's mail. Someone else in the office could open it and obtain your account numbers. If you notice that some of your mail has been opened or tampered with, report it to your local post office.

Large Scale Identity Theft

In recent years there have been more and more incidents where whole groups of credit card numbers are stolen from a store's computers. There is not much you can do to prevent this happening to you since it has to do with the store's security. However, should you find out that your credit card number is among those that have been stolen or breached, there are some steps you can take to protect yourself.

First, verify that your credit card number was among those stolen. Call the company or store and get details and verification. Find out when the theft happened. Next, notify your credit card company that yours was one of the cards stolen. You can ask that you be issued a new account number if you are very worried, or you can carefully monitor the charges on your statement and immediately report any activity you were not responsible for.

Online Scams

There are many online scams and it is important to be aware of them so that you can avoid them. Any email that seems to come from a bank or financial institution that you deal with that asks you to verify, update, or validate personal information is probably a scam. Identity thieves *spoof* email, making it appear to come from a legitimate source, but then use the information you provide for illegitimate purposes. Sometimes these emails include links to what appear to be real Web pages belonging to the financial institutions they are spoofing. If you have an eBay or Paypal account, you may also often get similar emails seeking information about your account. Report these types of emails to the site that is being spoofed. Do not reply to the emails. Never give out personal or financial information by email or on a Web page in this way. If you are concerned that this might be a real request, close your browser and email, type in the company's real Web address, and check your account or call and ask. Look to see that the Web address begins with "https" (meaning it is a secure site). A spam filter can help sort these emails for you.

You should also be aware of *phishing*, which uses pop-up messages while you are on the Internet to try to get you to disclose personal or financial information. If you receive any messages that you suspect are spoofs or phishing, forward them to the FTC at spam@ uce.gov.

It is important to have current antivirus software running on your computer and to use firewalls to prevent unauthorized access to your computer. Be careful about opening attachments in emails and only open those that come from people you know and people from whom you are expecting an attachment. Use passwords that contain letters and numbers and do not use the same password for everything. Do not use your birth date, marriage date, or Social Security number as a password. For more information about keeping your information safe and running protection software, visit **www.OnGuardOnline.gov**.

Do not get excited if you receive an email telling you that you have won a lottery. Lottery winners are never notified by email. Delete this email. Never respond to a request from someone who claims to be from another country and needs your help obtaining an inheritance or setting up a bank account in this country. Some of these emails can seem very honest and heartbreaking, but they are not real. If you want to help people, get involved with a bona fide charity.

Identity Theft Prevention Checklist

☐ Shred all credit card receipts, application copies, or bills you are disposing.

☐ Never give out account numbers or Social Security numbers by email.

☐ Only use secure servers when buying online.

☐ Do not leave outgoing or incoming mail sitting in a roadside mailbox.

☐ Consider using a post office box.

☐ Take all outgoing mail to a post office or drop box.

☐ Shred all credit card offers you are discarding.

☐ Avoid giving your Social Security number unless absolutely required.

☐ Obtain your credit report every year to check for accounts you did not open or balances you did not create.

☐ Never carry your Social Security card in your wallet or purse.

☐ Do not respond to email asking for your assistance in a financial matter.

☐ Do not write down your PIN numbers and especially do not write them on the cards or carry them on pieces of paper in your wallet or purse.

☐ Do not give your PIN number to anyone, even close friends or family.

☐ Pick PIN numbers that are random and do not stand for your birth date, anniversary, middle name, or anything of significance.

☐ Always check credit cards bills and bank statements for transactions or charges you did not incur. This can be your first clue to an identity theft problem.

Dealing with Identity Theft

Should identity theft happen to you, there are several steps you need to take. First, make sure it is in fact identity theft. If there is a charge on your credit card statement that you do not recognize, call the credit card company and get more information about it. You may have charged this item yourself and do not recognize the name, or the vendor may hold its credit card accounts in a different name than the one with which you are familiar. If there is a charge for a vendor or merchant from whom you have charged other items, this may be a duplicate charge made in error and not the result of identity theft. In this case, dispute the charge with the credit card company. If a vendor is listed in a city you have never visited, you cannot assume it is identity theft. Often vendors list their corporate or central offices on credit cards. If you are unsure, call the credit card company and ask where the charge was originated. Credit card companies can also tell you if the actual card was presented at the time of purchase or if just the number was supplied, such as for a phone or online order. If other charges appear with other vendors that you did not authorize, it is likely there has been identity theft.

Police Reports

Once you are certain that you did not incur the charges, the very first thing to do is to file a report with your local police. You will be asked questions and will need to sign a complaint. If your local police tell you they cannot take a report—if, for example, the identity thief used your information out of state—tell them how important the report will be as a record for you to use with your creditors to prove that the theft happened.

Remind them that under the voluntary *Police Report Initiative*, credit bureaus will automatically block the fraudulent accounts and bad debts from appearing on your credit report, but only if you can give them a copy of the police report. If you cannot get the local police to take a report, try your county sheriff or state police. If you are told that identity theft is not a crime under your state law, ask to file a *Miscellaneous Incident Report* instead. Give a copy of the report to creditors. Always make sure you retain a copy of the report for your records.

Practical Point

If you think you have been a victim of identity theft, visit **www.consumer.gov/idtheft** for immediate help. You can also call the FTC's Identity Theft hotline at: 877-ID-THEFT (438-4338), or write:

Federal Trade Commission
Consumer Response Center
600 Pennsylvania Avenue, NW
Washington, DC 20580

Creditors

Contact the creditor or loan company that was used by the thief. Notify the company in writing that you did not incur the charges and that your information was used illegally. Immediately close the account and open a new one with a PIN or security code attached to it. Ask that PINs be verified before changing the address on the accounts.

Contact all three of the credit reporting agencies and alert them that your identity has been stolen. Obtain current copies of your credit reports to check for other instances of identity theft. Ask that a *security alert* be placed on your credit file as well as a victim's statement asking that creditors call you before opening an account in your name. Request that inquiries made on behalf of the thief be removed from your file.

An *initial fraud alert* stays in your file for at least ninety days. An *extended alert* stays in your file for seven years. To place either of these alerts, a consumer credit reporting company will require you to provide appropriate proof of your identity, which may include your Social Security number. If you ask for an extended alert, you will have to provide an *identity theft report*. An *identity theft report* includes a copy of a report you have filed with a federal, state, or local law enforcement agency. For more detailed information about the identity theft report, visit **www.consumer.gov/idtheft**.

Note that once you notify one credit reporting agency of a fraud alert, it must contact the other two agencies with the information and have the same alert placed on those files as well. You may wish to follow up with the other two agencies to be sure they have actually placed the alert.

Here are important numbers to call to alert credit reporting agencies of fraud and identity theft.

Experian: 877-576-5734
Equifax: 888-397-3742
TransUnion: 800-680-7289

If you have a police report, send a copy to the three credit reporting agencies and ask that they block the information you are disputing (the charges you did not make) from your credit reports. They have thirty days to implement this. The credit bureaus can remove the block if they believe it was wrongly placed.

If your credit card is stolen or used without your permission, you are only liable for the first $50 charged if you report the theft within two business days. This also applies to ATM cards. If you wait more than two days, your liability increases, so it is important to report this kind of theft immediately. If your identity is stolen and someone applies for loans or credit cards using your information, it can be very difficult to prove that you are not liable. However, you cannot be held responsible if you can prove you were not the person incurring the debt. Should you learn that someone has used your identity, it is important to get your credit report immediately to find out if the thief has opened other accounts or tapped into other accounts of yours. Ask your credit reporting agency to assist you in contacting all your creditors about the situation. If there are creditors who insist you are responsible for the debts, you will need to hire an attorney.

Notify your employer of the identity theft and make sure the human resources department will not give out information from your personnel file without your permission.

Banks and Investments

Alert your bank that your identity has been stolen so that signatures for your accounts will be carefully verified. Close your accounts and open new PIN-verified accounts if your bank accounts have been accessed. Cancel your ATM or debit card and get a new one. The *Electronic Fund Transfer Act* gives you consumer protections for transactions involving an ATM or debit card or any other electronic debiting or crediting to an account (such as online transfers). It also limits your liability for unauthorized electronic fund transfers. Report lost or stolen ATM and debit cards immediately because the amount you can be held responsible for depends on how quickly you report the loss.

- If you report the loss or theft within two business days of discovering it, your losses are limited to $50.

- If you report it after two business days but within sixty days after a statement showing an unauthorized electronic fund transfer, you can be liable for up to $500 of what a thief withdraws.

- If you wait more than sixty days, you could be responsible for all the money that was taken from your account from the end of the sixty days to the time you reported your card missing.

If investments have been accessed by the thief, contact the *Securities and Exchange Commission* at:

100 F Street, NE
Washington, DC 20549
202-942-8088
www.sec.gov/investor.shtml

If checks have been stolen or used by the thief, stop payment on them. The following check verification companies can provide services (for a fee) to help you track down the checks.

- **SCAN:** 800-717-1245

- **TeleCheck:** 800-735-3362

- **CrossCheck:** 800-552-1900

If you have difficulty getting assistance from your bank, contact these agencies.

- *Federal Deposit Insurance Corporation (FDIC).* The FDIC supervises state-chartered banks that are not members of the Federal Reserve System and insures deposits at banks and savings and loans institutions. Contact the FDIC at:

Federal Deposit Insurance Corporation
Division of Compliance and Consumer Affairs
550 17th Street, NW
Washington, DC 20429
800-925-4618 (Consumer Call Center)
www.fdic.gov

- FDIC publications that may be helpful to you include:

  - Classic Cons...and How to Counter Them: **www.fdic. gov/consumers/consumer/news/cnsprg98/cons.html**

  - A Crook Has Drained Your Account. Who Pays?: **www.fdic.gov/consumers/consumer/news/cnsprg98/ crook.html**

  - Your Wallet: A Loser's Manual: **www.fdic.gov/ consumers/consumer/news/cnfall97/wallet.html**

- *Federal Reserve System (Fed).* The Fed supervises state-chartered banks that are members of the Federal Reserve System. Contact the Fed at:

Federal Reserve Board
20th Street and Constitution Avenue NW
Washington, DC 20551
202-452-3693
www.federalreserve.gov

- *Local Federal Reserve Bank in your area.* The twelve Reserve Banks are located in Boston, New York, Philadelphia, Cleveland, Richmond, Atlanta, Chicago, St. Louis, Minneapolis, Kansas City, Dallas, and San Francisco.

- *National Credit Union Administration (NCUA).* The NCUA charters and supervises federal credit unions and insures deposits at federal credit unions and many state credit unions. Contact the NCUA at:

National Credit Union Administration
1775 Duke Street
Alexandria, VA 22314
703-518-6300
www.ncua.gov

- *Office of the Comptroller of the Currency (OCC).* The OCC charters and supervises national banks. If the word *national* appears in the name of a bank, or the initials N.A. follow its name, the OCC oversees its operations. Contact the OCC at:

Customer Assistance Group
1301 McKinney Street
Suite 3450
Houston, TX 77010
800-613-6743
www.occ.treas.gov

- OCC publications that may be helpful to you include:

  - Check Fraud: A Guide to Avoiding Losses: **www.occ. treas.gov/chckfrd/chckfrd.pdf**

  - How to Avoid Becoming a Victim of Identity Theft: **www.occ.treas.gov/idtheft.pdf**

  - Identity Theft and Pretext Calling Advisory Letter 2001-4: **www.occ.treas.gov/ftp/advisory/2001-4.doc**

- *Office of Thrift Supervision (OTS)*. The OTS is the primary regulator of all federal, and many state-chartered, thrift institutions, which include savings banks and savings and loan institutions. Contact the OTS at:

Office of Thrift Supervision
1700 G Street, NW
Washington, DC 20552
202-906-6000
www.ots.treas.gov

Telephones and Utilities

If the identity thief has set up a phone line or account in your name—either a land line or a cell phone—or is using your accounts, call your phone service provider to report this. Close your current accounts and set up new ones with new PIN numbers and account numbers.

For help with local service problems, call your state public utility commission listed in the government guide of your phone book. For help with long distance or cell phones or cable or satellite issues, contact the *Federal Communications Commission* (FCC) at:

Federal Communications Commission
Consumer Information Bureau
445 12th Street SW
Washington, DC 20554
888-CALL-FCC

You can file complaints via the online complaint form at **www.fcc. gov**, or email questions to fccinfo@fcc.gov.

Other Agencies

Contact your state Department of Motor Vehicles (DMV) to find out if your driver's license is being used by the identity thief. Ask that your DMV files be flagged for fraud, so that any activity is carefully monitored and verified. If your state uses your Social Security number as your driver's license number, ask to use another number, because if the thief has your Social Security number, then he or she can access your DMV file.

If your mail has been stolen or tampered with, contact your local post office. You can get more information at **www.usps.gov/ websites/depart/inspect**.

If you suspect your passport has been used or tampered with, contact the U.S. Department of State. Check the government guide of your phone book for your local office. You can read more online at **www.travel.state.gov/passport/passport_1738.html**.

If your Social Security number was used by the thief, contact the *Social Security Administration's Fraud Hotline*. It is possible to obtain a new one.

Social Security Fraud Hotline
P.O. Box 17768
Baltimore, MD 21235
800-269-0271
www.ssa.gov/oig/hotline/index.htm

Once you have a new number, request a Social Security Earnings report to verify that all the information is now correct. (You can do so on the Social Security Administration's website.)

For more information, read these Social Security Administration (SSA) publications.

- Report Fraud to the Hotline: **www.ssa.gov/oig/hotline/ index.htm**

- Your Social Security Number and Card (SSA Pub. No. 05-10002): **www.ssa.gov/pubs/10002.html**

- Identity Theft and Your Social Security Number (SSA Pub. No. 05-10064): **www.ssa.gov/pubs/10064.html**

If you believe that the identity thief has used your identity to file tax returns, you need to contact both the Internal Revenue Service (IRS) as well as your state income tax agency (see the government guide of your phone book). Contact the IRS Taxpayer Advocate Office at 877-777-4778.

If the perpetrator has been caught, talk to an attorney about a lawsuit to compensate you for the costs and problems you have faced. The thief is not only criminally responsible, but can be sued in a civil case as well.

If one of your credit accounts has been used, you need to contact the security department of the credit card company. Close the account and open a new one with a new number. Request that a password be required on the new account. File a police report and get copies of it. You may need these copies to prove you have been a victim of identity theft when dealing with credit reporting agencies or other creditors.

If your wallet or purse was stolen, you must close every single account for which you had a card in your wallet, and have new cards issued with new account numbers. Make sure you notify the creditor and the credit reporting agencies in writing that you are a victim of identity theft. Include copies of all supporting documents. Use the IDENTITY THEFT TRACKING SHEET to track all your activity and notifications. (see form 38, p.402.)

ID Theft Affidavit

The FTC has created an ID THEFT AFFIDAVIT, a form you can complete and submit to everyone you need to contact about the theft of your identity. (see form 39, p.403.) This form is accepted by many banks, credit card companies, and other lenders, and it reduces the amount of paperwork you need to complete to report identity theft. A copy of the form with instructions can also be found at **www.ftc.gov/bcp/conline/pubs/credit/affidavit.pdf**.

You will be required to prove that your Social Security number has been stolen before a new one will be issued.

Bankruptcy

While it might sound strange, it is possible that the identity thief could file for bankruptcy in your name in order to wipe out existing debts so that he or she can get more credit in your name. If you suspect this has happened—if a creditor tells you a bankruptcy is showing up on a credit report or if you receive any communication from a bankruptcy court about debts in your name—you need to contact the U.S. Trustee in your area (look in the government pages of your phone book under U.S. Government Bankruptcy Administration). You can also find a list of offices online at: **www.usdoj.gov/ust**.

Send a letter to the office following up on your phone call. Use the LETTER TO U.S. BANKRUPTCY TRUSTEE for this. (see form 37, p.401.) Your letter should describe the situation and provide proof of your identity. The U.S. Trustee, if appropriate, will make a criminal referral to law enforcement authorities if you provide appropriate documentation to substantiate your claim. You also may want to file a complaint with the U.S. attorney general or the FBI in the city where the bankruptcy was filed. You may need to hire an attorney to help convince the bankruptcy court that the filing is fraudulent. The U.S. Trustee does not provide consumers with free copies of court documents. Those documents are available from the bankruptcy clerk's office for a fee.

Crimes in Your Name

If the identity thief has been arrested while pretending to be you or criminal complaints have been filed against him or her while he or she was impersonating you, you need to contact that law enforcement agency that made the arrest or took the complaint. There may be outstanding warrants for your arrest or scheduled court dates in your name. File an *impersonation report*. Ask to have your identity confirmed by taking fingerprints and photos, as well as copies of your license. Ask the police to compare the prints and photos with those of the thief to establish your innocence. If the arrest warrant is from a state or county other than where you live, ask your local police department to send the impersonation report to the police department in the jurisdiction where the arrest warrant, traffic citation, or criminal conviction originated.

Ask the agency to search the FTC Consumer Sentinel database for other complaints in your community that fit the pattern. If there are related crimes, there will be more resources used to investigate.

The law enforcement agency should recall any warrants and issue a *clearance letter* or *certificate of release* (if you were arrested and booked). You will need to keep this document with you at all times in case you are wrongly arrested. Also, ask the law enforcement agency to file, with the district attorney's office and the court where the crime took place, the record of the follow-up investigation establishing your innocence. This will result in an amended complaint being issued. Once your name is recorded in a criminal database, it is unlikely that it will be completely removed from the official record. Ask that the *key name*, or *primary name*, be changed from your name to the imposter's name (or to "John Doe" if the imposter's true identity is not known), with your name noted only as an alias.

You will also need to clear your name in the court records. Talk to an attorney to find out what your state laws are about this. If your state has no formal procedure for clearing your record, contact the district attorney's office in the county where the case was originally prosecuted and ask for the court records needed to clear your name.

Looking at the Identity Theft Risk Realistically

While identity theft is a problem many people face, you can protect yourself by being careful about how you give out information. The best way to deal with identity theft is to prevent it from occurring at all. Unless you have an ongoing problem with recurring identity theft, there is no reason to cancel all your credit cards, close your bank accounts, and stop making online purchases.

Having your identity stolen or your personal information accessed and used by someone else is a terrible feeling. You may feel violated, frightened, nervous, depressed, and very angry. The best way to deal with these feelings is to take active steps to deal with the theft. Keep good records, protect your information from future would-be thieves, and always remember that it is not your fault. You did not bring this on yourself, you did not do anything wrong, and you are not the criminal. If you find you are having a hard time coping with the aftermath of identity theft, think about talking with a counselor or therapist. It is not uncommon to experience depression or anxiety after being the victim of a crime like this. Here are some additional resources to assist you if you have been a victim of identity theft.

Identity Theft Clearinghouse
Federal Trade Commission
600 Pennsylvania Avenue, NW
Washington, DC 20580
FTC Identity Theft Hotline
877-ID-THEFT (438-4338)
www.consumer.gov/idtheft

Identity Theft Resource Center
P.O. Box 26833
San Diego CA 92196
858-693-7935
www.idtheftcenter.org

Privacy Rights Clearinghouse
3100 5th Avenue
Suite B
San Diego, CA 92103
619-298-3396
www.privacyrights.org

Call for Action, Inc.
5272 River Road
Suite 300
Bethesda, MD 20816
866-ID-HOTLINE
(866-434-6854)
www.callforaction.org

Checklist for Lost or Stolen Purse or Wallet

☐ File a report with the police immediately.

☐ Get a copy of the report in case your bank, credit card company, or insurance company needs proof of the crime.

☐ Cancel each credit and charge card that was in the purse or wallet by calling the companies and notifying them of the theft.

☐ Get new cards with new account numbers.

☐ Call the fraud departments of the major credit reporting agencies—Equifax (877-576-5734), Experian (888-397-3742), and TransUnion (800-680-7289)—and ask them to put a *fraud alert* on your account and add a *victim's statement* to your file requesting that creditors contact you before opening new accounts in your name.

☐ Ask the credit bureaus for copies of your credit reports.

☐ Review your reports carefully to make sure no additional fraudulent accounts have been opened in your name or unauthorized changes made to your existing accounts.

☐ In a few months, order new copies of your reports to verify your corrections and changes, and to make sure no new fraudulent activity has occurred.

☐ Report the loss to your bank if your wallet or purse contained bank account information, including account numbers, ATM cards, or checks.

☐ Cancel checking and savings accounts and open new ones.

☐ Stop payments on outstanding checks you did not write.

☐ Get a new ATM card, account number, and personal identification number (PIN) or password.

☐ Report your missing driver's license to the department of motor vehicles. If your state uses your Social Security number as your driver's license number, ask to substitute another number.

☐ Change the locks on your home and car if your keys were taken. Do not give an identity thief access to even more personal property and information.

CREATING A GOOD CREDIT RECORD | 10

Now that you have begun to work on your credit record and have started to get your debts in order, you should consider what you can proactively do to purposefully create a good credit record for yourself. It is important to remember that just as it took time to build up debt and poor credit, it will take a long time to create a credit record that will benefit you. Even if you have fairly good credit, it is important that you learn how to protect and maintain it.

IT'S A FACT!

The majority of consumers have good credit. Forty-five percent of consumers have a credit score between 700 and 799, and 13% have a credit score above 800, according to statistics from Fair Isaac.

Understanding Credit Terms

There are some basic terms to understand when you are working with credit.

- **Finance charges.** There are two types of finance charges. *Annual percentage rate* (APR) is the amount of interest you will pay each year on your balance, such as 19%. *Monthly periodic rate* is simply the APR divided by twelve months.

  To understand how much you are paying in interest, multiply the amount of your monthly payment by the number of months you will pay on the loan. This shows the total amount you will pay. Subtract the amount you borrowed from this number, and it will show you how much you will be paying in interest alone over the life of the loan.

  To understand how interest on your credit cards is calculated, contact your credit card company's customer service department and it can give you a computer-generated calculation of how interest will accrue and be paid on your credit card debt. You can also calculate interest using an online calculation, such as the one at **www.bankrate.com/brm/popcalcz.asp**.

- **Annual fees.** Some credit cards charge you a yearly fee just to use the card. The fee appears on your statement once a year and can range from $30 and up. Many companies will waive this fee if you ask. There are cards that do not charge this type of fee, so shop around.

- **Grace period.** Some credit cards offer a grace period. This is the time between the date the billing cycle closes and the date you have to pay the balance to avoid any finance charges.

- **Fees.** There are myriad fees you can encounter with credit cards. There are late payment fees, cash advance fees, fees for checks that bounce, fees for exceeding your credit limit, etc. One type of fee to avoid is a *transaction fee*. If your card has a *transaction fee*, you will be charged a small amount each time you use the card. This can really add up, so avoid it whenever possible.

Obtaining New Credit

If you have a bankruptcy or other poor credit entries on your record, you need to understand that you cannot walk out tomorrow and easily get a new credit card. Most creditors are going to turn you down. Even though you have now turned over a new leaf and have your financial situation under control, credit card companies are going to see you as a bad risk. Even if you have good credit, it is important to understand how to maintain your good credit standing.

Credit Agreements

There are some credit card companies that will eventually give you credit. You can often get a credit card within two years of bankruptcy. When you do apply for credit, read the agreements carefully and be sure to notice the interest rate and monthly fees proposed. Find out if there is a fee for cash advances, how the interest is calculated, and how often credit limits are reviewed. If you are offered a terrific deal, such as no payments for six months, be sure to find out if interest accrues during this period and find out what the interest rate will shoot up to after this introductory period.

Merchant Accounts

If you find that you are having difficulty being approved for new credit, try applying for credit with a local merchant, such as a department store. These types of cards are much easier to qualify for and can help you begin to build a good history so that you can then apply for a major credit card. Do not bother with catalog company credit cards. These cards have high interest rates and are not usually reported to credit reporting agencies, thus they do nothing to improve your credit rating.

Debit Cards

Debit cards are a great substitute for credit cards. A debit card appears on its face like a credit card. When you make a purchase with a debit card, the amount of the purchase is automatically deducted from your bank account and paid to the debit card company. Any purchase over the amount of funds in the account is denied. This type of card limits you to money you actually have, but can still be abused when it is used to withdraw the money you are supposed to be saving for rent or utilities.

Secured Cards

A *secured card* is similar to a debit card; however, the money you deposit remains untouched, earning interest. Your credit limit equals the amount you deposit with the bank. You are billed for your purchases and charged interest on them. If you fail to pay, the money you have deposited is kept by the bank. Make sure that the bank you deposit the money in is a federally insured bank and that the card can be converted to an unsecured card after eighteen months. Be sure you know the finance rate. Confirm that the company will report your account to credit reporting agencies since doing so will help establish good credit. Also be sure that if there is an application fee for this type of card, it is refundable if your application is denied.

Cosignors

If you cannot qualify for a credit card on your own and do not have the cash to set up a debit or secured card, you may wish to ask a family member or friend to cosign for you on a credit card or loan. The other person promises to pay the lender if you cannot pay and gives the lender the extra protection desired.

User Accounts

Another alternative is to have a friend or relative set up a credit card in his or her own name and then request that a card is issued to you. You can use the card, but the other person will be responsible for payment. Request that the bank report the card on your credit report. This will not have much impact on your credit rating, but it will get you access to credit.

Credit Report References

When you apply for credit, if you know that one of your credit reports from one of the big three reporting agencies appears more favorable than the others, ask the potential creditor to use that report. Attach anything to your credit application that may be favorable, such as tax returns or information about your assets. Be sure to completely fill in applications—you can be denied for failing to complete the application.

Frequent Application

Do not apply for credit too often. Every time you apply, an inquiry is made on your credit report and the inquiry is recorded on your report. Reports that have too many inquiries are not regarded favorably. Future creditors will feel you have been turned down frequently or that you are seeking too much credit.

Reapplication

If you apply for credit, and your application is denied, ask that it be sent to the reapplications department. Most major creditors have such departments where they will seriously reevaluate an application.

Fine Print

When you apply for credit, be sure to carefully read all the fine print. Some cards charge many different fees that will add up substantially when using the card. You would also be wise to shop around for a low finance rate on the card if you plan to carry a balance.

Equal Credit Opportunity Act

The *Equal Credit Opportunity Act* protects consumers from discrimination when they apply for credit. Consumers may not be denied credit because of age, race, religion, national origin, or because they receive public assistance, alimony, or child support, or if they work part-time.

Under this law, creditors have thirty days from the date of receiving all your information to notify you if you have been accepted or rejected. You must be notified in writing if you are rejected. You are entitled to a reason as to why you have been rejected—this may be in the letter, or the company may give you a phone number to call to get the information—as well the name and address of the credit reporting bureau from which your report was obtained.

The Internet can be a fast, convenient way to obtain information about the true costs of credit and to find credit cards. For example, you can use an online calculator to help you understand the true costs of any credit card offer (or other loans you are considering). One is available at **www.bankrate.com/brm/rate/calc_home.asp**. Other sites available to find credit cards include the following.

- http://moneycentral.msn.com/banking/services/ creditcard.asp

- www.bankrate.com/brm/rate/cc_home.asp

- www.credit-land.com

- www.lowcards.com

Improving Current Credit

If you have current credit cards, there are steps you can take to improve your credit with them. To increase your line of credit, maintain a good payment history for a minimum of three months and then ask for an increase in your limit. Paying more than the minimum each month will also improve your chances of getting an increase. Avoid going over your credit limit, as this will count against you. Paying on time is important, but you should know that most credit cards do not report delinquencies until they are at least two payments behind.

Statement of Circumstances

If you know you have some items on your credit report that are negative and you have been denied credit because of them, you may need to start submitting a STATEMENT OF CIRCUMSTANCES along with your application (see form 40, p.410). This statement allows you to offer an explanation for what happened, for example, if you have been ill and unable to work and overcome with medical bills. This statement also allows you to explain to the creditor in writing how your situation has changed and the steps you have taken to improve your situation. This could help convince a creditor to offer you credit you really need.

Account Closings

If you have many credit cards, you should close the ones you do not use regularly and leave yourself no more than two or three cards. A long list of open accounts makes many lenders nervous, even if the accounts are inactive. At any time, you could decide to use them and charge more than you can pay.

How to Use Your New Credit Cards

Now that you are working toward repairing your credit, if you have been able to obtain new credit cards, or if you still have your old cards, you must develop a new attitude about them. You need to think of the credit cards as a convenience and not as an extension of your spending capabilities. You should use your credit cards if you are able to do so in a controlled and reasonable way, but you should be certain to pay the entire balance off each month and not let interest accrue on the account. Using the cards and paying them off responsibly will help improve your credit rating. The creditors will report that you are paying as agreed and on time. You should never use your credit card unless you have cash in the bank or in your possession to pay for it at the time of purchase. A credit card should be a convenience, not a necessity. Pay careful attention to the due date on each bill and pay it on time.

If you find that you simply are not able to control your credit card spending, think about putting your cards in the freezer or your home safe. If you want to use them, you will have to make a point to get them out. Some people who have real difficulty with credit card spending keep their cards in a block of ice. It takes time and attention to chip them out or wait for it to melt—plenty of time to rethink your purchase.

Payments

Most credit cards offer a thirty-day grace period on purchases. Purchases made on June 1 will not incur interest until July 1. This means you can borrow money from your credit card company interest free each month for thirty days. Grace periods only apply if you have no outstanding balance. If you are carrying a balance on your card, interest will be charged on new purchases as well as the old balance. Getting your payment in on time is important. As suggested earlier in this book, to be sure your payment is made on time, mail it back as soon as you get it, or schedule the online payment immediately. It is to your advantage to pay off your credit card balances each month. If you already have an outstanding balance, you should attempt to pay some money each month toward the principal that you owe so you can gradually eliminate the balance.

Maintaining Accounts

Avoid obtaining too many credit cards. One or two really should be more than enough, particularly if you have had a past history of overusing them, not paying them on time, or just misusing them. It can be tempting to open more when you receive an offer in the mail for a card with an initial low interest rate, but remember that these initial rates always go up. Often these cards do not offer the best terms or interest rates available. If you do receive them, cut them up and send a letter to the bank rejecting them. The more accounts you have open, the more you can charge and end up owing. The best way to control credit card spending is to have a small number of cards that you use sparingly and in a controlled fashion.

Practical Point

The more open accounts you have on your credit report, the less likely you are to obtain new credit.

Choosing a Card

If you are trying to choose which accounts to keep and which accounts to close, consider the interest rates as well as any cash back or special discount programs the cards offer. Some cards offer a rebate (usually 1%) on purchases made with the card. Other cards allow you to accumulate frequent flyer miles or other special discounts. Avoid cards that require an annual fee, although often you can convince the company to waive the fee. If you plan on carrying a balance, the interest rate is the most important factor, since even a small difference can save you lots of money. If you plan to pay your card off each month, then the interest rate should not matter.

When comparing cash back offers or rewards programs, get the details on the rules. They may say they offer 1% back in cash, but in reality you may only get the 1% over a certain total charged. You can get rewards that offer you products you can "buy" with points you earn. If you are a frequent traveler, you might be interested in air miles. You can even choose a card that pays money into a retirement account.

There are lots of reward options and it is important to compare dollars spent to rewards earned and consider how often you would use the rewards offered. Rewards are great; however, a $50 cash reward does not justify buying something expensive and extravagant. It can be easy to fall into the trap of thinking, "Well, I'm not really spending that much since I'm getting a reward." Compare dollars spent to rewards earned and you will see you are earning a very insignificant amount.

REAL LIFE CREDIT

Elizabeth spent several years cleaning up her credit, getting out of debt, and improving her financial situation. She worked hard to get herself to a point where she was no longer at the mercy of her bills. She was so proud to have paid off all her debt. She felt like she was making a fresh start. Part of that fresh start was learning how to make good choices when it came to credit. She was ready to apply for new credit, but did not want to make any of the same mistakes she made in the past. The first thing she did was decide that she would use credit only as a convenience. She did not plan to carry any balances on her cards. Because of this she was not concerned with interest rates, but she was interested in getting a card that would benefit her the most. She compared many cards to get an understanding of their rewards programs, online payment policies, and other benefits. Based on this, she selected one card and applied for it. She used it only to make life easier. She never got cash advances and she never charged more than she could pay off at the next payment date.

Cash Advances

Be aware that cash advances are not *free* money. Most credit cards charge transaction fees, and interest begins accumulating immediately on these transactions. You are better off charging something than to take a cash advance and pay cash. If you need cash, you are far better off using your ATM card. If you do not have cash and need cash immediately, remember that a cash advance is really just a high-interest loan. You might be able to borrow cash from a family member or friend instead.

Tracking Your Cards

Keep a list of all your credit cards, including account numbers and phone numbers for customer service, so that you know at all times what credit you have available and also so that you can easily make a report if your cards are stolen. It is also helpful to keep track of your credit limits so you do not exceed them. Use the CREDIT CARD LIST (form 36, p.400.) It is also a good idea to photocopy the front and back of all your cards and keep this photocopy with your list.

IT'S A FACT!

According to the Federal Reserve, 25% of U.S. households have no credit card debt and 30% pay off their balances each month.

Obtaining Loans

After you have had debt problems or after your credit report has had negative information placed on it that cannot be removed, you may despair over not being able to get a car loan or a mortgage, let alone a personal loan. There are, in fact, ways to get loans after experiencing these difficulties. Remember, never take out a loan if you will not be able to pay it back. A loan does not mean free cash, but is instead a responsibility to make regular payments.

One strategy to obtain a loan is to make a large down payment on the car or home and pay a higher interest rate. When you put cash down for a car, the lender already holds a substantial amount in its hand and may be willing to lend you money. When you put a large down payment on a home, the bank can see that there will be plenty of equity in the home should a foreclosure happen, and therefore the bank will certainly get its money out.

Be willing to accept loans with higher than average interest rates. Everything has a price. Lending money to someone who is a credit risk has a higher price than lending it to someone with a spotless report. Use a *cosignor*. When you take out the loan or mortgage, someone else—perhaps a friend or relative—agrees to sign the loan and accept financial responsibility for it if you are ever unable to pay. The creditor now has someone else it can count on to get its money, and it may be willing to give you a chance.

Some other strategies that may allow you to purchase a home include rent-to-own leases, owner-financed mortgages, and purchasing a U.S. Department of Housing and Urban Development (HUD) home.

If you already own a home, a home equity loan gives you an available credit line by giving the bank a security interest in your home. You can only get a home equity loan if you have enough equity in your home. This means that you must have either put down a large deposit or paid off a portion of the original mortgage. A second mortgage is usually more difficult to get than a home equity loan because they are generally for larger amounts.

Remember that when you use a home equity loan, you are taking value away from what you own in your home. Home equity loans are a great way to finance remodeling projects and can also be useful for paying off high-interest credit card loans. But you are putting your home at risk, so it only makes sense if you are going to be able to pay it back.

Bank Accounts

To develop good credit, it is important to have stable bank accounts. You should have a savings and a checking account. Shop around for the bank that will offer you the best package—low fees, free checks, etc. Also check with any credit unions you belong to or are eligible to join. Many credit unions have opened up their membership requirements, so it pays to ask. Often a credit union will offer its members better rates than traditional banks. Some banks also offer overdraft protection to good customers. Overdraft protection means that if you accidentally write a check when there is not enough money in the account, the bank will pay the check, but note it as an overdraft and charge you a fee for it. The check will not bounce.

Use your savings account as a place to really save money, even if it is only a small amount. Use your checking account as the central organizing point for your monthly income and debts. Deposit your income, with deductions for savings, in the checking account. Write checks to pay bills from the account. Never write a check if you do not have the funds to cover it in the account.

It may also be a good idea to set up a separate savings account that you will use for vacation savings or to put money away toward a large purchase or holiday gifts. It is too easy to dip into your regular savings account, but if you have a separate account that is only for these special items, you will know you can take the money from that.

Sending a check that will bounce to a creditor as a way to delay payment or to temporarily get the creditor off your back is never a good idea. It will only cost you more money and add negative ratings to your credit report. The bank fees for bounced checks can be quite high when you add up the fee from your bank and the charge from the lender.

When using a bank account, consider using one of the computer software programs available to help you manage your account. These types of programs will automatically balance your account for you, so you do not have to worry about making math errors.

You may also want to find out information about the online banking services offered by your bank. With these services you can transfer money between accounts and pay bills online. You may also be able to set up automatic transfers, so bills, like your mortgage payment, will always be on time, since they will be automatically deducted from your account on a specific date each month. You have to be careful to make sure you have the needed funds in the account should you use automatic payments.

Another important tool is *direct deposit*. Find out if your employer offers this. Direct deposit often gets your earned wages in the account a day or two sooner than it would if you had to physically deposit the check yourself. Having direct deposit may make you eligible for perks on your account, such as no fees. If you have your bank accounts and mortgage with one bank and have direct deposit, you are in an even better position to negotiate rates and fees.

Practical Point

Maintaining bank accounts will demonstrate to creditors that you are able to manage money and that you are able to save funds.

Name and Address Changes

When you are trying to improve your credit rating, you want to appear as stable as possible. Moving often will make you appear unstable. Try to maintain your residence at one address for at least a year if you can. If you do move, be sure to notify all creditors of your new address. It is important to remember that your credit report is linked to you by your Social Security number and that it will follow you wherever you move.

Changing your name for reasons other than marriage or divorce is also not recommended while you are trying to build a good credit history. While you might have a legitimate reason for doing so, creditors will not know what that reason is, and they will become suspicious.

Negotiation with Past Creditors

If you have negative entries on your credit report, you do not have to just live with them.

Contact the creditor and offer to pay a sum of money in exchange for having the negative entry removed. You can still do this even if you have had a judgment obtained against you. (See Chapter 5 for more information.)

Scams to Avoid

There is no quick fix to credit and debt problems. Anyone who promises you that there is one is either lying or is offering an illegal plan. There are attorneys who advertise that they can cut your debts in half without bankruptcy. You may find yourself paying a large amount of money for an attorney to do just what you can do yourself—negotiate with creditors.

There are also scams that tell you to obtain a federal employer identification number and use it as a *new* Social Security number so that you can apply for credit and not be linked to your old credit report. Other scams involve transposing the numbers in your Social Security number, or applying for credit using someone else's name.

Do not try any of these plans. They are illegal and will make you liable for fraud and criminal prosecution. You should also remember that if you follow one of these illegal plans, you cheat yourself out of future Social Security benefits since your earnings will not be linked.

You cannot buy a clean credit report. The only report you are entitled to is your own, so anyone offering to sell you a clean credit report is offering you something illegal. Avoid anyone who requires payment before providing any services, does not tell you your rights, or does not point out what you can do yourself for free. A scam is brewing if you are told not to contact credit reporting agencies yourself or if you are told that you should dispute all the information in your credit report. The *Credit Repair Organizations Act* sets rules for credit repair agencies. Report any suspicious agency to your local attorney general and to the Federal Trade Commission.

Reducing Unsolicited Offers for Credit

It is likely that you receive many unsolicited offers for credit in the mail. Most of these companies get your name and basic information from the credit reporting agencies. They contact the agencies and are given nonconfidential information about you.

It can be very tempting to overspend if you constantly receive offers for credit in the mail, and it can also be annoying. Many people feel it violates their privacy when credit reporting agencies give out information about them. You can contact the credit reporting agencies and indicate that you wish to *opt-out* of these offers and not have any of your information disclosed. To opt-out, you need to send a letter, REQUEST TO OPT-OUT (see form 41, p.411), to one or all of the credit reporting agencies at a special address designated for this purpose. The addresses are as follows.

Equifax

Equifax, Inc.
P.O. Box 740123
Atlanta, GA 30374

Experian

Attn: Consumer Services Department
901 West Bond
Lincoln, NE 68521

TransUnion

TransUnion Name Removal Option
P.O. Box 505
Woodlyn, PA 19094

If you want to stop getting prescreened credit offers in the mail, call the opt-out phone line, 888-5-OPTOUT (888-567-8688), which notifies the big three agencies of your opt-out decision.

The Direct Marketing Association's (DMA) *Mail Preference Service* lets you opt-out of receiving direct mail marketing from many national companies for five years. When you register with this service, your name will be put on a delete file and made available to direct-mail marketers. However, your registration will not stop mailings from organizations that are not registered with the DMA's Mail Preference Service. Register with DMA online at **www.the-dma.org/consumers/offmailinglist.html**.

The DMA also has an *E-Mail Preference Service* to help you reduce unsolicited commercial emails. To opt-out of receiving unsolicited commercial email, use the online form at **www.dmaconsumers.org/offemaillist.html**. Your online request will be effective for one year.

Practical Point

Contact **www.dmachoice.org** in order to remove your name from many email offers.

If you want to reduce the number of catalogs you receive in the mail, go to **www.catalogchoice.org**. You can use this site to reduce duplicate mailings—for example, if you currently always receive two copies of the Plow & Hearth catalog, you just complete the information and the company will stop the duplicate—or to stop catalogs you don't want to receive at all. Receiving fewer catalogs reduces the urge to spend money you don't have.

BUDGETING

A *budget* is a way to organize your expenses and income so that you can anticipate the amount of funds you will have coming in and the funds you will have to pay out. If you find that you are having trouble seeing where all your money goes, you will want to track your actual expenditures.

A budget is the most important tool you can have if you are trying to improve your finances. Using a budget will help you completely understand where all your money goes and help you find ways to control your cash flow.

Why You Should Have a Budget

A budget is your most essential financial tool. It helps you pinpoint how much you have to spend all together, how much you can spend on nonessentials, and anticipate when you will receive money. A budget gives you a plan and a visual mapping of how you will use your money. A budget gives you little room to make impulse buys and helps you keep your finances on target. A budget is a way to make a financial contract with yourself.

Some people do not like the idea of a budget. They say it feels restrictive, like a diet. The best way to think about it is that a budget allows you to control your money, instead of allowing your money to control you. A budget is simply a way to make educated choices about your money. It does not mean you cannot spend money on fun things and it does not mean you have to save every dime. Instead, it helps you see what your planned expenses are so that you can understand how much money you have available for other things.

Creating a Budget

Use the **BUDGET** form at the back of this book. (see form 42, p.412.) Make several copies of it since you will be making estimated and actual budgets for each month. Complete the form as follows.

- Fill in all your regular, unchanging expenses, such as rent or mortgage, electric, water, phone, cable, etc.

- Estimate your average monthly costs for essentials like food, gas, clothing, etc.

- Estimate the nonessential expenses, such as entertainment, eating out, gifts, decorative home items, etc.

- Fill in the monthly amounts for loans and credit cards.

- Note how much you saved and how much you spent on education expenses.

- Fill in the yearly expenses. First you need to total what the yearly cost of these items are. Then divide by twelve so you can estimate accurately.

- Total your expenses.

- Complete the monthly income section of the budget and total that.

- Compare the two figures. If your expenses are greater than your income, you need to make some adjustments.

- Eliminate some of those nonessential expenses. These are the ones that often wind up on credit cards.

- Look at the rest of your expenses to see what can be trimmed. (Refer to the list in Chapter 6 about increasing your cash for some ideas.)

Once you have completed the form, you will have what is your *estimated budget*. This is your best guess as to what your expenses are. It is important to create this form so that you can look at how you think you spend your money.

Now that you have estimated your budget, you need to find out what your actual expenses are. Starting on the first day of the month, use the SPENDING LOG to record every penny you spend, whether you do so with cash, check, credit, debit, and so on. (see form 43, p.416.) Make sure to record those small expenditures like coffee, newspapers, fast food, and so on. You will be surprised at how quickly these add up.

Use a new SPENDING LOG for each week in the month. When the month is over, sit down with your SPENDING LOGS, tally them up, and use them to complete a new budget form. This will be your actual budget and will show, on a monthly basis, how your money is spent.

Making Changes to Your Budget

Now that you know exactly where your money is going, look back at your estimated monthly budget. There are probably areas you underestimated and a few you overestimated. Look closely at your actual spending and think about ways you can reduce or eliminate expenses. (See Chapter 6 for ideas for saving money.) You may be surprised at how much you find you can cut from your spending.

If you are wondering how your expenses compare to others, use the *Family Budget Analyzer* at **www.finaid.org/calculators/budget.phtml**. It will allow you to compare your budgeted item amounts to those of other families, as reported by the Bureau of Labor Statistics.

It is important to remember that budgets are always in flux. Your electric bill may be higher in the summer because you ran a fan or used air conditioning. Your food expenses may be less over the holidays if you go and stay with your family, but your travel costs will go up. Despite these fluctuations, it is essential that you plan out where your money is going to go, while leaving enough money in your miscellaneous expenses or by putting money into a savings account to cover these unexpected fluctuations.

When budgeting, it is a good idea to sit down at the beginning of each year and think about your plans for the year. If your car is in bad shape, you should anticipate a lot of repairs or even the expense of having to purchase another car. If you are starting a class in August, save up for tuition and books. The farther ahead you can foresee these things, the better you can plan for and save money to cover them.

REAL LIFE CREDIT

Jon needed a budget. He never had enough money to pay all his bills, but he could not figure out where all his cash was going. He took one month and wrote down everything he spent money on. He was shocked to see the following expenses:

- $200 a month on bar expenses

- $40 on takeout pizza

- $50 on coffee drinks

- $150 for gas

- $50 on recreational reading

These expenses were much more than Jon anticipated for these items. He decided to make some changes. First, he stopped buying takeout. Next, he learned how to make good coffee at home and took it with him to work and school. He began to use public transportation to cut down on gas costs. He stopped going to bars every weekend with friends, and instead instituted a BYOB get-together every Friday night at his place. He stopped buying every book that interested him and instead borrowed the ones he wanted to read from his local library. With these simple steps, Jon was able to make a huge impact on his monthly budget.

If you are having difficulty completing the BUDGET (form 42, p.412) or SPENDING LOG (form 43, p.416) forms or you find that your expenses consistently exceed your income, contact a consumer credit counseling service (see Chapter 7) for assistance in creating a workable budget.

Remember that a budget is a guideline to help you plan where your money will go. It is not an exact science by any means, so it is important to build some wiggle room into your budget. If you have your monthly income planned down to the last dime and then your refrigerator needs an expensive repair, you are going to be in trouble and have to put it on credit. For this reason, it is a good idea to have some extra cash built into your budget. If you do not use it, put it in savings. The general rule of thumb is that you should be saving 10% of your income. If you are in a tough spot, trying to pay off big credit card debt, this might be hard for you to do. Make sure you regularly save some money, though, no matter how bad your situation.

Getting Organized

In order to be able to budget well and be in control of your finances, you need to get all your information organized. Follow these steps to get everything together.

- Locate all your bills, financial statements, and pay stubs.

- Create a separate file for each account, credit card, loan, utility, and other expenses, such as medical bills or child care bills. Create a separate file for pay stubs and each bank account, CD, or other investment or asset you own.

- Use individual file folders or one big expandable file folder that is divided into sections.

- File items as soon as you are done with them. When you pay a bill, file the bill. When you cash your pay check, file the pay stub.

- Create a separate folder to hold your yearly taxes as well as one to store product and manufacturer warranties.

- Store important items, such as bonds, birth certificates, Social Security cards, real estate titles, marriage licenses, cash, and other valuable items in a fireproof safe (small household safe boxes can be purchased at discount and office supply stores for under $40). Keep this locked at all times and place the key somewhere where you will not lose it.

- When you withdraw money at an ATM machine, always get a receipt. Once a week, deduct these withdrawals from your checkbook or savings account register.

Paying Your Bills

If you toss all your bills on your kitchen counter or desk when they arrive, it is unlikely that you are going to remember to pay them on time. You need to devise a system that will help you pay your bills on time. Late payments mean late fees—something you want to avoid at all cost because they are expensive and because they adversely affect your credit rating.

- Purchase a monthly folder or box. These have pockets or slots for each day of the month in numerical order.

- When you receive a bill, place it in the pocket for the date it is due.

- Sit down with your weekly organizer on a set day each week and check to see what is due and when.

- It is important to get your payments in the mail far in advance before the due date. Be sure to allow adequate time.

- If you have payments automatically deducted from your bank account, write the date and amount of the deduction on a piece of paper and place it in the slot for the appropriate date so that you will be sure to have enough money in your account to cover it.

- Keep a supply of stamps in the folder or box, or nearby.

- File the bill in the appropriate spot after you have paid it.

- When you write a check, record it immediately in the register with the check number, name of payee, amount, and the date. Balance your checking account monthly.

- When you make an online payment, note the confirmation number, amount, and the date in your checkbook register.

Following Your Budget

You have created a budget that allows you to pay all your bills using your current income. Now you have to stick to it. This is the hard part. Next week you may see a sweater you have to have. Your friends may want you to go to a concert with them. You might become sick and have to pay for a doctor and medication even though you do not have medical insurance. If you are able to place some money each month in your emergency fund, you will be able to handle expenses like these occasionally. This takes willpower and self-deprivation. Remind yourself that if you exceed your budget, you are not going to be able to pay your rent, or that awful things like repossession can occur.

Living on a Budget and Using Credit

Some financial advisors recommend not using credit at all if you are having trouble living on a budget. If a credit card in your pocket is like a license to spend and you cannot stop yourself, you should not use credit cards. However, it is possible to live on a budget and use credit responsibly. Doing so means thinking about what you are buying and how it fits into your budget. You must also resolve to always pay off your entire balance each month and never put more on your credit card than you can pay off. You must adjust your thinking so that a credit card is a convenience, not a free pass to buy anything you want.

Tips for Using Credit Responsibly

- Consider using your credit card only for true emergencies, such as car repairs, medical bills, or other unexpected and necessary items. This will limit unnecessary expenses.

- To control your credit card spending, use the card only to buy things that you have the money to pay for. This way, the card gives you the convenience of being able to avoid carrying large amounts of cash while preventing you from overspending. If you have to, write down your bank account balance every day on a sticky note and attach it to your credit card so you know exactly how much money you have each day.

- Pay your account balance each month in full. Interest charges are the problem with carrying a balance and they accrue quickly.

- Pay your credit card bills on time. Late fees add up and can throw off a careful budget.

- Think of your credit card as a convenience you must be careful with, not as an excuse to go into debt.

- Cancel all but one or two credit card accounts. It is difficult to keep a handle on the balances if you have too many cards.

- Cancel all your merchant accounts. Store-specific credit cards are never a good deal, even if they offer you a reward for signing up. The interest rates are higher, and they do not carry as much weight on your credit report as big bank cards.

- Switch to a debit card if you find that you cannot use credit responsibly. A debit card gives you the freedom and convenience of a credit card but the same sense of responsibility as using a check or cash.

FACING THE FUTURE | 12

This book has helped you deal with your debt problems, understand and improve your credit rating, and manage your money more effectively. However, there is still some work left to do.

Changing Your Outlook and Mind-Set about Money

You have experienced some difficulties with handling debt or keeping a clean credit report. Now that those problems are cleared up, you need to think about how you can avoid repeating them in the future. Many of the solutions offered in this book will only work once. For example, you cannot always go back to the same creditor and keep renegotiating the debt you owe. You have one shot.

You need to be very careful to follow your budget. (see Chapter 11.) Keep it on your refrigerator or in your wallet if it will help you stay on track. Your budget is a reminder of how you are supposed to be allocating the money you earn. You have set responsibilities each month and you must be sure you have the money available to pay for those before you buy a round of drinks for your friends.

It is time to change the way you deal with money. Become a penny-pincher. This does not mean being stingy, but it does mean being in charge of your money. Keep track of where every cent goes. Use credit cards cautiously. Do not allow yourself to use a credit card without first understanding how and where you are going to get the money to pay for the purchase.

Give yourself a break occasionally. You are going to go off your budget just as you go off your diet occasionally when you diet. But just as with a diet, you have to make up the difference somewhere else, or you are going to be in trouble. Be aware of how you allow yourself to be lenient. It is one thing to spend a little extra to buy yourself an espresso on the way to work, but quite another to splurge on a new couch. Each of these will have to be compensated for in a completely different way. As long as you are prepared to find the money for it, it is okay to spend it.

Dealing with Changes

You have a budget that works for you given your current expenses and income. However, it is unlikely that all of these are going to remain the same in your life forever. You might get a lower or higher paying job. Gas prices could keep going up. You might need to buy a newer car, or rent a different apartment with a different rent amount.

If your income or expenses change, you will need to adjust your budget accordingly. If your income goes down, you are going to need to find some way to cut your expenses or increase your income, or you will end up over your head in debt. If your income goes up, you might want to consider leaving your expenses at the level they are now and save the extra income. Place it in a bank account, CD, or even an investment account. Watch your money grow so that you can buy a house, take a vacation, or have a safety net for the future.

Keep in mind that if you do change jobs, you are under no obligation to notify your creditors. If you want a higher credit limit and your income is higher, you may wish to notify them. However, if you take a pay cut, they do not need to know as long as you adjust your expenses so that you can pay all your bills. Remember to notify creditors if you move so that you can continue to get your statements on time and pay your bills on time.

Dealing with Self-Esteem and Compulsion Issues

Most people have difficulty handling debt at one point or another in their lives. You are not alone. You may have ended up in this situation because of unexpected misfortune, like a divorce, illness, or layoff. Accept that some things in life just happen and that the best you can do is deal with the repercussions. Look to the future. Make plans for how you are going to get ahead and pursue them.

Practical Point

As you look to the future, think of money as an important but potentially dangerous tool that you must use carefully.

If you have ended up in this situation because of your own mistakes, look at what happened, find out how to change yourself or your habits, and follow through. You may find you have a spending compulsion. If this is the case, seek assistance from a mental health professional or debt professional. Perhaps you are simply terrible with numbers. Have your spouse or a good friend help you follow a budget. Do not be afraid to look around you for help.

Educating Children about Debt

Although debt is one of the biggest problems Americans face, very little is done to educate children and teens about money management. While some schools offer classes and instruction about avoiding pregnancy, parenting, and other life skills, very few take the time to teach budgeting or to explain credit, loans, bank accounts, interest, and other financial matters. If you have children, take the time to talk to them about money and debt. Giving an allowance is a good way to help children learn to manage money. Setting up a savings account for your child is an important way to encourage saving and to teach the basics of account balancing. Kids can have a budget too, so help your child set one up. You might encourage your child to save half of his or her allowance and spend the other half in a controlled and planned way. Encourage your child to avoid becoming an impulse shopper.

If you have a teen, take the time to talk to him or her about credit cards. Many young adults head off to college and are bombarded with credit card offers. This free money can seem like a bonanza to a young adult who is on his or her own for the first time. Work with your college student so he or she learns to manage money and expenses. You may be able to help your on-campus college student control spending with a school debit card. You load a certain amount on the card each month and the student must control his or her on-campus spending within the budget.

A great way to help a teen or college student learn to manage credit is with a card the parent cosigns on. This means mom or dad has the right to access the account and find out what is going on. This is an easy way to monitor how your child is doing with credit and step in when there is trouble—before it becomes insurmountable.

IT'S A FACT!

Only 40% of teens pay off their credit card balances each month, even though many may be financially able to.

Be honest with your kids about the mistakes you have made and involve them in the changes you are making to get on the right track. Setting a good example and teaching kids essential money management skills will ensure that debt problems do not spread to the next generation.

Moving Forward

Whatever problems you have had with debt, credit, or bankruptcy are in the past. You must always be careful to make sure you do not end up in a similar situation again, but you need to let go of those past problems. Stop blaming yourself and feeling guilty or inadequate. Remind yourself that you have developed a new plan to manage your finances and that you control the future. You have the power to approach the future with a positive mind-set! You can make decisions and take actions that will make your financial life better suited to your needs. Change is yours for the making!

GLOSSARY

A

alimony. Support money paid to an ex-spouse on a regular basis after a divorce; ordered by the court.

annual fee. A yearly amount charged by credit card companies for the privilege of holding the card.

annual percentage rate (APR). The amount of interest you will pay each year on your outstanding credit balance.

asset. Property or money you own.

B

balance. The total amount owed on an account.

bankruptcy. A legal process that freezes all actions by creditors against a debtor. If the petition for bankruptcy is approved, all the debt will be discharged or excused.

budget. A way to organize expenses and income so that you can control your spending.

C

cancellation. When a loan is forgiven.

child support. An amount of money paid by one parent to another under court order to assist in financially supporting a child.

collection agency. A company that collects debts on behalf of creditors.

consolidation. Combining several loans into one with a lower monthly payment. Most often used with student loans.

Consumer Credit Counseling. A service that will assist you in combining your debts into one monthly payment.

contingency payment. A form of payment to an attorney. The attorney agrees to accept a percentage of your winnings instead of a fee you pay up front.

correspondence. Any letters or items that you have sent or received through the mail, email, or fax.

cosignor. Someone who agrees to be responsible for a debt if the debtor does not make payments.

credit card. A card that allows you to charge items to your account. Interest is charged on balances not paid off during the billing cycle.

credit history. Your past credit reports that indicate how much of a risk you are to loan money to.

credit limit. The total amount you are authorized to charge on a credit card.

creditor. A person loaning money.

credit report. A document that lists all your debts and their status.

credit reporting agencies. Companies that create credit reports by gathering information from creditors.

credit score. A numerical rating of your overall credit issued by credit reporting agencies.

D

debit card. A type of card in which the user deposits money with the bank and then uses that money to directly pay for the items purchased.

debt. An amount of money owed.

debt collector. A person whose job it is to collect money owed on debts.

debtor. A person who owes money.

deferment. Putting a loan on hold without payments becoming due. Usually only applies to student loans.

delinquent. Late or overdue.

E

eviction. A legal process through which a tenant is forced to move out of a rental unit by a landlord.

F

finance charge. Fees charged for borrowing money, often stated as a percentage.

forbearance. Occurs when the lender allows you to postpone or make temporary reductions in your payments.

foreclosure. Occurs when a person fails to make mortgage payments on a home and the bank takes the property and sells it, forcing the homeowner to move out.

G

garnishment. A court order that directly deducts money from a person's wages to pay a debt.

grace period. The time between the date the billing cycle closes and the date by which the customer has to pay the balance to avoid any finance charges.

graduated payments. Loan payments that begin low and increase over time, often beginning with interest-only payments.

I

identity theft. The problem that occurs when someone else uses your accounts or opens new accounts using your personal information.

income. Money earned from a job or interest on money that is saved or invested.

income-based payments. Loan payments that are determined by income, which go up or down as your income does.

interest. A percentage of the balance that is charged by the creditor as a fee for borrowing the money, or a percentage you earn on money you have saved.

J

joint account. An account that is equally owned by two people.

judgment. A court order determining that a person owes a sum of money.

judgment proof. Someone who has little or no assets so that a judgment against him or her has little effect since there is nothing that can be taken.

L

lien. A formal judgment of debt that is entered into court and county records, indicating that you owe a creditor a certain amount and attaching the debt to a piece of real property so that if it is ever sold the debt must be paid.

M

minimum payment. The lowest amount you can pay to keep an account current.

monthly periodic rate. The annual percentage rate divided by twelve months.

mortgage. A loan for the purchase of real estate that gives the bank a security interest in the property.

N

negotiation. The process of resolving a dispute to a mutually acceptable solution.

P

postdated check. A check dated with a future date.

prioritizing. Placing things in order of importance.

R

repossession. Occurs when a creditor seizes a piece of personal property to pay off a loan secured by the property.

S

secured credit card. A credit card in which the debtor gives a certain amount of money to the bank to be used as a security. The debtor charges items and repays them, and the security interest is held in case there is a failure to pay.

secured loan. A loan in which you borrow money or buy a certain item and give the creditor a security interest or collateral in an item, e.g., a car loan.

secured property. Items purchased or financed through a loan that gives the creditor a security interest in them.

security interest. The right maintained by a creditor to repossess or take back an item a person borrowed money to buy if he or she fails to make payments.

settlement. An agreement that is reached between a debtor and a creditor that solves or eliminates the dispute.

state banking authority. An agency that governs the banks and financial institutions within a state.

student loan. An unsecured loan that is usually offered through a bank or loan agency and backed by the government in order to pay for college. Student loans cannot be discharged in bankruptcy and are often a source of credit problems.

U

unsecured loan. A loan in which the creditor does not hold a security interest in an item you own. Most credit cards are unsecured.

user accounts. A credit card account set up in one person's name that has a card issued to another person so that he or she may charge against the account. The person who holds the account is ultimately responsible for payments.

STATE-BY-STATE RESOURCES

This appendix contains a state-by-state listing of attorneys general, banking authorities, and consumer protection agencies. These can answer questions, help you solve problems, and provide assistance for problems involving discrimination, credit concerns, hate crimes, and housing problems. (The names of the officials are not included since these change often.)

Alabama

Attorney General
11 South Union Street
3rd Floor
Montgomery, AL 36130

Banking Authority
State of Alabama
State Banking Department
401 Adams Avenue
Suite 680
Montgomery, AL 36104
334-242-3452
www.banking.alabama.gov

Consumer Protection Agency
Office of the Attorney General
Consumer Affairs
11 South Union Street
3rd Floor
Montgomery, AL 36130
334-242-7334
www.ago.state.al.us

Alaska

Attorney General
State Capitol
P.O. Box 110300
Juneau, AK 99811

Banking Authority
Department of Commerce,
Community, and Economic
Development
P.O. Box 110807
Juneau, AK 99811
907-465-2521
www.dced.state.ak.us

Consumer Protection Agency
Office of the Attorney General
Civil Division
1031 West 4th Avenue
Suite 200
Anchorage, AK 99501
907-269-5100
www.law.state.ak.us

Arizona

Attorney General
1275 West Washington Street
Phoenix, AZ 85007

Banking Authority
Arizona State Banking
Department
2910 North 44th Street
Suite 310
Phoenix, AZ 85018
602-255-4421
www.azdfi.gov

Consumer Protection Agency
Office of the Attorney General
Consumer Information and
Complaints
1275 West Washington Street
Phoenix, AZ 85007
602-542-5763
www.azag.gov/consumer

Office of the Attorney General
Consumer Information and
Complaints
400 West Congress
South Building, Suite 315
Tucson, AZ 85701
520-628-6504
www.azag.gov/consumer

Arkansas

Attorney General
323 Center Street
Suite 200
Little Rock, AR 72201

Banking Authority
Arkansas State Bank
Department
400 Hardin Road
Suite 100
Little Rock, AR 72211
501-324-9019
www.arkansas.gov/bank

Consumer Protection Agency
Office of the Attorney General
Consumer Protection Division
323 Center Street
Suite 200
Little Rock, AR 72201
501-682-2007
www.ag.state.ar.us

California

Attorney General
California Department of
Justice
P.O. Box 944255
Sacramento, CA 94244

Banking Authority
State Department of Financial
Institutions
111 Pine Street
Suite 1100
San Francisco, CA 94111
415-263-8555
www.dfi.ca.gov

Consumer Protection Agency
California Department of
Consumer Affairs
Consumer Information
Division
1625 North Market Blvd.
Suite N 112

Sacramento, CA 95834
916-445-1254
www.dca.ca.gov

Colorado

Attorney General
1525 Sherman Street
7th Floor
Denver, CO 80203

Banking Authority
Division of Banking
Department of Regulatory
Agencies
Division of Banking
1560 Broadway
Suite 975
Denver, CO 80202
303-894-7575
www.dora.state.co.us/banking

Consumer Protection Agency
Colorado Attorney General's
Office
Consumer Protection Division
1525 Sherman Street
7th Floor
Denver, CO 80203
303-866-5189

Connecticut

Attorney General
55 Elm Street
Hartford, CT 06106

Banking Authority
Connecticut Department of
Banking
260 Constitution Plaza
Hartford, CT 06103
860-240-8299
www.state.ct.us/dob

Consumer Protection Agency
Department of Consumer
Protection
165 Capitol Avenue
Hartford, CT 06106
860-713-6050
www.state.ct.us/dcp

Delaware

Attorney General
Carvel State Office Building
820 North French Street
Wilmington, DE 19801

Banking Authority
State Bank Commissioner
555 East Loockerman Street
Suite 210
Dover, DE 19901

302-739-4235
www.state.de.us/bank

Consumer Protection Agency
Office of the Attorney General
Consumer Protection Unit
820 North French Street
5th Floor
Wilmington, DE 19801
302-577-8600

District of Columbia

Attorney General
441 4th Street, NW
Suite 1060 N
Washington, DC 20001

Banking Authority
Department of Insurance,
Securities and Banking
1400 L Street, NW
Washington, DC 20005
202-727-1563
www.dbfi.dc.gov

**Consumer Protection and
Antitrust**
441 4th Street, NW
Suite 1060 N
Washington, DC 20001
202-442-9828

Florida

Attorney General
The Capitol, PL-01
Tallahassee, FL 32399

Banking Authority
Department of Financial
Services
200 East Gaines Street
Tallahassee, FL 32399
850-413-3100
www.fldfs.com

Consumer Protection Agency
Office of the Attorney General
PL-01 The Capitol
Tallahassee, FL 32399
850-414-3990

Economic Crimes Division
Office of the Attorney General
The Capitol, PL-01
Tallahassee, FL 32399
850-414-3300

**Department of Agriculture
    and Consumer Services**
Division of Consumer Services
Terry L Rhodes Building
2005 Apalachee Parkway
Tallahassee, FL 32399
850-488-2221
www.800helpfla.com

Georgia

Attorney General
40 Capitol Square, SW
Atlanta, GA 30334

Banking Authority
Department of Banking and
Finance
2990 Brandywine Road
Suite 200
Atlanta, GA 30341
770-986-1633

Consumer Protection Agency
Governor's Office of Consumer
Affairs
2 Martin Luther King Jr. Drive
SE
Suite 356
Atlanta, GA 30334
404-651-8600
http://consumer.georgia.gov

Hawaii

Attorney General
425 Queen Street
Honolulu, HI 96813

Banking Authority
Division of Financial
Institutions

Department of Commerce and
Consumer Affairs
P.O. Box 2054
Honolulu, HI 96805
808-586-2820

Consumer Protection Agency
Department of Commerce and
Consumer Affairs
Office of Consumer Protection
345 Kekuanaoa Street
Suite 12
Hilo, HI 96720
808-933-0910

Office of Consumer Protection
Department of Commerce and
Consumer Affairs
Leiopapa A. Kamehameha
Building
235 South Beretania Street
Suite 801
Honolulu, HI 96813
808-586-2630

Office of Consumer Protection
Department of Commerce and
Consumer Affairs
1063 Lower Main Street
Suite C-216
Wailuku, HI 96793
808-984-8244
www.state.hi.us/dcca

Idaho

Attorney General
P.O. Box 83720
Boise, ID 83720

Banking Authority
State of Idaho Department of
Finance
P.O. Box 83720
Boise, ID 83720
208-332-8000
http://finance.idaho.gov

Consumer Protection Agency
Consumer Protection Division
Idaho Attorney General's
Office
700 West Jefferson Street
Boise, ID 83720
208-334-2424
www2.state.id.us/ag

Illinois

Attorney General
100 West Randolph St.
Chicago, IL 60601

Banking Authority
Division of Banks and Real
Estate
122 South Michigan Avenue
Suite 1900

Chicago, IL 60603
312-793-3000
www.idfpr.com

Consumer Protection Agency
Office of the Attorney General
1001 East Main Street
Carbondale, IL 62901
618-529-6400

Consumer Fraud Bureau
100 West Randolph
12th Floor
Chicago, IL 60601
312-814-3000
www.ag.state.il.us

**Governor's Office of Citizens
    Assistance**
222 South College
Room 106
Springfield, IL 62706
217-782-0244

Indiana

Attorney General
Indiana Government Center
South
302 West Washington Street
Indianapolis, IN 46204

Banking Authority
Department of Financial
Institutions
30 South Meridian Street
Suite 300
Indianapolis, IN 46204
317-232-3955
www.in.gov/dfi

Consumer Protection Agency
Office of the Attorney General
Consumer Protection Division
Indiana Government Center
South
302 West Washington Street
5th Floor
Indianapolis, IN 46204
317-232-6330
www.in.gov/attorneygeneral

Iowa

Attorney General
1305 East Walnut Street
Des Moines, IA 50319

Banking Authority
Iowa Division of Banking
200 East Grand
Suite 300

Des Moines, IA 50309
515-281-4014
www.idob.state.ia.us

Consumer Protection Agency
Consumer Protection Division
Office of the Attorney General
1305 East Walnut Street
2nd Floor
Des Moines, IA 50319
515-281-5926
www.IowaAttorneyGeneral.org

Kansas

Attorney General
120 SW 10th Street
Memorial Hall, 2nd Floor
Topeka, KS 66612

Banking Authority
Office of the State Bank
Commissioner
700 Jackson Street
Suite 300
Topeka, KS 66603
785-296-2266
www.osbckansas.org

Consumer Protection Agency
Consumer Protection &
Antitrust Division

Office of the Attorney General
120 SW 10th Street
2nd Floor
Topeka, KS 66612
785-296-3751
www.ksag.org

Kentucky

Attorney General
The Capitol
Suite 118
700 Capitol Avenue
Frankfort, KY 40601

Banking Authority
Department of Financial
Institutions
1025 Capitol Center Drive
Suite 200
Frankfort, KY 40601
502-573-3390
www.dfi.state.ky.us

Consumer Protection Agency
Office of the Attorney General
Office of Consumer Protection
1024 Capital Center Drive
Suite 200
Frankfort, KY 40601
502-696-5389
http://ag.ky.gov

Office of the Attorney General
Consumer Protection Division
8911 Shelbyville Road
Louisville, KY 40222
502-429-7134

Louisiana

Attorney General
P.O. Box 94005
Baton Rouge, LA 70804

Banking Authority
LA Office of Financial
Institutions
P.O. Box 94095
Baton Rouge, LA 70804
225-925-4660
www.ofi.state.la.us

Consumer Protection Agency
Consumer Protection Section
Office of the Attorney General
P.O. Box 94005
Baton Rouge, LA 70804
800-351-4889
www.ag.state.la.us

Maine

Attorney General
6 State House Station
Augusta, ME 04333

Banking Authority
Bureau of Financial Institutions
36 State House Station
Augusta, ME 04333
207-624-8570
www.mainebankingreg.org

Consumer Protection Agency
Bureau of Consumer Credit
Protection
35 State House Station
Augusta, ME 04333
207-624-8527
www.mainecreditreg.org

Consumer Protection Division
Office of the Attorney General
Division Chief
6 State House Station
Augusta, ME 04333
207-626-8800

Maryland

Attorney General
200 Saint Paul Place
Baltimore, MD 21202

Banking Authority
Financial Regulation
500 North Calvert Street
Suite 402
Baltimore, MD 21202
410-230-6100
www.dllr.state.md.us/finance

Consumer Protection Agency
Consumer Protection Division
Office of the Attorney General
200 Saint Paul Place
16th Floor
Baltimore, MD 21202
410-528-8662
www.oag.state.md.us/consumer

Massachusetts

Attorney General
One Ashburton Place
Boston, MA 02108

Banking Authority
MA Division of Banks
One South Station
Boston, MA 02110
617-956-1500
www.mass.gov/dob

Consumer Protection Agency
Executive Office of Consumer
Affairs and Business Regulation
10 Park Plaza
Suite 5170
Boston, MA 02116
617-973-8787
www.mass.gov/consumer

Consumer Protection and
    Antitrust Division
Office of the Attorney General
One Ashburton Place
Boston, MA 02114
617-727-8400
www.mass.gov/ago

Michigan

Attorney General
G. Mennen Williams Building
525 West Ottawa Street
7th Floor
Lansing, MI 48909

Banking Authority
Office of Financial and
Insurance Services
P.O. Box 30220
Lansing, MI 48933
517-373-0220
www.michigan.gov/ofis

Consumer Protection Agency
Consumer Protection Division
Office of the Attorney General
P.O. Box 30213
Lansing, MI 48909
517-373-1140

Minnesota

Attorney General
1400 Bremer Tower
445 Minnesota Street
St. Paul, MN 55101

Banking Authority
Financial Examinations
Division
Minnesota Department of
Commerce
85 Seventh Place East
Suite 500
St. Paul, MN 55101
651-296-2715
www.commerce.state.mn.us

Consumer Protection Agency
Consumer Services Division
Minnesota Attorney General's
Office
1400 Bremer Tower
445 Minnesota Street
St. Paul, MN 55101
651-296-3353
www.ag.state.mn.us

Mississippi

Attorney General
P.O. Box 220
Jackson, MS 39205

Banking Authority
Department of Banking and
Consumer Finance
P.O. Box 23729
Jackson, MS 39225
601-359-1031
www.dbcf.state.ms.us

Consumer Protection Agency
Consumer Protection Division
of the
Mississippi Attorney General's
Office
P.O. Box 22947
Jackson, MS 39225
601-359-4230
www.ago.state.ms.us

Missouri

Attorney General
Supreme Court Building
207 West High Street
Jefferson City, MO 65102

Banking Authority
Department of Finance
301 West High Street
Room 630
Jefferson City, MO 65102
573-751-3242
www.missouri-finance.org

Consumer Protection Agency
Consumer Protection Division
P.O. Box 899
Jefferson City, MO 65102
573-751-3321
www.ago.mo.gov

Montana

Attorney General
Department of Justice
P.O. Box 201401
Helena, MT 59620

Banking Authority
Division of Banking &
Financial Institutions
301 South Park Avenue
Suite 316
Helena, MT 59620
406-841-2920
www.banking.mt.gov

Consumer Protection Agency
Montana Office of Consumer
Protection
Department of Justice
1219 8th Avenue
Helena, MT 59620
406-444-4500

Nebraska

Attorney General
2115 State Capitol
Lincoln, NE 68509

Banking Authority
Department of Banking &
Finance
1230 "O" Street
Commerce Court
Suite 400
Lincoln, NE 68509
402-471-2171
www.ndbf.org

Consumer Protection Agency
Office of the Attorney General
Department of Justice
2115 State Capitol
Lincoln, NE 68509
402-471-2682
www.ago.state.ne.us

Nevada

Attorney General
100 North Carson Street
Carson City, NV 89701

Banking Authority
Financial Institutions Division

Department of Business &
Industry
2785 East Desert Inn Road
Suite 180
Las Vegas, NV 89121
702-486-4563
www.fid.state.nv.us

Consumer Protection Agency
Bureau of Consumer Protection
Office of the Attorney General
1000 North Carson Street
Carson City, NV 89707
775-684-1180
www.ag.state.nv.us

Nevada Consumer Affairs
    Division
1850 East Sahara Avenue
Suite 101
Las Vegas, NV 89104
702-486-7355
www.fyiconsumer.org

Bureau of Consumer Protection
555 East Washington Avenue
Suite 3900
Las Vegas, NV 89101
702-486-3420

Consumer Affairs Division

Department of Business and
Industry
Deputy Chief Investigator
4600 Kietzke Lane
Building B
Suite 113
Reno, NV 89502
775-688-1800

New Hampshire

Attorney General
33 Capitol Street
Concord, NH 03301

Banking Authority
State of New Hampshire
Banking Department
64B Old Suncook Road
Concord, NH 03301
603-271-3561
www.state.nh.us/banking

Consumer Protection Agency
Consumer Protection and
Antitrust Bureau
New Hampshire Attorney
General's Office
33 Capitol Street
Concord, NH 03301
603-271-3641

www.doj.nh.gov/consumer/
index.html

New Jersey

Attorney General
P.O. Box 080
Trenton, NJ 08625

Banking Authority
Department of Banking and
Insurance
20 West State Street
Trenton, NJ 08625
609-292-3420
www.njdobi.org

Consumer Protection Agency
Division of Consumer Affairs
Department of Law and Public
Safety
P.O. Box 45027
Newark, NJ 07101
973-504-6200
www.state.nj.us/lps/ca/home.
htm

New Mexico

Attorney General
P.O. Drawer 1508
Santa Fe, NM 87504

Banking Authority
Financial Institutions Division
Regulation and Licensing
Department
2550 Cerrillos Road
3rd Floor
Santa Fe, NM 87501
505-476-4885
www.rld.state.nm.us/FID

Consumer Protection Agency
Consumer Protection Division
407 Galisteo
Santa Fe, NM 87504
505-827-6060
www.ago.state.nm.us

New York

Attorney General
The Capitol
Albany, NY 12224

Banking Authority
New York State Banking
Department
Consumer Help Unit
One State Street
New York, NY 10004
212-709-5470
www.banking.state.ny.us

Consumer Protection Agency
Bureau of Consumer Frauds and
Protection
Office of the Attorney General
State Capitol
Albany, NY 12224
518-474-5481
www.oag.state.ny.us

New York State Consumer
    Protection Board
Office of the Attorney General
5 Empire State Plaza
Suite 2101
Albany, NY 12223
518-474-2474
www.nyconsumer.gov

Consumer Frauds and
    Protection Bureau
Office of the Attorney General
120 Broadway
3rd Floor
New York, NY 10271
212-416-8300

North Carolina

Attorney General
9001 Mail Service Center
Raleigh, NC 27699

Banking Authority
North Carolina Commissioner
of Banks
4309 Mail Service Center
Raleigh, NC 27699
919-733-3016
www.nccob.org

Consumer Protection Agency
Consumer Protection Division
Office of the Attorney General
9001 Mail Service Center
Raleigh, NC 27699
919-716-6000
www.ncdoj.com

North Dakota

Attorney General
State Capitol
600 East Boulevard Avenue
Department 125
Bismarck, ND 58505

Banking Authority
ND Department of Financial
Institutions
2000 Schafer Street
Suite G
Bismarck, ND 58501
701-328-9933
www.nd.gov/dfi

Consumer Protection Agency
Consumer Protection and
Antitrust Division
Office of the Attorney General
600 East Boulevard Avenue
Department 125
Bismarck, ND 58505
701-328-3404
www.ag.state.nd.us

Ohio

Attorney General
State Office Tower
30 East Broad Street
17th Floor
Columbus, OH 43215

Banking Authority
Department of Commerce—
State of Ohio
Financial Institutions Division
77 South High Street
21st Floor
Columbus, OH 43215
614-728-8400
www.com.ohio.gov/fiin

Consumer Protection Agency
Ohio Consumers' Counsel
10 West Broad Street, 18th
Floor

Suite 1800
Columbus, OH 43215
614-466-8574
www.pickocc.org

Consumer Protection Section
30 East Broad Street
17th Floor
Columbus, OH 43215
614-466-8831
www.ag.state.oh.us

Oklahoma

Attorney General
313 NE 21st Street
Oklahoma City, OK 73105

Banking Authority
OK State Banking Department
4545 North Lincoln Boulevard
Suite 164
Oklahoma City, OK 73105
405-521-2782
www.osbd.state.ok.us

Consumer Protection Agency
Department of Consumer
Credit
4545 North Lincoln Boulevard
#104
Oklahoma City, OK 73105
405-521-3653

Consumer Protection Unit
Oklahoma Attorney General
313 NE 21st Street
Oklahoma City, OK 73105
405-521-2029
www.oag.state.ok.us

Oregon

Attorney General
1162 Court Street NE
Salem, OR 97301

Banking Authority
Department of Consumer &
Business Services
Division of Finance &
Corporate Securities
350 Winter Street NE
Room 410
Salem, OR 97310
503-378-4140
http://dfcs.oregon.gov

Consumer Protection Agency
Financial Fraud/Consumer
Protection Section
Department of Justice
1162 Court Street NE
Salem, OR 97310
503-947-4333
www.doj.state.or.us

Pennsylvania

Attorney General
Pennsylvania Office of
Attorney General
16th Floor
Strawberry Square
Harrisburg, PA 17120

Banking Authority
Department of Banking
17 North Second Street
Suite 1300
333 Market Street
16th Floor
Harrisburg, PA 17101
717-787-6991
www.banking.state.pa.us

Consumer Protection Agency
Bureau of Consumer Protection
Office of Attorney General
16th Floor
Strawberry Square
Harrisburg, PA 17120
717-787-3391
www.attorneygeneral.gov

**Office of the Consumer
    Advocate**
Office of the Attorney General
555 Walnut Street
Forum Place, 5th Floor

Harrisburg, PA 17101
800-684-6560
www.oca.state.pa.us

Rhode Island

Attorney General
150 South Main Street
Providence, RI 02903

Banking Authority
Division of Banking
Department of Business
Regulation
233 Richmond Street
Suite 231
Providence, RI 02903
401-222-2246

Consumer Protection Agency
Consumer Protection Unit
Department of Attorney
General
150 South Main Street
Providence, RI 02903
401-274-4400

South Carolina

Attorney General
P.O. Box 11549
Columbia, SC 29211

Banking Authority
State Board of Financial
Institutions
1015 Sumter Street
Room 309
Columbia, SC 29201
803-734-2001
www.state.sc.us/treas/index2.
htm

Consumer Protection Agency
Office of the Attorney General
P.O. Box 11549
Columbia, SC 29211
803-734-3970
www.scattorneygeneral.org

**SC Department of Consumer
    Affairs**
Administrator/Consumer
Advocate
3600 Forest Drive
Suite 300
Columbia, SC 29250
803-734-4200
www.scconsumer.gov

South Dakota

Attorney General
1302 East Highway 14

Suite 1
Pierre, SD 57501

Banking Authority
SD Division of Banking
217 1/2 West Missouri Avenue
Pierre, SD 57501
605-773-3421
www.state.sd.us/banking

Consumer Protection Agency
Consumer Affairs
Office of the Attorney General
1302 East Highway 14
Suite 3
Pierre, SD 57501
605-773-4400

Tennessee

Attorney General
P.O. Box 20207
Nashville, TN 37202

Banking Authority
Department of Financial
Institutions
Consumer Resources Division
Nashville City Center
511 Union Street, 4th Floor
Nashville, TN 37219
615-253-2023
www.tennessee.gov/tdfi

Consumer Protection Agency
Division of Consumer Affairs
500 James Robertson Parkway,
5th Floor
Nashville, TN 37243
615-741-4737
www.state.tn.us/consumer

Consumer Advocate and
    Protection Division
Tennessee Attorney General's
Office
P.O. Box 20207
Nashville, TN 37202
615-741-1671

Texas

Attorney General
P.O. Box 12548
Austin, TX 78711

Banking Authority
Texas Department of Banking
2601 North Lamar Boulevard
Austin, TX 78705
512-475-1300
www.banking.state.tx.us

Consumer Protection Agency
Austin Regional Office
P.O. Box 12548
Austin, TX 78711

512-463-2100
www.oag.state.tx.us

Utah

Attorney General
Utah State Capitol Complex
P.O. Box 142320
Salt Lake City, UT 84114

Banking Authority
Department of Financial
Institutions
P.O. Box 146800
Salt Lake City, UT 84114
801-538-8830
www.dfi.utah.gov

Consumer Protection Agency
Division of Consumer
Protection
Department of Commerce
160 East 300 South
Salt Lake City, UT 84114
801-530-6601
www.consumerprotection.utah.
gov

Vermont

Attorney General
109 State Sreet
Montpelier, VT 05609

Banking Authority
Department of Banking,
Insurance, Securities and
Health Care Administration
89 Main Street
Drawer 20
Montpelier, VT 05620
802-828-3301
www.bishca.state.vt.us

Consumer Protection Agency
Consumer Assistance Program
104 Morrill Hall
UVM
Burlington, VT 05405
802-656-3183
www.atg.state.vt.us

Virginia

Attorney General
900 East Main Street
Richmond, VA 23219

Banking Authority
Bureau of Financial Institutions
1300 East Main Street
Suite 800
Richmond, VA 23219
804-371-9657
www.scc.virginia.gov

Consumer Protection Agency
Antitrust and Consumer
Litigation Section
Office of the Attorney General
900 East Main Street
Richmond, VA 23219
804-786-2116
www.oag.state.va.us

Office of Consumer Affairs
Department of Agriculture and
Consumer Services
Oliver W. Hill Building
102 Governor Street
Richmond, VA 23219
804-786-2042
www.vdacs.virginia.com

Washington

Attorney General
1125 Washington Street, S.E.
P.O. Box 40100
Olympia, WA 98504

Banking Authority
Department of Financial
Institutions
P.O. Box 41200
Olympia, WA 98504
360-902-8700
www.dfi.wa.gov

Consumer Protection Agency
Bellingham Consumer
Resource Center
Office of the Attorney General
103 East Holly Street
Suite 308
Bellingham, WA 98225
360-738-6185

Kennewick Consumer Resource
Center
Office of the Attorney General
500 North Morain Street
Suite 1250
Kennewick, WA 99336
509-734-7140

Seattle Consumer Resource
Center
Office of the Attorney General
900 Fourth Avenue
Suite 2000
Seattle, WA 98164
206-464-6684
www.atg.wa.gov

Spokane Consumer Resource
Center
Office of the Attorney General
1116 West Riverside
Spokane, WA 99201
509-456-3123

Tacoma Consumer Resource
   Center
Office of the Attorney General
Consumer Protection Division
P.O. Box 2317
Tacoma, WA 98401
253-593-2904
www.atg.wa.gov

Vancouver Consumer Resource
   Center
Office of the Attorney General
1220 Main Street
Suite 549
Vancouver, WA 98660
360-759-2150
www.atg.wa.gov/consumer

West Virginia

Attorney General
State Capitol Building 1
Room 26-E
Charleston, WV 25305

Banking Authority
Division of Banking
State Capitol Complex
Building 3, Room 311
1900 Kanawha Boulevard East
Charleston, WV 25305

304-558-2294
www.wvdob.org

Consumer Protection Agency
Consumer Protection Division
Office of the Attorney General
P.O. Box 1789
Charleston, WV 25326
304-558-8986
www.wvago.us

Wisconsin

Attorney General
Wisconsin Department of
Justice
P.O. Box 7857
Madison, WI 53707

Banking Authority
Department of Financial
Institutions
345 West Washington Avenue
4th Floor
Madison, WI 53703
608-264-7969
www.wdfi.org

Consumer Protection Agency

Bureau of Consumer Protection

Department of Agriculture,
    Trade & Consumer
    Protection

200 North Jefferson Street

Suite 146A

Green Bay, WI 54301

920-448-5110

http://datcp.state.wi.us

**Division of Agriculture, Trade
    and Consumer Protection**

2811 Agriculture Drive

P.O. Box 8911

Madison, WI 53708

608-224-4949

http://datcp.state.wi.us

Wyoming

Attorney General

123 Capitol Building

200 W. 24th Street

Cheyenne, WY 82002

Banking Authority

Division of Banking

Herschler Building

122 West 25th Street

3rd Floor, East

Cheyenne, WY 82002

307-777-3555

Consumer Protection Agency

Consumer Protection Unit

Office of the Attorney General

123 Capitol

200 W. 24th Street

Cheyenne, WY 82002

307-777-7841

http://attorneygeneral.state.
wy.us

STATE-BY-STATE CRIMINAL LAW STATUTES REGARDING IDENTITY THEFT

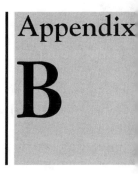

Appendix

B

This appendix provides a list of state-by-state criminal law statutes regarding identity theft, part of the language from the statutes defining identity theft, and a Web address for finding the full text of the statutes (where available).

Alabama

Ala. Code Sec. 13A-8-190 through 201
www.legislature.state.al.us/Search/SearchText.htm

> (a) A person commits the crime of identity theft if, without the authorization, consent, or permission of the victim, and with the intent to defraud for his or her own benefit or the benefit of a third person, he or she does any of the following:
>
> > (1) Obtains, records, or accesses identifying information that would assist in accessing financial resources, obtaining identification documents, or obtaining benefits of the victim.
> >
> > (2) Obtains goods or services through the use of identifying information of the victim.

(3) Obtains identification documents in the victim's name.

(b) Identity theft in which there is a financial loss of greater than five hundred dollars ($500) or the defendant has previously been convicted of identity theft constitutes identity theft in the first degree. Identity theft in the first degree is a Class C felony.

(c) Identity theft in which the defendant has not previously been convicted of identity theft and there is no financial loss or the financial loss is five hundred dollars ($500) or less constitutes identity theft in the second degree. Identity theft in the second degree is a Class A misdemeanor.

(d) This section shall not apply when a person obtains the identity of another person to misrepresent his or her age for the sole purpose of obtaining alcoholic beverages, tobacco, or another privilege denied to minors. (Act 2001-312, p. 399, §3.)

Restitution for financial loss.

Upon conviction for any crime in this article, in addition to any other punishment, a person found guilty shall be ordered by the court to make restitution for financial loss caused by the criminal violation of this article to any person whose identifying information was appropriated. Financial loss may include any costs incurred by the victim in correcting the credit history or credit rating of the victim or any costs incurred in connection with any civil or administrative proceeding to satisfy any debt, lien, or other obligations resulting from the theft of the victim's identification documents or identifying information, including lost wages and attorney's fees. The court may order restitution for financial loss to any other person or entity that suffers a loss from the violation. Additionally, persons convicted of violation of this article shall be assessed an amount of twenty-five dollars ($25) per day and medical expenses for time spent in county or municipal jails or in a state prison facility.

Order to correct records.

(a) Upon a conviction for any crime in violation of this article and at the victim's request, the sentencing court shall issue any orders necessary to correct any public or private record that contains false information as a result of a criminal violation of this article. Any order shall be under seal and may be released only as prescribed by this section. The order shall include the following information:

(1) Information about financial accounts affected by the crime, including, but not limited to, the name of the financial institution, the account number, amount of money involved in the crime, and the date of the crime.

(2) The specific identifying information and identification documents used to commit the crime.

(3) A description of the perpetrator of the crime.

(b) The victim may release the orders as follows:

(1) The victim may submit this order in any civil proceeding to set aside a judgment against the victim involving the specific account and amounts as determined by the criminal sentencing court. The order shall remain sealed in the civil proceeding.

(2) The victim may submit the order to any governmental entity or private business as proof that any financial accounts therein created or altered were a result of the crime and not the actions of the victim.

Alaska

Alaska Stat Sec. 11.46.565
www.legis.state.ak.us/folhome.htm
Click on "The Current Alaska Statutes" and navigate to citation.

Criminal impersonation in the first degree.

(a) A person commits the crime of criminal impersonation in the first degree if the person

(1) possesses an access device or identification document of another person;

(2) without authorization of the other person, uses the access device or identification document of another person to obtain a false identification document, open an account at a financial institution, obtain an access device, or obtain property or services; and

(3) recklessly damages the financial reputation of the other person.

(b) Criminal impersonation in the first degree is a class B felony.

Arizona

Ariz. Rev. Stat. Sec. 13-2008
www.azleg.state.az.us/ars/13/02008.htm

Taking identity of another person or entity; classification.

A. A person commits taking the identity of another person or entity if the person knowingly takes, purchases, manufactures, records, possesses or uses any personal identifying information or entity identifying information of another person or entity, including a real or fictitious person or entity, without the consent of that other person or entity, with the intent to obtain or use the other person's or entity's identity for any unlawful purpose or to cause loss to a person or entity whether or not the person or entity actually suffers any economic loss as a result of the offense.

B. On the request of a person or entity, a peace officer in any jurisdiction in which an element of the offense is committed, a result of the offense occurs or the person or entity whose identity is taken resides or is located shall take a report. The peace officer may provide a copy of the report to any other law enforcement agency that is located in a jurisdiction in which a violation of this section occurred.

C. If a defendant is alleged to have committed multiple violations of this section within the same county, the prosecutor may file a complaint charging all of the violations and any related charges under other sections that have not been previously filed in any precinct in which a violation is alleged to have occurred. If a defendant is alleged to have committed multiple violations of this section within the state, the prosecutor may file a complaint charging all of the violations and any related charges under other sections that have not been previously filed in any county in which a violation is alleged to have occurred.

D. This section does not apply to a violation of section 4-241 by a person who is under twenty-one years of age.

E. Taking the identity of another person or entity is a class 4 felony.

Arkansas

Ark. Code Ann. Sec. 5-37-227
www.arkleg.state.ar.us/data/ar_code.asp
Click on "Arkansas Code" and then enter the citation.

Financial identity fraud—Nonfinancial identity fraud—Restitution—Venue.

(a) A person commits financial identity fraud if, with the intent to:

(1) Create, obtain, or open a credit account, debit account, or other financial resource for his or her benefit or for the benefit of a third party, he or she accesses, obtains, records, or submits to a financial institution another person's identifying information for the purpose of opening or creating a credit account, debit account, or financial resource without the authorization of the person identified by the information; or

(2) Appropriate a financial resource of another person to his or her own use or to the use of a third party without the authorization of that other person, the actor:

(A) Uses a scanning device; or
(B) Uses a re-encoder.

(b) A person commits nonfinancial identity fraud if he or she knowingly obtains another person's identifying information without the other person's authorization and uses the identifying information for any unlawful purpose, including without limitation:

   (1) To avoid apprehension or criminal prosecution;

   (2) To harass another person; or

   (3) To obtain or to attempt to obtain a good, service, real property, or medical information of another person.

(c) As used in this section:

   (1) "Disabled person" means the same as defined in § 4-88-201;

   (2) "Elder person" means the same as defined in § 4-88-201;

   (3) "Financial institution" includes, but is not limited to, a credit card company, bank, or any other type of lending or credit company or institution;

   (4) "Financial resource" includes, but is not limited to, a credit card, debit card, or any other type of line of credit or loan;

   (5) "Identifying information" includes, but is not limited to, a:

      (A) Social Security number;

      (B) Driver's license number;

      (C) Checking account number;

      (D) Savings account number;

(E) Credit card number;

(F) Debit card number;

(G) Personal identification number;

(H) Electronic identification number;

(I) Digital signature; or

(J) Any other number or information that can be used to access a person's financial resources;

(6) "Re-encoder" means an electronic device that places encoded information from the magnetic strip or stripe of a payment card onto the magnetic strip or stripe of a different card; and

(7) "Scanning device" means a scanner, reader, or any other electronic device that is used to access, read, scan, obtain, memorize, or store, temporarily or permanently, information encoded on the magnetic strip or stripe of a payment card.

(d) The provisions of this section do not apply to any person who obtains another person's driver's license or other form of identification for the sole purpose of misrepresenting the actor's age.

(e) (1) Except as provided in subdivision (e)(2) of this section, financial identity fraud is a Class C felony.

(2) Financial identify fraud is a Class B felony if the victim is an elder person or a disabled person.

(f) (1) Except as provided in subdivision (f)(2) of this section, nonfinancial identity fraud is a Class D felony.

(2) Nonfinancial identity fraud is a Class C felony if the victim is an elder person or a disabled person.

(g) (1) In addition to any penalty imposed under this section, a violation of this section constitutes an unfair or deceptive act or practice as defined by the Deceptive Trade Practices Act, § 4-88-101 et seq.

(2) Any remedy, penalty, or authority granted to the Attorney General or another person under the Deceptive Trade Practices Act, § 4-88-101 et seq., is available to the Attorney General or that other person for the enforcement of this section.

(h) (1) (A) In addition to any penalty imposed under this section, upon conviction for financial identity fraud or nonfinancial identity fraud, a court may order the defendant to make restitution to any victim whose identifying information was appropriated or to the estate of the victim under § 5-4-205.

(B) In addition to any other authorized restitution, the restitution order described in subdivision (h)(1)(A) of this section may include without limitation restitution for the following financial losses:

(i) Any costs incurred by the victim in correcting the credit history or credit rating of the victim; and

(ii) Any costs incurred in connection with any civil or administrative proceeding to satisfy any debt, lien, or other obligation resulting from the theft of the victim's identifying information, including lost wages and attorney's fees.

(C) The court also may order restitution for financial loss to any other person or entity that suffers a financial loss from a violation of subsection (a) or (b) of this section.

(2) A judgment entered under this section and § 5-4-205 does not bar a remedy available in a civil action to recover damages relating to financial identity fraud or nonfinancial identity fraud.

(i) Venue for any criminal prosecution under this section or any civil action to recover damages relating to financial identity fraud or nonfinancial identity fraud is proper in any of the following venues:

(1) In the county where the violation occurred;

(2) If the violation was committed in more than one (1) county, or if the elements of the offense were committed in more than one (1) county, then in any county where any violation occurred or where an element of the offense occurred;

(3) In the county where the victim resides; or

(4) In the county where property that was fraudulently used or attempted to be used was located at the time of the violation.

California

Cal. Penal Code Sec. 530.5-8

www.leginfo.ca.gov/calaw.html

Click on "Penal Code" and navigate to citation.

530.5.

(a) Every person who willfully obtains personal identifying information, as defined in subdivision (b) of Section 530.55, of another person, and uses that information for any unlawful purpose, including to obtain, or attempt to obtain, credit, goods, services, real property, or medical information without the consent of that person, is guilty of a public offense, and upon conviction therefor, shall be punished by a fine, by imprisonment in a county jail not to exceed one year, or by both a fine and imprisonment, or by imprisonment in the state prison.

(b) In any case in which a person willfully obtains personal identifying information of another person, uses that information to commit a crime in addition to a violation of subdivision (a), and is convicted of that crime, the court records shall reflect that the person whose identity was falsely used to commit the crime did not commit the crime.

(c) (1) Every person who, with the intent to defraud, acquires or retains possession of the personal identifying information, as defined in subdivision (b) of Section 530.55, of another person is guilty of a public offense, and upon conviction therefor, shall be punished by a fine, by imprisonment in a county jail not to exceed one year, or by both a fine and imprisonment.

(2) Every person who, with the intent to defraud, acquires or retains possession of the personal identifying information, as defined in subdivision (b) of Section 530.55, of another person, and who has previously been convicted of a violation of this section, upon conviction therefor shall be punished by a fine, by imprisonment in a county jail not to exceed one year, or by both a fine and imprisonment, or by imprisonment in the state prison.

(3) Every person who, with the intent to defraud, acquires or retains possession of the personal identifying information, as defined in subdivision (b) of Section 530.55, of 10 or more other persons is guilty of a public offense, and upon conviction therefor, shall be punished by a fine, by imprisonment in a county jail not to exceed one year, or by both a fine and imprisonment, or by imprisonment in the state prison.

(d) (1) Every person who, with the intent to defraud, sells, transfers, or conveys the personal identifying information, as defined in subdivision (b) of Section 530.55, of another person is guilty of a public offense, and upon conviction therefor, shall be punished by a fine, by imprisonment in a county jail not to exceed one year, or by both a fine and imprisonment, or by imprisonment in the state prison.

(2) Every person who, with actual knowledge that the personal identifying information, as defined in subdivision (b) of Section 530.55, of a specific person will be used to commit a violation of subdivision (a), sells, transfers, or conveys that same personal identifying information is guilty of a public offense, and upon

conviction therefor, shall be punished by a fine, by imprisonment in the state prison, or by both a fine and imprisonment.

(e) Every person who commits mail theft, as defined in Section 1708 of Title 18 of the United States Code, is guilty of a public offense, and upon conviction therefor shall be punished by a fine, by imprisonment in a county jail not to exceed one year, or by both a fine and imprisonment. Prosecution under this subdivision shall not limit or preclude prosecution under any other provision of law, including, but not limited to, subdivisions (a) to (c), inclusive, of this section.

(f) An interactive computer service or access software provider, as defined in subsection (f) of Section 230 of Title 47 of the United States Code, shall not be liable under this section unless the service or provider acquires, transfers, sells, conveys, or retains possession of personal information with the intent to defraud.

530.6.

(a) A person who has learned or reasonably suspects that his or her personal identifying information has been unlawfully used by another, as described in subdivision (a) of Section 530.5, may initiate a law enforcement investigation by contacting the local law enforcement agency that has jurisdiction over his or her actual residence or place of business, which shall take a police report of the matter, provide the complainant with a copy of that report, and begin an investigation of the facts. If the suspected crime was committed in a different jurisdiction, the local law enforcement agency may refer the matter to the law enforcement agency where the suspected crime was committed for further investigation of the facts.

(b) A person who reasonably believes that he or she is the victim of identity theft may petition a court, or the court, on its own motion or upon application of the prosecuting attorney, may move, for an expedited judicial determination of his or her factual innocence, where the perpetrator of the identity theft was arrested for, cited for, or convicted of a crime under the victim's identity, or where a criminal complaint has been filed against the perpetrator in the victim's name, or where the victim's identity has been mistakenly associated with a record of criminal conviction. Any judicial determination of factual innocence made pursuant to this section may be heard and determined upon declarations, affidavits, police reports, or other material, relevant, and reliable information submitted by the parties or ordered to be part of the record by the court. Where the court determines that the petition or motion is meritorious and that there is no reasonable cause to believe that the victim committed the offense for which the perpetrator of the identity theft was arrested, cited, convicted, or subject to a criminal complaint in the victim's name, or that the victim's identity has been mistakenly associated with a record of criminal conviction, the court shall find the victim factually innocent of that offense. If the victim is found factually innocent, the court shall issue an order certifying this determination.

(c) After a court has issued a determination of factual innocence pursuant to this section, the court may order the name and associated personal identifying information contained in court records, files, and indexes accessible by the public deleted, sealed, or labeled to show that the data is impersonated and does not reflect the defendant's identity.

(d) A court that has issued a determination of factual innocence pursuant to this section may at any time vacate that determination if the petition, or any information submitted in support of the petition, is found to contain any material misrepresentation or fraud.

Colorado

Colo. Rev. Stat Sec. 18-5-902
www.michie.com/colorado/lpext.dll?f=templates&fn=main-h.htm
&cp=

Identity Theft.

(1) A person commits identity theft if he or she:

(a) Knowingly uses the personal identifying information, financial identifying information, or financial device of another without permission or lawful authority to obtain cash, credit, property, services, or any other thing of value or to make a financial payment.

(b) Knowingly possesses the personal identifying information, financial identifying information, or financial device of another without permission or lawful authority, with the intent to use or to aid or permit some other person to use such information or device to obtain cash, credit, property, services, or any other thing of value or to make a financial payment;

(c) With the intent to defraud, falsely makes, completes, alters, or utters a written instrument or financial device containing any personal identifying information or financial identifying information of another;

(d) Knowingly possesses the personal identifying information or financial identifying information of another without permission or lawful authority to use in applying for or completing an application for a financial device or other extension of credit;

(e) Knowingly uses or possesses the personal identifying information of another without permission or lawful authority with the intent to obtain a government-issued document; or

(f) Attempts, conspires with another, or solicits another to commit any of the acts set forth in paragraphs (a) to (e) of this subsection (1).

(2) Identity theft is a class 4 felony.

Delaware

Del. Code Ann. tit. II, Sec. 854
http://delcode.delaware.gov/title11/c005/sc03/index.shtml

Identity theft; class D felony.

(a) A person commits identity theft when the person knowingly or recklessly obtains, produces, possesses, uses, sells, gives or transfers personal identifying information belonging or pertaining to another person without the consent of the other person and with intent to use the information to commit or facilitate any crime set forth in this title.

(b) A person commits identity theft when the person knowingly or recklessly obtains, produces, possesses, uses, sells, gives or transfers personal identifying information belonging or pertaining to another person without the consent of the other person, thereby knowingly or recklessly facilitating the use of the information by a third person to commit or facilitate any crime set forth in this title.

(c) For the purposes of this section, "personal identifying information" includes name, address, birth date, Social Security number, driver's license number, telephone number, financial services account number, savings account number, checking account number, credit card number, debit card number, identification document or false identification document, electronic identification number, educational record, health care record, financial record, credit record, employment record, e-mail address, computer system password, mother's maiden name or similar personal number, record or information.

(d) Identity theft is a class D felony.

(e) When a person is convicted of or pleads guilty to identity theft, the sentencing judge shall order full restitution for monetary loss, including documented loss of wages and reasonable attorney fees, suffered by the victim.

District of Columbia

(Does not have specific identity theft law.)

Florida

Fla. Stat. Ann. Sec. 817.568
www.leg.state.fl.us/statutes/index.cfm?App_mode=Display_
Statute&Search_String=&URL=Ch0817/SEC568.HTM&Title=-
>2000->Ch0817->Section 568

Criminal use of personal identification information.

(2) (a) Any person who willfully and without authorization
fraudulently uses, or possesses with intent to fraudulently use, personal identification information
concerning an individual without first obtaining
that individual's consent, commits the offense of
fraudulent use of personal identification information, which is a felony of the third degree, punishable as provided in s. 775.082, s. 775.083, or s.
775.084.

(b) Any person who willfully and without authorization
fraudulently uses personal identification information
concerning an individual without first obtaining
that individual's consent commits a felony of the
second degree, punishable as provided in s. 775.082,
s. 775.083, or s. 775.084, if the pecuniary benefit, the
value of the services received, the payment sought
to be avoided, or the amount of the injury or fraud
perpetrated is $5,000 or more or if the person fraudu-
lently uses the personal identification information of
10 or more individuals, but fewer than 20 individuals,
without their consent. Notwithstanding any other
provision of law, the court shall sentence any person
convicted of committing the offense described in this

paragraph to a mandatory minimum sentence of 3 years' imprisonment.

(c) Any person who willfully and without authorization fraudulently uses personal identification information concerning an individual without first obtaining that individual's consent commits a felony of the first degree, punishable as provided in s. 775.082, s. 775.083, or s. 775.084, if the pecuniary benefit, the value of the services received, the payment sought to be avoided, or the amount of the injury or fraud perpetrated is $50,000 or more or if the person fraudulently uses the personal identification information of 20 or more individuals, but fewer than 30 individuals, without their consent. Notwithstanding any other provision of law, the court shall sentence any person convicted of committing the offense described in this paragraph to a mandatory minimum sentence of 5 years' imprisonment. If the pecuniary benefit, the value of the services received, the payment sought to be avoided, or the amount of the injury or fraud perpetrated is $100,000 or more, or if the person fraudulently uses the personal identification information of 30 or more individuals without their consent, notwithstanding any other provision of law, the court shall sentence any person convicted of committing the offense described in this paragraph to a mandatory minimum sentence of 10 years' imprisonment.

(4) Any person who willfully and without authorization possesses, uses, or attempts to use personal identification information concerning an individual without first

obtaining that individual's consent, and who does so for the purpose of harassing that individual, commits the offense of harassment by use of personal identification information, which is a misdemeanor of the first degree, punishable as provided in s. 775.082 or s. 775.083.

(5) If an offense prohibited under this section was facilitated or furthered by the use of a public record, as defined in s. 119.011, the offense is reclassified to the next higher degree as follows:

(a) A misdemeanor of the first degree is reclassified as a felony of the third degree.

(b) A felony of the third degree is reclassified as a felony of the second degree.

(c) A felony of the second degree is reclassified as a felony of the first degree.

(6) Any person who willfully and without authorization fraudulently uses personal identification information concerning an individual who is less than 18 years of age without first obtaining the consent of that individual or of his or her legal guardian commits a felony of the second degree, punishable as provided in s. 775.082, s. 775.083, or s. 775.084.

(7) Any person who is in the relationship of parent or legal guardian, or who otherwise exercises custodial authority over an individual who is less than 18 years of age, who willfully and fraudulently uses personal identification information of that individual commits a felony of the second degree, punishable as provided in s. 775.082, s. 775.083, or s. 775.084.

(8)(a) Any person who willfully and fraudulently uses, or possesses with intent to fraudulently use, personal identification information concerning a deceased individual commits the offense of fraudulent use or possession with intent to use personal identification information of a deceased individual, a felony of the third degree, punishable as provided in s. 775.082, s. 775.083, or s. 775.084.

(b) Any person who willfully and fraudulently uses personal identification information concerning a deceased individual commits a felony of the second degree, punishable as provided in s. 775.082, s. 775.083, or s. 775.084, if the pecuniary benefit, the value of the services received, the payment sought to be avoided, or the amount of injury or fraud perpetrated is $5,000 or more, or if the person fraudulently uses the personal identification information of 10 or more but fewer than 20 deceased individuals. Notwithstanding any other provision of law, the court shall sentence any person convicted of committing the offense described in this paragraph to a mandatory minimum sentence of 3 years' imprisonment.

(c) Any person who willfully and fraudulently uses personal identification information concerning a deceased individual commits the offense of aggravated fraudulent use of the personal identification information of multiple deceased individuals, a felony of the first degree, punishable as provided in s. 775.082, s. 775.083, or s. 775.084, if the pecuniary benefit, the value of the services received, the payment sought to be avoided, or the amount of injury or fraud perpetrated is $50,000 or more, or if the person fraudulently uses the personal identification information of 20 or more but fewer than 30 deceased individuals. Notwithstanding any other provision of law, the court shall sentence any person convicted of the offense described in this paragraph to a minimum mandatory sentence of 5 years' imprisonment. If the pecuniary benefit, the value of the services received, the payment sought to be avoided, or the amount of the injury or fraud perpetrated is $100,000 or more, or if the person fraudulently uses the personal identification information of 30 or more deceased individuals, notwithstanding any other provision of law, the court shall sentence any person convicted of an offense described in this paragraph to a mandatory minimum sentence of 10 years' imprisonment.

(9) Any person who willfully and fraudulently creates or uses, or possesses with intent to fraudulently use, counterfeit or fictitious personal identification information concerning a fictitious individual, or concerning a real individual without first obtaining that real individual's consent, with intent to use such counterfeit or fictitious personal identification information for the purpose of committing or facilitating the commission of a fraud on another person, commits the offense of fraudulent creation or use, or possession with intent to fraudulently use, counterfeit or fictitious personal identification information, a felony of the third degree, punishable as provided in s. 775.082, s. 775.083, or s. 775.084.

Georgia

Ga. Code Ann. Sec. 16-9-120, through 128
www.legis.state.ga.us
Click on "Georgia Code," then navigate to citation.

Elements of offense

(a) A person commits the offense of identity fraud when he or she willfully and fraudulently:

(1) Without authorization or consent, uses or possesses with intent to fraudulently use, identifying information concerning an individual;

(2) Uses identifying information of an individual under 18 years old over whom he or she exercises custodial authority;

(3) Uses or possesses with intent to fraudulently use, identifying information concerning a deceased individual;

(4) Creates, uses, or possesses with intent to fraudulently use, any counterfeit or fictitious identifying information concerning a fictitious individual with intent to use such counterfeit or fictitious identification information for the purpose of committing or facilitating the commission of a crime or fraud on another person; or

(5) Without authorization or consent, creates, uses, or possesses with intent to fraudulently use, any counterfeit or fictitious identifying information

concerning a real individual with intent to use such counterfeit or fictitious identification information for the purpose of committing or facilitating the commission of a crime or fraud on another person.

(b) A person commits the offense of identity fraud by receipt of fraudulent identification information when he or she willingly accepts for identification purposes identifying information which he or she knows to be fraudulent, stolen, counterfeit, or fictitious. In any prosecution under this subsection it shall not be necessary to show a conviction of the principal thief, counterfeiter, or fraudulent user.

Penalty for violations.

(a) A violation of this article, other than a violation of Code Section 16-9-122, shall be punishable by imprisonment for not less than one nor more than ten years or a fine not to exceed $100,000.00, or both. Any person who commits such a violation for the second or any subsequent offense shall be punished by imprisonment for not less than three nor more than 15 years, a fine not to exceed $250,000.00, or both.

(b) A violation of this article which does not involve the intent to commit theft or appropriation of any property, resource, or other thing of value that is committed by a person who is less than 21 years of age shall be punishable by imprisonment for not less than one nor more than three years or a fine not to exceed $5,000.00, or both.

(c) Any person found guilty of a violation of this article may be ordered by the court to make restitution to any consumer victim or any business victim of such fraud.

Hawaii

HI Rev. Stat. Sec. 708-839.6 through Sec. 708-839.8
www.capitol.hawaii.gov/hrscurrent/Vol14_Ch0701-0853

Find and click on "HRS0708" then "-0839_0006," "-0839_0007," or "-0839_0008."

Identity theft in the first degree.

(1) A person commits the offense of identity theft in the first degree if that person makes or causes to be made, either directly or indirectly, a transmission of any personal information of another by any oral statement, any written statement, or any statement conveyed by any electronic means, with the intent to:

(a) Facilitate the commission of a murder in any degree, a class A felony, kidnapping, unlawful imprisonment in any degree, extortion in any degree, any offense under chapter 134, criminal property damage in the first or second degree, escape in any degree, any offense under part VI of chapter 710, any offense under section 711-1103, or any offense under chapter 842; or

(b) Commit the offense of theft in the first degree from the person whose personal information is used, or from any other person or entity.

(2) Identity theft in the first degree is a class A felony.

Identity theft in the second degree.

(1) A person commits the offense of identity theft in the second degree if that person makes or causes to

be made, either directly or indirectly, a transmission of any personal information of another by any oral statement, any written statement, or any statement conveyed by any electronic means, with the intent to commit the offense of theft in the second degree from any person or entity.

(2) Identity theft in the second degree is a class B felony.

Identity theft in the third degree.

(1) A person commits the offense of identity theft in the third degree if that person makes or causes to be made, either directly or indirectly, a transmission of any personal information of another by any oral statement, any written statement, or any statement conveyed by any electronic means, with the intent to commit the offense of theft in the third or fourth degree from any person or entity.

(2) Identity theft in the third degree is a class C felony.

Idaho

Idaho Code Sec. 18-3126 (criminal)
www3.state.id.us/cgi-bin/newidst?sctid=180310026.K

Misappropriation of Personal Identifying Information.

It is unlawful for any person to obtain or record personal identifying information of another person without the authorization of that person, with the intent that the information be used to obtain, or attempt to obtain, credit, money, goods or services in the name of the other person without the consent of that person.

Illinois

720 ILCS 5/16 G-15
www.ilga.gov/legislation/ilcs/ilcs.asp
Click on "CHAPTER 720 - CRIMINAL OFFENSES" then "720 ILCS 5/ - Criminal Code of 1961" then "Article 16 - Theft And Related Offenses."

Identity Theft.

(a) A person commits the offense of identity theft when he or she knowingly:

(1) uses any personal identifying information or personal identification document of another person to fraudulently obtain credit, money, goods, services, or other property, or

(2) uses any personal identification information or personal identification document of another with intent to commit any felony theft or other felony violation of State law not set forth in paragraph (1) of this subsection (a), or

(3) obtains, records, possesses, sells, transfers, purchases, or manufactures any personal identification information or personal identification document of another with intent to commit or to aid or abet another in committing any felony theft or other felony violation of State law, or

(4) uses, obtains, records, possesses, sells, transfers, purchases, or manufactures any personal identification information or personal identification document of another knowing that such personal identification

information or personal information documents were stolen or produced without lawful authority, or

(5) uses, transfers, or possesses document-making implements to produce false identification or false documents with knowledge that they will be used by the person or another to commit any felony theft or other felony violation of State law, or

(6) uses any personal identification information or personal identification document of another to portray himself or herself as that person, or otherwise, for the purpose of gaining access to any personal identification information or personal identification document of that person, without the prior express permission of that person, or

(7) uses any personal identification information or personal identification document of another for the purpose of gaining access to any record of the actions taken, communications made or received, or other activities or transactions of that person, without the prior express permission of that person.

Indiana

Ind. Code Sec. 35-43-5-3.5
www.state.in.us/legislative/ic/code/title35/ar43/ch5.html

Identity deception.

(a) Except as provided in subsection (c), a person who knowingly or intentionally obtains, possesses, transfers, or uses the identifying information of another person, including the identifying information of a person who is deceased:

(1) without the other person's consent; and

(2) with intent to:

    (A) harm or defraud another person;

    (B) assume another person's identity; or

    (C) profess to be another person; commits identity deception, a Class D felony.

(b) However, the offense defined in subsection (a) is a Class C felony if:

    (1) a person obtains, possesses, transfers, or uses the identifying information of more than one hundred (100) persons; or

    (2) the fair market value of the fraud or harm caused by the offense is at least fifty thousand dollars ($50,000).

(c) The conduct prohibited in subsections (a) and (b) does not apply to:

    (1) a person less than twenty-one (21) years of age who uses the identifying information of another person to acquire an alcoholic beverage (as defined in IC 7.1-1-3-5);

    (2) a minor (as defined in IC 35-49-1-4) who uses the identifying information of another person to acquire:

        (A) a cigarette or tobacco product (as defined in IC 6-7-2-5);

(B) a periodical, a videotape, or other communication medium that contains or depicts nudity (as
defined in IC 35-49-1-5);

(C) admittance to a performance (live or film) that
prohibits the attendance of the minor based on
age; or

(D) an item that is prohibited by law for use or
consumption by a minor; or

(3) any person who uses the identifying information for
a lawful purpose.

(d) It is not a defense in a prosecution under subsection (a)
or (b) that no person was harmed or defrauded.

Iowa

Iowa Code Sec. 715A.8
http://nxtsearch.legis.state.ia.us/NXT/gateway.dll? f=templates&
fn=default.htm

Identity theft.

2. A person commits the offense of identity theft if the
person fraudulently uses or attempts to fraudulently
use identification information of another person, with
the intent to obtain credit, property, services, or other
benefit.

3. If the value of the credit, property, or services exceeds one
thousand dollars, the person commits a class "D" felony.
If the value of the credit, property, or services does not
exceed one thousand dollars, the person commits an
aggravated misdemeanor.

4. A violation of this section is an unlawful practice under section 714.16.

5. Violations of this section shall be prosecuted in any of the following venues:

   a. In the county in which the violation occurred.

   b. If the violation was committed in more than one county, or if the elements of the offense were committed in more than one county, then in any county where any violation occurred or where an element of the offense occurred.

   c. In the county where the victim resides.

   d. In the county where the property that was fraudulently used or attempted to be used was located at the time of the violation.

6. Any real or personal property obtained by a person as a result of a violation of this section, including but not limited to any money, interest, security, claim, contractual right, or financial instrument that is in the possession of the person, shall be subject to seizure and forfeiture pursuant to chapter 809A. A victim injured by a violation of this section, or a financial institution that has indemnified a victim injured by a violation of this section, may file a claim as an interest holder pursuant to section 809A.11 for payment of damages suffered by the victim including costs of recovery and reasonable attorney fees.

7. A financial institution may file a complaint regarding a violation of this section on behalf of a victim and shall have the same rights and privileges as the victim if the financial institution has indemnified the victim for such violations.

8. Upon the request of a victim, a peace officer in any jurisdiction described in subsection 5 shall take a report regarding an alleged violation of this section and shall provide a copy of the report to the victim. The report may also be provided to any other law enforcement agency in any of the jurisdictions described in subsection 5.

Kansas

Kan. Stat. Ann. Sec. 21-4018
www.kslegislature.org/legsrv-statutes/getStatuteInfo.do

Identity theft; identity fraud.

(a) Identity theft is knowingly and with intent to defraud for any benefit, obtaining, possessing, transferring, using or attempting to obtain, possess, transfer or use, one or more identification documents or personal identification number of another person other than that issued lawfully for the use of the possessor.

(b) "Identification documents" has the meaning provided in K.S.A. 21-3830, and amendments thereto.

(c) Except as provided further, identity theft is a severity level 8, nonperson felony. If the monetary loss to the victim or victims is more than $100,000, identity theft is a severity level 5, nonperson felony.

(d) Identity fraud is:

(1) Willfully and knowingly supplying false information intending that the information be used to obtain an identification document;

(2) making, counterfeiting, altering, amending or mutilating any identification document:

   (A) Without lawful authority; and

   (B) with the intent to deceive; or

(3) willfully and knowingly obtaining, possessing, using, selling or furnishing or attempting to obtain, possess or furnish to another for any purpose of deception an identification document.

(e) Identity fraud is a severity level 8, nonperson felony.

Kentucky

Ky. Rev. Stat. Ann. Sec. 514.160
http://162.114.4.13/KRS/514-00/160.PDF

Theft of identity.

(1) A person is guilty of the theft of the identity of another when he or she knowingly possesses or uses any current or former identifying information of the other person or family member or ancestor of the other person, such as that person's or family member's or ancestor's name, address, telephone number, electronic mail address, Social Security number, driver's license number, birth date, personal identification number or code, and any other information which could be used to identify the person, including unique biometric data, with the intent to represent that he or she is the other person for the purpose of:

(a) Depriving the other person of property;

(b) Obtaining benefits or property to which he or she would otherwise not be entitled;

(c) Making financial or credit transactions using the other person's identity;

(d) Avoiding detection; or

(e) Commercial or political benefit.

(2) Theft of identity is a Class D felony. If the person violating this section is a business that has violated this section on more than one (1) occasion, then that person also violates the Consumer Protection Act, KRS 367.110 to 367.300.

(3) This section shall not apply when a person obtains the identity of another to misrepresent his or her age for the purpose of obtaining alcoholic beverages, tobacco, or another privilege denied to minors.

Louisiana

La. Rev. Stat. Ann. Sec. 14:67.16
www.legis.state.la.us/lss/lss.asp?doc=78613

Identity theft.

B. Identity theft is the intentional use or possession or transfer or attempted use with fraudulent intent by any person of any personal identifying information of another person to obtain, possess, or transfer, whether contemporaneously or not, credit, money, goods, services, or anything else of value without the authorization or consent of the other person.

F. The provisions of this Section shall not apply to any person who obtains another's driver's license or other form of identification for the sole purpose of misrepresenting his age.

G.(1) Any person who has learned or reasonably suspects that his personal identifying information has been unlawfully used by another in violation of any provision of this Section may initiate a law enforcement investigation by contacting the local law enforcement agency that has jurisdiction over the area of his residence. Any law enforcement agency which is requested to conduct an investigation under the provisions of this Subsection shall take a police report of the matter from the victim, provide the complainant with a copy of such report, and begin an investigation of the facts. If the crime was committed in a different jurisdiction, the agency preparing the report shall refer the matter, with a copy of the report, to the local law enforcement agency having jurisdiction over the area in which the alleged crime was committed for an investigation of the facts.

(2) Any officer of any law enforcement agency who investigates an alleged violation in compliance with the provisions of this Subsection shall make a written report of the investigation that includes the name of the victim; the name of the suspect, if known; the type of personal identifying information obtained, possessed, transferred, or used in violation of this Section; and the results of the investigation. At the request of the victim who has requested the

investigation, the law enforcement agency shall provide to such victim the report created under the provisions of this Paragraph. In providing the report, the agency shall eliminate any information that is included in the report other than the information required by this Paragraph.

Maine

ME Rev. Stat. Ann. tit. 17-A Sec. 905-A

http://janus.state.me.us/legis/statutes/17-A/title17-Asec905-A.html

Misuse of identification.

1. A person is guilty of misuse of identification if, in order to obtain confidential information, property or services, the person intentionally or knowingly:

   A. Presents or uses a credit or debit card that is stolen, forged, canceled or obtained as a result of fraud or deception; [1999, c. 190, §3 (NEW).]

   B. Presents or uses an account, credit or billing number that that person is not authorized to use or that was obtained as a result of fraud or deception; or

   C. Presents or uses a form of legal identification that that person is not authorized to use.

2. It is an affirmative defense to prosecution under this section that the person believed in good faith that the person was authorized to present or use the card, number or legal identification.

3. Proof of actual or constructive notice of cancellation gives rise to a permissible inference under the Maine Rules of

Evidence, Rule 303 that the person who presented the canceled credit or debit card knew it had been canceled.

5. Misuse of identification is a Class D crime.

Maryland

Md. Code Ann. Sec. 8-301
www.michie.com/maryland/lpext.dll?f=templates&fn=main-h.htm
&2.0

Identity Fraud.

(b) *Prohibited—Obtaining personal identifying information without consent.*—A person may not knowingly, willfully, and with fraudulent intent possess, obtain, or help another to possess or obtain any personal identifying information of an individual, without the consent of the individual, in order to use, sell, or transfer the information to get a benefit, credit, good, service, or other thing of value in the name of the individual.

(c) *Same—Assuming identity of another.*—A person may not knowingly and willfully assume the identity of another:

(1) to avoid identification, apprehension, or prosecution for a crime; or

(2) with fraudulent intent to:

(i) get a benefit, credit, good, service, or other thing of value; or

(ii) avoid the payment of debt or other legal obligation.

(d) *Representation without authorization prohibited.*—A person may not knowingly and willfully claim to represent another person without the knowledge and consent of that person, with the intent to solicit, request, or take any other action to otherwise induce another person to provide personal identifying information or a payment device number.

(g) *Restitution and costs.*—In addition to restitution under Title 11, Subtitle 6 of the Criminal Procedure Article, a court may order a person who pleads guilty or nolo contendere or who is found guilty under this section to make restitution to the victim for reasonable costs, including reasonable attorney's fees, incurred.

Massachusetts

Mass. Gen. Laws ch. 266, Sec. 37E
www.mass.gov/legis/laws/mgl/266-37e.htm

Use of personal identification of another; identity fraud; penalty; restitution.

(b) Whoever, with intent to defraud, poses as another person without the express authorization of that person and uses such person's personal identifying information to obtain or to attempt to obtain money, credit, goods, services, anything of value, any identification card or other evidence of such person's identity, or to harass another shall be guilty of identity fraud and shall be punished by a fine of not more than $5,000 or imprisonment in a house of correction for not more than two and one-half years, or by both such fine and imprisonment.

(c) Whoever, with intent to defraud, obtains personal identifying information about another person without the express authorization of such person, with the intent to pose as such person or who obtains personal identifying information about a person without the express authorization of such person in order to assist another to pose as such person in order to obtain money, credit, goods, services, anything of value, any identification card or other evidence of such person's identity, or to harass another shall be guilty of the crime of identity fraud and shall be punished by a fine of not more than $5,000 or imprisonment in a house of correction for not more than two and one-half years, or by both such fine and imprisonment.

(d) A person found guilty of violating any provisions of this section shall, in addition to any other punishment, be ordered to make restitution for financial loss sustained by a victim as a result of such violation. Financial loss may include any costs incurred by such victim in correcting the credit history of such victim or any costs incurred in connection with any civil or administrative proceeding to satisfy any debt or other obligation of such victim, including lost wages and attorney's fees.

(e) A law enforcement officer may arrest without warrant any person he has probable cause to believe has committed the offense of identity fraud as defined in this section.

(f) A law enforcement officer shall accept a police incident report from a victim and shall provide a copy to such victim, if requested, within 24 hours. Such police incident reports may be filed in any county where a victim resides, or in any county where the owner or license holder of personal information stores or maintains said personal information, the owner's or license holder's principal place of business or any county in which the breach of security occurred, in whole or in part.

Michigan

(Does not have specific identity theft law.)

Minnesota

Minn. Stat. Ann. Sec. 609.527
www.revisor.leg.state.mn.us/statutes/?id=609.527

Identity Theft.

Subd. 2. **Crime.** A person who transfers, possesses, or uses an identity that is not the person's own, with the intent to commit, aid, or abet any unlawful activity is guilty of identity theft and may be punished as provided in subdivision 3.

Subd. 3. **Penalties.** A person who violates subdivision 2 may be sentenced as follows:

(1) if the offense involves a single direct victim and the total, combined loss to the direct victim and any indirect victims is $250 or less, the person may be sentenced as provided in section 609.52, subdivision 3, clause (5);

(2) if the offense involves a single direct victim and the total, combined loss to the direct victim and any indirect victims is more than $250 but not more than $500, the person may be sentenced as provided in section 609.52, subdivision 3, clause (4);

(3) if the offense involves two or three direct victims or the total, combined loss to the direct and indirect victims is more than $500 but not more than $2,500, the person may be sentenced as provided in section 609.52, subdivision 3, clause (3);

(4) if the offense involves more than three but not more than seven direct victims, or if the total combined loss to the direct and indirect victims is more than $2,500, the person may be sentenced as provided in section 609.52, subdivision 3, clause (2); and

(5) if the offense involves eight or more direct victims; or if the total, combined loss to the direct and indirect victims is more than $35,000; or if the offense is related to possession or distribution of pornographic work in violation of section 617.246 or 617.247; the person may be sentenced as provided in section 609.52, subdivision 3, clause (1).

Subd. 4. **Restitution; items provided to victim.**

(a) A direct or indirect victim of an identity theft crime shall be considered a victim for all purposes, including any rights that accrue under chapter 611A and rights to court-ordered restitution.

(b) The court shall order a person convicted of violating subdivision 2 to pay restitution of not less than $1,000 to each direct victim of the offense.

(c) Upon the written request of a direct victim or the prosecutor setting forth with specificity the facts and circumstances of the offense in a proposed order, the court shall provide to the victim, without cost, a certified copy of the complaint filed in the matter, the judgment of conviction, and an order setting forth the facts and circumstances of the offense.

Mississippi

Miss. Code Ann. Sec. 97-19-85
www.mscode.com/free/statutes/97/019/0085.htm

Fraudulent use of identity, Social Security number or other identifying information to obtain thing of value.

(1) Any person who shall make or cause to be made any false statement or representation as to his or another person's identity, Social Security account number or other identifying information for the purpose of fraudulently obtaining or with the intent to obtain goods, services or any thing of value, shall be guilty of a misdemeanor and upon conviction thereof shall be fined not more than five thousand dollars ($5,000.00) or imprisoned for a term not to exceed one (1) year, or both.

(2) A person is guilty of fraud under subsection (1) who:

    (a) Shall furnish false information wilfully, knowingly and with intent to deceive anyone as to his true identity or the true identity of another person;

    (b) Wilfully, knowingly, and with intent to deceive, uses a Social Security account number to establish and maintain business or other records; or

    (c) With intent to deceive, falsely represents a number to be the Social Security account number assigned to him or another person, when in fact the number is not the Social Security account number assigned to him or such other person; or

(d) Knowingly alters a Social Security card, buys or sells a Social Security card or counterfeit or altered Social Security card, counterfeits a Social Security card, or possesses a Social Security card or counterfeit Social Security card with intent to sell or alter it.

Missouri

Mo. Rev. Stat. Sec. 570.223
www.moga.state.mo.us/statutes/c500-599/5700000223.htm

Identity theft—penalty—restitution—other civil remedies available—exempted activities.

1. A person commits the crime of identity theft if he or she knowingly and with the intent to deceive or defraud obtains, possesses, transfers, uses, or attempts to obtain, transfer or use, one or more means of identification not lawfully issued for his or her use.

3. A person found guilty of identity theft shall be punished as follows:

   (1) Identity theft or attempted identity theft which does not result in the theft or appropriation of credit, money, goods, services, or other property is a class B misdemeanor;

   (2) Identity theft which results in the theft or appropriation of credit, money, goods, services, or other property not exceeding five hundred dollars in value is a class A misdemeanor;

(3) Identity theft which results in the theft or appropriation of credit, money, goods, services, or other property exceeding five hundred dollars and not exceeding five thousand dollars in value is a class C felony;

(4) Identity theft which results in the theft or appropriation of credit, money, goods, services, or other property exceeding five thousand dollars and not exceeding fifty thousand dollars in value is a class B felony;

(5) Identity theft which results in the theft or appropriation of credit, money, goods, services, or other property exceeding fifty thousand dollars in value is a class A felony.

4. In addition to the provisions of subsection 3 of this section, the court may order that the defendant make restitution to any victim of the offense. Restitution may include payment for any costs, including attorney fees, incurred by the victim:

(1) In clearing the credit history or credit rating of the victim; and

(2) In connection with any civil or administrative proceeding to satisfy any debt, lien, or other obligation of the victim arising from the actions of the defendant.

7. Civil actions under this section must be brought within five years from the date on which the identity of the wrongdoer was discovered or reasonably should have been discovered.

Montana

Mon. Code Ann. Sec. 45-6-332
http://data.opi.state.mt.us/bills/mca/45/6/45-6-332.htm

Theft of identity.

(1) A person commits the offense of theft of identity if the person purposely or knowingly obtains personal identifying information of another person and uses that information for any unlawful purpose, including to obtain or attempt to obtain credit, goods, services, financial information, or medical information in the name of the other person without the consent of the other person.

(2) (a) A person convicted of the offense of theft of identity if no economic benefit was gained or was attempted to be gained or if an economic benefit of less than $1,000 was gained or attempted to be gained shall be fined an amount not to exceed $1,000, imprisoned in the county jail for a term not to exceed 6 months, or both.

(b) A person convicted of the offense of theft of identity if an economic benefit of $1,000 or more was gained or attempted to be gained shall be fined an amount not to exceed $10,000, imprisoned in a state prison for a term not to exceed 10 years, or both.

(4) If restitution is ordered, the court may include, as part of its determination of an amount owed, payment for any costs incurred by the victim, including attorney fees and any costs incurred in clearing the credit history or credit rating of the victim or in connection with any civil or

administrative proceeding to satisfy any debt, lien, or other obligation of the victim arising as a result of the actions of the defendant.

Nebraska

NE Rev. Stat. Sec. 28-608 & 620
http://uniweb.legislature.ne.gov/QS/laws.php?mode=view_sta&sta= s2806008000

Criminal impersonation; penalty; restitution.

(1) A person commits the crime of criminal impersonation if he or she:

(a) Assumes a false identity and does an act in his or her assumed character with intent to gain a pecuniary benefit for himself, herself, or another or to deceive or harm another;

(b) Pretends to be a representative of some person or organization and does an act in his or her pretended capacity with the intent to gain a pecuniary benefit for himself, herself, or another and to deceive or harm another;

(c) Carries on any profession, business, or any other occupation without a license, certificate, or other authorization required by law; or

(d) Without the authorization or permission of another and with the intent to deceive or harm another:

(i) Obtains or records personal identification documents or personal identifying information; and

(ii) Accesses or attempts to access the financial resources of another through the use of a personal identification document or personal identifying information for the purpose of obtaining credit, money, goods, services, or any other thing of value.

(2) (a) Criminal impersonation is a Class III felony if the credit, money, goods, services, or other thing of value that was gained or was attempted to be gained was one thousand five hundred dollars or more.

(b) Criminal impersonation is a Class IV felony if the credit, money, goods, services, or other thing of value that was gained or was attempted to be gained was five hundred dollars or more but less than one thousand five hundred dollars.

(c) Criminal impersonation is a Class I misdemeanor if the credit, money, goods, services, or other thing of value that was gained or was attempted to be gained was two hundred dollars or more but less than five hundred dollars. Any second or subsequent conviction under this subdivision is a Class IV felony.

(d) Criminal impersonation is a Class II misdemeanor if no credit, money, goods, services, or other thing of value was gained or was attempted to be gained, or if the credit, money, goods, services, or other thing of value that was gained or was attempted to be gained was less than two hundred dollars. Any second conviction under this subdivision is a Class

I misdemeanor, and any third or subsequent conviction under this subdivision is a Class IV felony.

(e) A person found guilty of violating this section may, in addition to the penalties under this subsection, be ordered to make restitution pursuant to sections 29-2280 to 29-2289.

Unauthorized use of a financial transaction device; penalties; prosecution of offense.

(1) A person commits the offense of unauthorized use of a financial transaction device if such person uses such device in an automated banking device, to imprint a sales form, or in any other manner:

(a) For the purpose of obtaining money, credit, property, or services or for making financial payment, with intent to defraud;

(b) With notice that the financial transaction device is expired, revoked, or canceled;

(c) With notice that the financial transaction device is forged, altered, or counterfeited; or

(d) When for any reason his or her use of the financial transaction device is unauthorized either by the issuer or by the account holder.

(2) For purposes of this section, notice shall mean either notice given in person or notice given in writing to the account holder, by registered or certified mail, return receipt requested, duly stamped and addressed to such account holder at his or her last address known to the

issuer. Such notice shall be evidenced by a returned receipt signed by the account holder which shall be prima facie evidence that the notice was received.

(3) Any person committing the offense of unauthorized use of a financial transaction device shall be guilty of:

(a) A Class II misdemeanor if the total value of the money, credit, property, or services obtained or the financial payments made are less than two hundred dollars within a six-month period from the date of the first unauthorized use;

(b) A Class I misdemeanor if the total value of the money, credit, property, or services obtained or the financial payments made are two hundred dollars or more but less than five hundred dollars within a six-month period from the date of the first unauthorized use;

(c) A Class IV felony if the total value of the money, credit, property, or services obtained or the financial payments made are five hundred dollars or more but less than one thousand five hundred dollars within a six-month period from the date of the first unauthorized use; and

(d) A Class III felony if the total value of the money, credit, property, or services obtained or the financial payments made are one thousand five hundred dollars or more within a six-month period from the date of the first unauthorized use.

(4) Any prosecution under this section may be conducted in any county where the person committed the offense or any one of a series of offenses to be aggregated.

(5) Once aggregated and filed, no separate prosecution for an offense arising out of the same series of offenses aggregated and filed shall be allowed in any county.

Nevada

Nev. Rev. State. Sec. 205.463-465
www.leg.state.nv.us/NRS/NRS-205.html

Obtaining and using personal identifying information of another person to harm or impersonate person, to obtain certain nonpublic records or for other unlawful purpose; penalties; rebuttable inference that possessor of personal identifying information intended to unlawfully use such information.

1. Except as otherwise provided in subsections 2 and 3, a person who knowingly:

    (a) Obtains any personal identifying information of another person; and

    (b) With the intent to commit an unlawful act, uses the personal identifying information:

        (1) To harm that other person;

        (2) To represent or impersonate that other person to obtain access to any personal identifying information of that other person without the prior express consent of that other person;

        (3) To obtain access to any nonpublic record of the actions taken, communications made or

received by, or other activities or transactions of that other person without the prior express consent of that other person; or

(4) For any other unlawful purpose, including, without limitation, to obtain credit, a good, a service or anything of value in the name of that other person, is guilty of a category B felony and shall be punished by imprisonment in the state prison for a minimum term of not less than 1 year and a maximum term of not more than 20 years, and may be further punished by a fine of not more than $100,000.

2. Except as otherwise provided in subsection 3, a person who knowingly:

(a) Obtains any personal identifying information of another person; and

(b) Uses the personal identifying information to avoid or delay being prosecuted for an unlawful act, is guilty of a category C felony and shall be punished as provided in NRS 193.130.

3. A person who violates:

(a) Subsection 1 or 2 by obtaining and using the personal identifying information of an older person or a vulnerable person;

(b) Subsection 1 or 2 by obtaining and using the personal identifying information of five or more persons;

(c) Subsection 1 or 2 by causing another person to suffer a financial loss or injury of $3,000 or more as a result of the violation; or

(d) Subsection 2 to avoid or delay being prosecuted for an unlawful act that is punishable as a category A felony or category B felony is guilty of a category B felony and shall be punished by imprisonment in the state prison for a minimum term of not less than 3 years and a maximum term of not more than 20 years, and may be further punished by a fine of not more than $100,000.

4. In addition to any other penalty, the court shall order a person convicted of violating subsection 1 to pay restitution, including, without limitation, any attorney's fees and costs incurred to:

(a) Repair the credit history or rating of the person whose personal identifying information he obtained and used in violation of subsection 1; and

(b) Satisfy a debt, lien or other obligation incurred by the person whose personal identifying information he obtained and used in violation of subsection 1.

5. Proof of possession of the personal identifying information of five or more persons in a manner not set forth in NRS 205.4655 permits a rebuttable inference that the possessor intended to use such information in violation of this section.

Possession or sale of document or personal identifying information to establish false status or identity; penalties; rebuttable inference that possessor of personal identifying information intended to unlawfully use such information.

1. It is unlawful for a person to possess, sell or transfer any document or personal identifying information for the purpose of establishing a false status, occupation, membership, license or identity for himself or any other person.

2. Except as otherwise provided in subsection 3, a person who:

   (a) Sells or transfers any such document or personal identifying information in violation of subsection 1; or

   (b) Possesses any such document or personal identifying information in violation of subsection 1 to commit any of the crimes set forth in NRS 205.085 to 205.217, inclusive, 205.473 to 205.513, inclusive, or 205.610 to 205.810, inclusive, is guilty of a category C felony and shall be punished as provided in NRS 193.130.

3. A person who violates subsection 2 by:

   (a) Selling or transferring the personal identifying information of an older person or a vulnerable person;

   (b) Selling or transferring the personal identifying information of five or more persons; or

   (c) Causing another person to suffer a financial loss or injury of $3,000 or more as a result of the violation, is guilty of a category B felony and shall be punished by imprisonment in the state prison for a minimum term of not less than 1 year and a maximum term of not more than 20 years, and may be further punished by a fine of not more than $100,000.

4. Except as otherwise provided in this subsection and subsections 2 and 3, a person who possesses any such document or personal identifying information in violation of subsection 1 is guilty of a category E felony and shall be punished as provided in NRS 193.130. If a person possesses any such document or personal identifying information in violation of subsection 1 for the sole purpose of establishing false proof of age, including, without limitation, establishing false proof of age to game, purchase alcoholic beverages or purchase cigarettes or other tobacco products, the person is guilty of a misdemeanor.

New Hampshire

N.H. Rev. Stat. Ann. Sec. 638:26
www.gencourt.state.nh.us/rsa/html/LXII/638/638-26.htm

Identity Fraud.

I. A person is guilty of identity fraud when the person:

(a) Poses as another person with the purpose to defraud in order to obtain money, credit, goods, services, or anything else of value;

(b) Obtains or records personal identifying information about another person without the express authorization of such person, with the intent to pose as such person;

(c) Obtains or records personal identifying information about a person without the express authorization of such person in order to assist another to pose as such person; or

(d) Poses as another person, without the express authorization of such person, with the purpose of obtaining confidential information about such person that is not available to the general public.

II. Identity fraud is a class A felony.

III. A person found guilty of violating any provisions of this section shall, in addition to the penalty under paragraph II, be ordered to make restitution for economic loss sustained by a victim as a result of such violation.

New Mexico

N.M. Stat. Ann. Sec. 30-16-24.1
www.conwaygreene.com/nmsu/lpext.dll?f=templates&fn=main-hit-h.htm&2.0

Theft of identity; obtaining identity by electronic fraud.

A. Theft of identity consists of willfully obtaining, recording or transferring personal identity information of another person without the authorization or consent of that person and with the intent to defraud that person or another.

B. Obtaining identity by electronic fraud consists of knowingly and willfully soliciting, requesting or taking any action by means of a fraudulent electronic communication with intent to obtain the personal identifying information of another.

D. Whoever commits theft of identity is guilty of a fourth-degree felony.

E. Whoever commits obtaining identity by electronic fraud is guilty of a fourth-degree felony.

H. A person found guilty of theft of identity or of obtaining identity by electronic fraud shall, in addition to any other punishment, be ordered to make restitution for any financial loss sustained by a person injured as the direct result of the offense. In addition to out-of-pocket costs, restitution may include payment for costs, including attorney fees, incurred by that person in clearing the person's credit history or credit rating or costs incurred in connection with a civil or administrative proceeding to satisfy a debt, lien, judgment or other obligation of that person arising as a result of the offense.

New York

NY CLS Penal Sec. 190.77 through 190.84
http://public.leginfo.state.ny.us/menugetf.cgi?
COMMONQUERY=LAWS

Offenses involving theft of identity; definitions.

1. For the purposes of sections 190.78, 190.79 and 190.80 of this article "personal identifying information" means a person's name, address, telephone number, date of birth, driver's license number, Social Security number, place of employment, mother's maiden name, financial services account number or code, savings account number or code, checking account number or code, brokerage account

number or code, credit card account number or code, debit card number or code, automated teller machine number or code, taxpayer identification number, computer system password, signature or copy of a signature, electronic signature, unique biometric data that is a fingerprint, voice print, retinal image or iris image of another person, telephone calling card number, mobile identification number or code, electronic serial number or personal identification number, or any other name, number, code or information that may be used alone or in conjunction with other such information to assume the identity of another person.

2. For the purposes of sections 190.78, 190.79, 190.80, 190.81, 190.82 and 190.83 of this article:

   a. "electronic signature" shall have the same meaning as defined in subdivision three of section three hundred two of the state technology law.

   b. "personal identification number" means any number or code which may be used alone or in conjunction with any other information to assume the identity of another person or access financial resources or credit of another person.

Identity theft in the third degree.

A person is guilty of identity theft in the third degree when he or she knowingly and with intent to defraud assumes the identity of another person by presenting himself or herself as that other person, or by acting as that other person or by using personal identifying information of that other person, and thereby:

1. obtains goods, money, property or services or uses credit in the name of such other person or causes financial loss to such person or to another person or persons; or

2. commits a class A misdemeanor or higher level crime.

Identity theft in the third degree is a class A misdemeanor.

Identity theft in the second degree.

A person is guilty of identify theft in the second degree when he or she knowingly and with intent to defraud assumes the identity of another person by presenting himself or herself as that other person, or by acting as that other person or by using personal identifying information of that other person, and thereby:

1. obtains goods, money, property or services or uses credit in the name of such other person in an aggregate amount that exceeds five hundred dollars; or

2. causes financial loss to such person or to another person or persons in an aggregate amount that exceeds five hundred dollars; or

3. commits or attempts to commit a felony or acts as an accessory to the commission of a felony; or

4. commits the crime of identity theft in the third degree as defined in section 190.78 of this article and has been previously convicted within the last five years of identity theft in the third degree as defined in section 190.78, identity theft in the second degree as defined in this section, identity theft in the first degree as defined in section 190.80, unlawful possession of personal identification information in the third degree as defined in section 190.81, unlawful

possession of personal identification information in the second degree as defined in section 190.82, unlawful possession of personal identification information in the first degree as defined in section 190.83, grand larceny in the fourth degree as defined in section 155.30, grand larceny in the third degree as defined in section 155.35, grand larceny in the second degree as defined in section 155.40 or grand larceny in the first degree as defined in section 155.42 of this chapter. Identity theft in the second degree is a class E felony.

Identity theft in the first degree.

A person is guilty of identity theft in the first degree when he or she knowingly and with intent to defraud assumes the identity of another person by presenting himself or herself as that other person, or by acting as that other person or by using personal identifying information of that other person, and thereby:

1. obtains goods, money, property or services or uses credit in the name of such other person in an aggregate amount that exceeds two thousand dollars; or

2. causes financial loss to such person or to another person or persons in an aggregate amount that exceeds two thousand dollars; or

3. commits or attempts to commit a class D felony or higher level crime or acts as an accessory in the commission of a class D or higher level felony; or

4. commits the crime of identity theft in the second degree as defined in section 190.79 of this article and has been previously convicted within the last five years of identity

theft in the third degree as defined in section 190.78, identity theft in the second degree as defined in section 190.79, identity theft in the first degree as defined in this section, unlawful possession of personal identification information in the third degree as defined in section 190.81, unlawful possession of personal identification information in the second degree as defined in section 190.82, unlawful possession of personal identification information in the first degree as defined in section 190.83, grand larceny in the fourth degree as defined in section 155.30, grand larceny in the third degree as defined in section 155.35, grand larceny in the second degree as defined in section 155.40 or grand larceny in the first degree as defined in section 155.42 of this chapter. Identity theft in the first degree is a class D felony.

New Jersey

N.J. Stat. Ann. Sec. 2C:21-17
http://lis.njleg.state.nj.us/cgi-bin/om_isapi.dll?clientID=24578030
&Depth=2&depth=2&expandheadings=on&headingswithhits=
on&hitsperheading=on&infobase=statutes.nfo&record={1647}
&softpage=Doc_Frame_PG42

Use of personal identifying information of another, certain; second degree crime.

5. a. A person is guilty of a crime of the second degree if, in obtaining or attempting to obtain a driver's license, birth certificate or other document issued by a governmental agency which could be used as a means of verifying a person's identity, age or any other personal identifying information, that person knowingly

exhibits, displays or utters a document or other writing which falsely purports to be a driver's license, birth certificate or other document issued by a governmental agency or which belongs or pertains to a person other than the person who possesses the document.

b. Notwithstanding the provisions of N.J.S.2C:1-8 or any other law, a conviction under this section shall not merge with a conviction of any other criminal offense, nor shall such other conviction merge with a conviction under this section, and the court shall impose separate sentences upon each violation of this section and any other criminal offense.

c. A violation of N.J.S.2C:28-7, constituting a disorderly persons offense, section 1 of P.L.1979, c.264 (C.2C:33-15), R.S.33:1-81 or section 6 of P.L.1968, c.313 (C.33:1-81.7) in a case where the person uses the personal identifying information of another to illegally purchase an alcoholic beverage or for using the personal identifying information of another to misrepresent his age for the purpose of obtaining tobacco or other consumer product denied to persons under 18 years of age shall not constitute an offense under this section if the actor received only that benefit or service and did not perpetrate or attempt to perpetrate any additional injury or fraud on another.

Trafficking in personal identifying information pertaining to another person, certain; crime degrees; terms defined.

6. a. A person who knowingly distributes, manufactures or possesses any item containing personal identifying information pertaining to another person, without that

person's authorization, and with knowledge that the actor is facilitating a fraud or injury to be perpetrated by anyone is guilty of a crime of the fourth degree.

b.(1) If the person distributes, manufactures or possesses 20 or more items containing personal identifying information pertaining to another person, or five or more items containing personal information pertaining to five or more separate persons, without authorization, and with knowledge that the actor is facilitating a fraud or injury to be perpetrated by anyone the person is guilty of a crime of the third degree.

(2) If the person distributes, manufactures or possesses 50 or more items containing personal identifying information pertaining to another person, or ten or more items containing personal identifying information pertaining to five or more separate persons, without authorization, and with knowledge that the actor is facilitating a fraud or injury to be perpetrated by anyone the person is guilty of a crime of the second degree.

c. Distribution, manufacture or possession of 20 or more items containing personal identifying information pertaining to another person or of items containing personal identifying information pertaining to five or more separate persons without authorization shall create an inference that the items were distributed, manufactured or possessed with knowledge that the actor is facilitating a fraud or injury to be perpetrated by anyone.

North Carolina

N.C. Gen. Stat. Sec. 14-113.20 through 23
www.ncga.state.nc.us/enactedlegislation/statutes/html/bysection/
chapter_14/gs_14-113.20.html

Identity theft.

(a) A person who knowingly obtains, possesses, or uses identifying information of another person, living or dead, with the intent to fraudulently represent that the person is the other person for the purposes of making financial or credit transactions in the other person's name, to obtain anything of value, benefit, or advantage, or for the purpose of avoiding legal consequences is guilty of a felony punishable as provided in G.S. 14 113.22(a).

(b) The term "identifying information" as used in this article includes the following:

(1) Social Security or employer taxpayer identification numbers.

(2) Driver's license, State identification card, or passport numbers.

(3) Checking account numbers.

(4) Savings account numbers.

(5) Credit card numbers.

(6) Debit card numbers.

(7) Personal Identification (PIN) Code as defined in G.S. 14 113.8(6).

(8) Electronic identification numbers, electronic mail names or addresses, Internet account numbers, or Internet identification names.

(9) Digital signatures.

(10) Any other numbers or information that can be used to access a person's financial resources.

(11) Biometric data.

(12) Fingerprints.

(13) Passwords.

(14) Parent's legal surname prior to marriage.

(c) It shall not be a violation under this article for a person to do any of the following:

(1) Lawfully obtain credit information in the course of a bona fide consumer or commercial transaction.

(2) Lawfully exercise, in good faith, a security interest or a right of offset by a creditor or financial institution.

(3) Lawfully comply, in good faith, with any warrant, court order, levy, garnishment, attachment, or other judicial or administrative order, decree, or directive, when any party is required to do so.

North Dakota

N.D. Criminal Code 12.1-23-11
http://www.legis.nd.gov/cencode/t121c23.pdf

Unauthorized use of personal identifying information - Penalty.

1. As used in this section, "personal identifying information" means any of the following information:

   a. An individual's name;

   b. An individual's address;

   c. An individual's telephone number;

   d. The distinguishing operator's license number assigned to an individual by the department of transportation under section 39-06-14;

   e. An individual's Social Security number;

   f. An individual's employer or place of employment;

   g. An identification number assigned to the individual by the individual's employer;

   h. The maiden name of the individual's mother;

   i. The identifying number of a depository account in a financial institution; or

   j. An individual's birth, death, or marriage certificate.

2. A person is guilty of an offense if the person uses or attempts to use any personal identifying information of an individual, living or deceased, to obtain credit, money, goods, services, or anything else of value without the authorization or consent of the individual and by representing that person is the individual or is acting with the authorization or consent of the individual. The offense is a class B felony if the credit, money, goods, services, or anything else of value exceeds one thousand

dollars in value, otherwise the offense is a class C felony. A second or subsequent offense is a class A felony.

3. A violation of this section, of a law of another state, or of federal law that is equivalent to this section and which resulted in a plea or finding of guilt must be considered a prior offense. The prior offense must be alleged in the complaint, information, or indictment. The plea or finding of guilt for the prior offense must have occurred before the date of the commission of the offense or offenses charged in the complaint, information, or indictment.

4. A prosecution for a violation of this section must be commenced within six years after discovery by the victim of the offense of the facts constituting the violation.

5. When a person commits violations of this section in more than one county involving either one or more victims or the commission of acts constituting an element of the offense, the multiple offenses may be consolidated for commencement of prosecution in any county where one of the offenses was committed.

Ohio

OH Revised Code 2913.49
http://codes.ohio.gov/orc/2913

Identity Fraud

(B) No person, without the express or implied consent of the other person, shall use, obtain, or possess any personal identifying information of another person with intent to do either of the following:

(1) Hold the person out to be the other person;

(2) Represent the other person's personal identifying information as the person's own personal identifying information.

(C) No person shall create, obtain, possess, or use the personal identifying information of any person with the intent to aid or abet another person in violating division (B) of this section.

(D) No person, with intent to defraud, shall permit another person to use the person's own personal identifying information.

(E) No person who is permitted to use another person's personal identifying information as described in division (D) of this section shall use, obtain, or possess the other person's personal identifying information with intent to defraud any person by doing any act identified in division (B)(1) or (2) of this section.

(I) (1) Whoever violates this section is guilty of identity fraud.

(2) Except as otherwise provided in this division or division (I)(3) of this section, identity fraud is a felony of the fifth degree. If the value of the credit, property, services, debt, or other legal obligation involved in the violation or course of conduct is five hundred dollars or more and is less than five thousand dollars, except as otherwise provided in division (I)(3) of this section, identity fraud is a felony of the fourth degree. If the value of the credit, property, services,

debt, or other legal obligation involved in the violation or course of conduct is five thousand dollars or more and is less than one hundred thousand dollars, except as otherwise provided in division (I)(3) of this section, identity fraud is a felony of the third degree. If the value of the credit, property, services, debt, or other legal obligation involved in the violation or course of conduct is one hundred thousand dollars or more, except as otherwise provided in division (I)(3) of this section, identity fraud is a felony of the second degree.

(3) If the victim of the offense is an elderly person or disabled adult, a violation of this section is identity fraud against an elderly person or disabled adult. Except as otherwise provided in this division, identity fraud against an elderly person or disabled adult is a felony of the fifth degree. If the value of the credit, property, services, debt, or other legal obligation involved in the violation or course of conduct is five hundred dollars or more and is less than five thousand dollars, identity fraud against an elderly person or disabled adult is a felony of the third degree. If the value of the credit, property, services, debt, or other legal obligation involved in the violation or course of conduct is five thousand dollars or more and is less than one hundred thousand dollars, identity fraud against an elderly person or disabled adult is a felony of the second degree. If the value of the credit, property, services, debt, or other legal obligation involved in the violation or course of conduct is one hundred thousand dollars or more,

identity fraud against an elderly person or disabled adult is a felony of the first degree.

Oklahoma

Okla. Stat. tit. 21, Sec. 1533.1
www.lsb.state.ok.us/osStatuesTitle.html
Click on "Title 21. Crimes and Punishments" and scroll to 21-1533.1.

Identity theft - Penalties - Civil action.

A. It is unlawful for any person to willfully and with fraudulent intent obtain the name, address, Social Security number, date of birth, place of business or employment, debit, credit or account numbers, driver's license number, or any other personal identifying information of another person, living or dead, with intent to use, sell, or allow any other person to use or sell such personal identifying information to obtain or attempt to obtain money, credit, goods, property, or service in the name of the other person without the consent of that person.

B. It is unlawful for any person to use with fraudulent intent the personal identity of another person, living or dead, or any information relating to the personal identity of another person, living or dead, to obtain or attempt to obtain credit or anything of value.

C. It is unlawful for any person with fraudulent intent to lend, sell, or otherwise offer the use of such person's own name, address, Social Security number, date of birth, or any other personal identifying information or document to any other person with the intent to allow such other person to use the personal identifying information or document to obtain or attempt to obtain any identifying document in the name of such other person.

D. It is unlawful for any person to willfully create, modify, alter or change any personal identifying information of another person with fraudulent intent to obtain any money, credit, goods, property, service or any benefit or thing of value, or to control, use, waste, hinder or encumber another person's credit, accounts, goods, property, title, interests, benefits or entitlements without the consent of that person.

E. Any person convicted of violating any provision of this section shall be guilty of identity theft. Identity theft is a felony offense punishable by imprisonment in the custody of the Department of Corrections for a term of not less than one (1) year nor more than five (5) years, or a fine not to exceed one hundred thousand dollars ($100,000.00), or by both such fine and imprisonment. Restitution to the victim may be ordered in addition to any criminal penalty imposed by the court. The victim of identity theft may bring a civil action for damages against any person participating in furthering the crime or attempted crime of identity theft.

Oregon

Or. Rev. Stat. Sec. 165.800
www.leg.state.or.us/ors/165.html

Identity theft.

(1) A person commits the crime of identity theft if the person, with the intent to deceive or to defraud, obtains, possesses, transfers, creates, utters or converts to the person's own use the personal identification of another person.

(2) Identity theft is a Class C felony.

(3) It is an affirmative defense to violating subsection (1) of this section that the person charged with the offense:

(a) Was under 21 years of age at the time of committing the offense and the person used the personal identification of another person solely for the purpose of purchasing alcohol;

(b) Was under 18 years of age at the time of committing the offense and the person used the personal identification of another person solely for the purpose of purchasing tobacco products; or

(c) Used the personal identification of another person solely for the purpose of misrepresenting the person's age to gain access to a:

(A) Place the access to which is restricted based on age; or

(B) Benefit based on age.

(4) As used in this section:

(a) "Another person" means a real person, whether living or deceased, or an imaginary person.

(b) "Personal identification" includes, but is not limited to, any written document or electronic data that does, or purports to, provide information concerning:

(A) A person's name, address or telephone number;

(B) A person's driving privileges;

(C) A person's Social Security number or tax identification number;

(D) A person's citizenship status or alien identification number;

(E) A person's employment status, employer or place of employment;

(F) The identification number assigned to a person by a person's employer;

(G) The maiden name of a person or a person's mother;

(H) The identifying number of a person's depository account at a "financial institution" or "trust company," as those terms are defined in ORS 706.008, or a credit card account;

(I) A person's signature or a copy of a person's signature;

(J) A person's electronic mail name, electronic mail signature, electronic mail address or electronic mail account;

(K) A person's photograph;

(L) A person's date of birth; and

(M) A person's personal identification number. [1999 c.1022 §1; 2001 c.870 §3; 2007 c.583 §1]

Pennsylvania

18 Pa. Cons. State Sec. 4120

Rhode Island

R.I. Gen. Laws Sec. 11-49.1-1
www.rilin.state.ri.us/Statutes/TITLE11/11-49.1/INDEX.HTM

Identity fraud.

(a) Any person who shall: (1) knowingly and without lawful authority produce an identification document or a false identification document; (2) knowingly transfer an identification document or a false identification document knowing that the document was stolen or produced without lawful authority; (3) knowingly possess with intent to use unlawfully or transfer unlawfully five (5) or more identification documents (other than those issued lawfully for the use of the possessor) or false identification documents; (4) knowingly possess an identification document (other than one issued lawfully for the use of the possessor) or a false identification document, or financial information with the intent that the document or financial information be used to defraud the United States, the State of Rhode Island, any political subdivision of it or any public or private entity; (5) knowingly transfer, or possess a document-making implement with the intent that the document-making implement will be used in the production of a false identification document or another document-making implement which will be so used; (6) knowingly possess a false identification document that is or appears to be a genuine identification document of the United States, the State of Rhode Island or any political subdivision of it or any public or private entity which is stolen or produced without lawful authority knowing that the document was stolen or produced without such authority; or (7) knowingly transfer or use with intent to defraud, without lawful authority, a means of identification or financial information of another person living or dead, with the intent to commit, or to aid or abet, any unlawful activity that constitutes a violation of federal, state or local law; shall be guilty of a felony and shall be subject to the penalties set forth in § 11-49.1-4.

(b) The provisions of this section shall not apply to any person who has not reached his or her twenty-first (21st) birthday who misrepresents or misstates his or her age through the presentation of any document in order to enter any premises licensed for the retail sale of alcoholic beverages for the purpose of purchasing or having served or delivered to him or her alcoholic beverages or attempting to purchase or have another person purchase for him or her any alcoholic beverage pursuant to § 3-8-6.

South Carolina

S.C. Code Ann. Sec. 16-13-500, 501

www.scstatehouse.net/code/t16c013.htm

"Financial identity fraud" and "identifying information" defined; penalty and restitution.

    (A) It is unlawful for a person to commit the offense of financial identity fraud.

    (B) A person is guilty of financial identity fraud when he, without the authorization or permission of another person and with the intent of unlawfully appropriating the financial resources of that person to his own use or the use of a third party:

        (1) obtains or records identifying information which would assist in accessing the financial records of the other person; or

        (2) accesses or attempts to access the financial resources of the other person through the use of identifying information as defined in subsection (C).

    (C) Identifying information includes, but is not limited to:

        (1) Social Security numbers;

        (2) driver's license numbers;

        (3) checking account numbers;

        (4) savings account numbers;

(5) credit card numbers;

(6) debit card numbers;

(7) personal identification numbers;

(8) electronic identification numbers;

(9) digital signatures;

(10) other numbers or information which may be used to access a person's financial resources; or

(11) identifying documentation that defines a person other than the person presenting the document. This includes, but is not limited to, passports, driver's licenses, birth certificates, immigration documents, and state-issued identification cards.

(D) A person who violates the provisions of this section is guilty of a felony and, upon conviction, must be fined in the discretion of the court or imprisoned not more than ten years, or both. The court may order restitution to the victim pursuant to the provisions of Section 17-25-322.

Identity fraud; penalty.

(B) A person who violates the provisions of this section is guilty of a felony and, upon conviction, must be fined in the discretion of the court or imprisoned not more than ten years, or both. The court may order restitution to the victim pursuant to the provisions of Section 17-25-322.

South Dakota

S.D. Codified Laws Sec. 22-30A-8.1, 22-40-08.
http://legis.state.sd.us/statutes/index.aspx?FuseAction=DisplayStat
ute&Statute=22-30A-3.1&Type=Statute

22-30A-8.1. Obtaining property or services with false credit card. Any person who, by use of a credit card issued to another person, without the consent of the person to whom issued, or by use of a credit card which has been revoked or canceled or has expired, or by use of a falsified, mutilated, altered, or counterfeit credit card obtains property or services on credit, is guilty of theft.

22-40-8. Identity theft—Felony. If any person, without the authorization or permission of another person and with the intent to deceive or defraud:

(1) Obtains, possesses, transfers, uses, attempts to obtain, or records identifying information not lawfully issued for that person's use; or

(2) Accesses or attempts to access the financial resources of that person through the use of identifying information; such person commits the crime of identity theft. Identity theft committed pursuant to this section is a Class 6 felony.

Tennessee

TCA Sec. 39-14-150
www.michie.com/tennessee/lpext.dll?f=templates&fn=main-h.
htm&cp

Identity theft victims' rights.

(b) A person commits the offense of identity theft who knowingly obtains, possesses, buys, or uses, the personal identifying information of another:

(1) With the intent to commit any unlawful act including, but not limited to, obtaining or attempting to obtain credit, goods, services, or medical information in the name of such other person; and

(2) (A) Without the consent of such other person; or

(B) Without the lawful authority to obtain, possess, buy or use that identifying information.

(3) For purposes of the offense of identity theft, an activity involving a possession, use or transfer that is permitted by the Tennessee Financial Records Privacy Act, codified in title 45, chapter 10…shall not be considered an "unlawful act."

(c) (1) A person commits the offense of identity theft who knowingly sells, transfers, gives, trades, loans or delivers, or possesses with the intent to sell, transfer, give, trade, loan or deliver, the personal identifying information of another:

(A) With the intent that the information be used by someone else to commit any unlawful act including, but not limited to, obtaining or attempting to obtain credit, goods, services or medical information in the name of another person; or

(B) Under circumstances such that the person should have known that the identifying information would be used by someone else to commit any unlawful act including, but not limited to obtaining or attempting to obtain credit, goods, services or medical information in the name of the other person; and

(C) The person does not have the consent of the person who is identified by the information to sell, transfer, give, trade, loan or deliver that information; and

(D) The person does not have lawful authority to sell, transfer, give, trade, loan or deliver the personal identifying information.

(d) In a prosecution under subsection (c), the trier of fact may infer from the defendant's simultaneous possession of the personal identifying information of five (5) or more different individuals that the defendant possessed the personal identifying information with the intent to sell, transfer, give, trade, loan or deliver the information. However, if the defendant had the consent of one (1) or more of the individuals to possess the personal identifying information of that individual, the consenting individual shall not be counted in determining whether an inference of possession for sale may be drawn by the trier of fact.

Texas

Tex. Penal Code Sec. 32.51
http://tlo2.tlc.state.tx.us/statutes/docs/PE/content/htm/pe.007.
00.000032.00.htm#32.51.00

Fraudulent Use or Possession of Identifying Information.

(b) A person commits an offense if the person, with intent to harm or defraud another, obtains, possesses, transfers, or uses identifying information of:

   (1) another person without the other person's consent; or

   (2) a child younger than 18 years of age.

(b) A person commits an offense if the person, with the intent to harm or defraud another, obtains, possesses, transfers, or uses:

   (1) identifying information of another person without the other person's consent; or

   (2) without legal authorization, information concerning a deceased person that would be identifying information of that person were that person alive.

(c) An offense under this section is:

   (1) a state jail felony if the number of items obtained, possessed, transferred, or used is less than five;

   (2) a felony of the third degree if the number of items obtained, possessed, transferred, or used is five or more but less than 10;

(3) a felony of the second degree if the number of items obtained, possessed, transferred, or used is 10 or more but less than 50; or

(4) a felony of the first degree if the number of items obtained, possessed, transferred, or used is 50 or more.

(d) If a court orders a defendant convicted of an offense under this section to make restitution to the victim of the offense, the court may order the defendant to reimburse the victim for lost income or other expenses, other than attorney's fees, incurred as a result of the offense.

Utah

Utah Code Ann. Sec. 76-6-1101 through 1104
http://le.utah.gov/~code/TITLE76/76_06.htm

Identity fraud crime.

(2) (a) A person is guilty of identity fraud when that person:

(i) obtains personal identifying information of another person whether that person is alive or deceased; and

(ii) knowingly or intentionally uses, or attempts to use, that information with fraudulent intent, including to obtain, or attempt to obtain, credit, goods, services, any other thing of value, or medical information.

(b) It is not a defense to a violation of Subsection (2) (a) that the person did not know that the personal information belonged to another person.

(3) Identity fraud is:

(a) except as provided in Subsection (3)(b)(ii), a third degree felony if the value of the credit, goods, services, or any other thing of value is less than $5,000; or

(b) a second degree felony if:

(i) the value of the credit, goods, services, employment, or any other thing of value is or exceeds $5,000; or

(ii) the use described in Subsection (2)(a)(ii) of personal identifying information results, directly or indirectly, in bodily injury to another person.

(4) Multiple violations may be aggregated into a single offense, and the degree of the offense is determined by the total value of all credit, goods, services, or any other thing of value used, or attempted to be used, through the multiple violations.

(5) When a defendant is convicted of a violation of this section, the court shall order the defendant to make restitution to any victim of the offense or state on the record the reason the court does not find ordering restitution to be appropriate.

(6) Restitution under Subsection (5) may include:

(a) payment for any costs incurred, including attorney fees, lost wages, and replacement of checks; and

(b) the value of the victim's time incurred due to the offense:

(i) in clearing the victim's credit history or credit rating;

(ii) in any civil or administrative proceedings necessary to satisfy or resolve any debt, lien, or other obligation of the victim or imputed to the victim and arising from the offense; and

(iii) in attempting to remedy any other intended or actual harm to the victim incurred as a result of the offense.

Vermont

(Does not have specific identity theft law.)

Virginia

Va. Code Ann. Sec. 18.2-186.3
http://leg1.state.va.us/cgi-bin/legp504.exe?000+cod+18.2-186.3

Identity theft; penalty; restitution; victim assistance.

A. It shall be unlawful for any person, without the authorization or permission of the person or persons who are the subjects of the identifying information, with the intent to defraud, for his own use or the use of a third person, to:

1. Obtain, record or access identifying information which is not available to the general public that would assist in accessing financial resources, obtaining identification documents, or obtaining benefits of such other person;

2. Obtain goods or services through the use of identifying information of such other person;

3. Obtain identification documents in such other person's name; or

4. Obtain, record or access identifying information while impersonating a law-enforcement officer or an official of the government of the Commonwealth.

B. It shall be unlawful for any person without the authorization or permission of the person who is the subject of the identifying information, with the intent to sell or distribute the information to another to:

1. Fraudulently obtain, record or access identifying information that is not available to the general public that would assist in accessing financial resources, obtaining identification documents, or obtaining benefits of such other person;

2. Obtain goods or services through the use of identifying information of such other person;

3. Obtain identification documents in such other person's name; or

4. Obtain, record or access identifying information while impersonating a law-enforcement officer or an official of the Commonwealth.

B 1. It shall be unlawful for any person to use identification documents or identifying information of another person, whether that person is dead or alive, or of a false or fictitious person, to avoid summons, arrest, prosecution or to impede a criminal investigation.

C. As used in this section, "identifying information" shall include but not be limited to: (i) name; (ii) date of birth; (iii) Social Security number; (iv) driver's license number; (v) bank account numbers; (vi) credit or debit card numbers; (vii) personal identification numbers (PIN); (viii) electronic identification codes; (ix) automated or electronic signatures; (x) biometric data; (xi) fingerprints; (xii) passwords; or (xiii) any other numbers or information that can be used to access a person's financial resources, obtain identification, act as identification, or obtain goods or services.

D. Violations of this section shall be punishable as a Class 1 misdemeanor. Any violation resulting in financial loss of greater than $200 shall be punishable as a Class 6 felony. Any second or subsequent conviction shall be punishable as a Class 6 felony. Any violation of subsection B where five or more persons' identifying information has been obtained, recorded, or accessed in the same transaction or occurrence shall be punishable as a Class 6 felony. Any violation of subsection B where 50 or more persons' identifying information has been obtained, recorded, or accessed in the same transaction or occurrence shall be punishable as a Class 5 felony. Any violation resulting in the arrest and detention of the person whose identification documents or identifying information were used to avoid summons, arrest, prosecution, or to impede a criminal investigation shall be punishable as a Class 6 felony. In any proceeding brought pursuant to this section, the crime shall be considered to have been committed in any locality where the person whose identifying information was appropriated resides, or in which any part of the offense took place, regardless of whether the defendant was ever actually in such locality.

E. Upon conviction, in addition to any other punishment, a person found guilty of this offense shall be ordered by the court to make restitution as the court deems appropriate to any person whose identifying information was appropriated or to the estate of such person. Such restitution may include the person's or his estate's actual expenses associated with correcting inaccuracies or errors in his credit report or other identifying information.

F. Upon the request of a person whose identifying information was appropriated, the Attorney General may provide assistance to the victim in obtaining information necessary to correct inaccuracies or errors in his credit report or other identifying information; however, no legal representation shall be afforded such person.

Washington

Wash. Rev. Code Sec. 9.35.020
http://apps.leg.wa.gov/rcw/default.aspx?Cite=9
Click on "9.35 Identity crimes."

Sec. 2.

(1) A person who has learned or reasonably suspects that his or her financial information or means of identification has been unlawfully obtained, used by, or disclosed

to another, as described in this chapter, may file an incident report with a law enforcement agency, by contacting the local law enforcement agency that has jurisdiction over his or her actual residence, place of business, or place where the crime occurred. The law enforcement agency shall create a police incident report of the matter and provide the complainant with a copy of that report, and may refer the incident report to another law enforcement agency.

(2) Nothing in this section shall be construed to require a law enforcement agency to investigate reports claiming identity theft. An incident report filed under this section is not required to be counted as an open case for purposes of compiling open case statistics.

Sec. 4.

(1) No person may knowingly obtain, possess, use, or transfer a means of identification or financial information of another person, living or dead, with the intent to commit, or to aid or abet, any crime.

(2) Violation of this section when the accused or an accomplice violates subsection (1) of this section and obtains credit, money, goods, services, or anything else of value in excess of one thousand five hundred dollars in value shall constitute identity theft in the first degree. Identity theft in the first degree is a class B felony punishable according to chapter 9A.20 RCW.

(3) A person is guilty of identity theft in the second degree when he or she violates subsection (1) of this section under circumstances not amounting to identity theft in

the first degree. Identity theft in the second degree is a class C felony punishable according to chapter 9A.20 RCW.

(4) Each crime prosecuted under this section shall be punished separately under chapter 9.94A RCW, unless it is the same criminal conduct as any other crime, under RCW 9.94A.589.

(5) Whenever any series of transactions involving a single person's means of identification or financial information which constitute identity theft would, when considered separately, constitute identity theft in the second degree because of value, and the series of transactions are a part of a common scheme or plan, then the transactions may be aggregated in one count and the sum of the value of p. 3 SB 5878.SL

West Virginia

W. Va. Code Sec. 61-3-54
www.legis.state.wv.us/WVCODE/Code.cfm
Use drop-down menu to go to "Chapter 61. Crimes and Their Punishment," then click "Crimes Against Property," and scroll down to 61-3-54.

Taking identity of another person; penalty.

Any person who knowingly takes the name, birth date, Social Security number or other identifying information of another person, without the consent of that other person, with the intent to fraudulently represent that he or she is the other person for the purpose of making financial or credit transactions in the other person's name, is guilty of a felony, and upon conviction, shall be punished by confinement in the penitentiary not more than five years, or fined not more than one thousand dollars, or both: *provided,* that the provisions of this section do not apply to any person who obtains another person's driver's license or other form of identification for the sole purpose of misrepresenting his or her age.

Wisconsin

Wis. Stat. Sec. 943.201
http://nxt.legis.state.wi.us/nxt/gateway.dll/?f=templates$fn=
default.htm
Search for section number.

Unauthorized use of an individual's personal identifying information or documents.

(2) Whoever, for any of the following purposes, intentionally uses, attempts to use, or possesses with intent to use any personal identifying information or personal identification document of an individual, including a deceased individual, without the authorization or consent of the individual and by representing that he or she is the individual, that he or she is acting with the authorization or consent of the individual, or that the information or document belongs to him or her is guilty of a Class H felony:

(a) To obtain credit, money, goods, services, employment, or any other thing of value or benefit.

(b) To avoid civil or criminal process or penalty.

(c) To harm the reputation, property, person, or estate of the individual.

(3) It is an affirmative defense to a prosecution under this section that the defendant was authorized by law to engage in the conduct that is the subject of the prosecution. A defendant who raises this affirmative defense has the burden of proving the defense by a preponderance of the evidence.

(4) If an individual reports to a law enforcement agency for the jurisdiction which is the individual's residence that personal identifying information or a personal identifying document belonging to the individual reasonably appears to be in the possession of another in violation of this section or that another has used or has attempted to use it in violation of this section, the agency shall prepare a report on the alleged violation. If the law enforcement agency concludes that it appears not to have jurisdiction to investigate the violation, it shall inform the individual which law enforcement agency may have jurisdiction. A copy of a report prepared under this subsection shall be furnished upon request to the individual who made the request, subject to payment of any reasonable fee for the copy.

Wyoming

Wyo. Stat. Ann. Sec. 6-3-901
http://legisweb.state.wy.us/statutes/statutes.aspx?file=titles/Title6/T6CH3AR9.htm

Unauthorized use of personal identifying information; penalties; restitution.

(a) Every person who willfully obtains personal identifying information of another person, and uses that information for any unlawful purpose, including to obtain, or attempt to obtain, credit, goods, services or medical information in the name of the other person without the consent of that person is guilty of theft of identity.

(b) As used in this section "personal identifying information," means the name, address, telephone number, driver's license number, Social Security number, place of employment, employee identification number, tribal identification card number, mother's maiden name, demand deposit account number, savings account number, or credit card number of an individual person.

(c) Theft of identity is:

(i) A misdemeanor punishable by imprisonment for not more than six (6) months, a fine of not more than seven hundred fifty dollars ($750.00), or both, if no economic benefit was gained or was attempted to be gained, or if an economic benefit of less than one thousand dollars ($1,000.00) was gained or was attempted to be gained by the defendant; or

(ii) A felony punishable by imprisonment for not more than ten (10) years, a fine of not more than ten thousand dollars ($10,000.00), or both, if an economic benefit of one thousand dollars ($1,000.00) or more was gained or was attempted to be gained by the defendant.

(d) If a restitution plan is ordered pursuant to W.S. 7-9-101 through 7-9-115, the court may include, as part of its determination of amount owed pursuant to W.S. 7-9-103, payment for any costs incurred by the victim, including attorney fees, any costs incurred in clearing the credit history or credit rating of the victim or in connection with any civil or administrative proceeding to satisfy any debt, lien or other obligation of the victim arising as a result of the actions of the defendant.

(e) In any case in which a person willfully obtains personal identifying information of another person, and without the authorization of that person uses that information to commit a crime in addition to a violation of subsection (a) of this section, and is convicted of that crime, the court records shall reflect that the person whose identity was falsely used to commit the crime did not commit the crime.

FORMS AND LETTERS

The forms in this appendix should be copied for use in case you make a mistake or need more than one copy. All the letters would serve you best if you put them on your own stationary or letterhead. Each of these forms is also available on the attached CD-ROM. The CD-ROM is compatible with both PC and Mac formats. A listing of the forms is contained on the CD-ROM to help you select the file you need.

Once selected, you can easily complete the form directly on your computer. Simply fill in the missing information. You can then have a document that is completely computer-generated and ready to be signed. You can, of course, also just print the blank forms from the disc and fill them in as you would the forms in the book.

TABLE OF FORMS

Form 1

VALIDATION OF DEBT

_____ [your name and address]
_____
_____

_____ [name and address of creditor/
_____ collection agency]
_____

_____ [date]

Dear Sir or Madam:

In accordance with Section 809 of the Fair Debt Collection Practices Act, I am requesting validation of the debt related to account #_____ . According to the statute, you must cease any debt collection activities until you have verified this debt.

Sincerely,

_____
[signature]

Form 2

DEBT ASSESSMENT

Fill in the blanks to list all your monthly debts. Total the items at the bottom to get the number for your total monthly debts.

Name of Creditor	Account Number	Total Due	Monthly Payment
_____	_____	_____	_____
_____	_____	_____	_____
_____	_____	_____	_____
_____	_____	_____	_____
_____	_____	_____	_____
_____	_____	_____	_____
_____	_____	_____	_____
_____	_____	_____	_____
_____	_____	_____	_____
_____	_____	_____	_____

Total amount due: _____

Total monthly payments due: _____

Form 3

ASSET ASSESSMENT

Salary:

Monthly amount earned: _____

Yearly amount earned: _____

Other Income (such as child support, alimony, etc.)

Monthly amount: _____

Yearly amount: _____

Other Income (include interest, unreported income, etc.):

Monthly amount: _____

Yearly amount: _____

Total Income:

Monthly: _____

Yearly: _____

Other Assets: List name of item, account number, if applicable, and value.

Name/Description	Account Number	Value
_____	_____	_____
_____	_____	_____
_____	_____	_____
_____	_____	_____
_____	_____	_____

Total value of other assets: _____

Form 4

TOTAL ASSESSMENT
(MONTHLY)

Total Monthly Income: _____

Total Monthly Debts: _____

Subtract debts from assets and you get this:

_____

If this is a negative number, you know you need to make some changes. If this is a positive number but is not enough to pay your expenses, such as food and gas, you need to make some changes.

Total Assets: _____

Total Debts: _____

Compare these two numbers. If your assets are larger than your debts, you are in good shape. If your debts are larger than your assets, you know this is something you need to work on.

Form 5

NEW ADDRESS LETTER

_____ [your name and address]

_____

_____

_____ [date]

Re: Account Number _____

Dear Sir or Madam:

This is to notify you that I am moving. Effective _____ [date], my address will be:

_____

_____

_____

Please direct all correspondence and bills to this address.

Thank you.

Sincerely,

_____

[signature]

Form 6

LETTER TO MERCHANT

_____ [your name and address]

_____

_____

_____ [merchant name and address]

_____

_____

_____ [date]

Dear Sir or Madam:

On _____ [date], I purchased [*or* had repaired] _____ [name of the product with the serial or model number or service performed]. I made this purchase at _____

[location, date, and other important details of the transaction].

Unfortunately, your product [*or* service] has not performed well [*or* the service was inadequate] because _____

_____

_____ [state the problem].

Therefore, to resolve the problem, I would appreciate your _____

_____ [state the specific action you want]. Enclosed are copies [copies, not originals] of my records [receipts, guarantees, warranties, cancelled checks, contracts, model and serial numbers, and any other documents].

I look forward to your reply and a resolution to my problem and will wait for _____ [set a time limit] before seeking third-party assistance. Please contact me at the above address or by phone at _____ [home or office numbers with area codes].

Thank you.

Sincerely,

_____

[signature]

_____

[account number]

LETTER COMPLAINING OF UNFAIR DEBT
COLLECTION PRACTICES

_____ [your name and address]

_____

_____

_____ [name and address of
_____ creditor/collection agency]

_____

_____ [date]

Dear Sir or Madam:

I am writing to inform you that your agency/company violated the
Fair Debt Collection Practices Act, a federal law, in your dealings
with me. The incident(s) occurred on _____ [date]
and was/were as follows: _____

_____

_____

_____ [state the problem].

I am requesting that you take steps to change your practices. I am
also forwarding a copy of this letter to the Federal Trade
Commission and the State Attorney General.

Sincerely,

_____

[signature]

cc: Federal Trade Commission
    State Attorney General

Form 8

LETTER REQUESTING CREDIT REPORT

_____ [your name and address]
_____
_____
_____ [name and address of
_____ creditor/collection agency]

_____ [date]

Dear Sir or Madam:

I am writing to request a copy of my credit report.

_____ I have been denied credit or employment in the last sixty days based on my credit report and request my free copy.

_____ I am enclosing $ _____ as required in my state and request that you send me my credit report.

Please use the following information for verification purposes:

Social Security #: _____
Employer: _____
My last previous address: _____
One credit card name and account number I hold: _____

Please forward my report to me at the above address.

Sincerely,

_____
[signature]

Form 9

LETTER REQUESTING MERGER OF SPOUSE'S REPORT

_____ [your name and address]

_____

_____

_____ [name and address of
_____ creditor/collection agency]

_____

_____ [date]

Dear Sir or Madam:

Please merge my spouse's credit report with mine. I am enclosing a certified copy of our marriage license.

My Social Security #: _____

Number of my file or report number from your agency: _____

My spouse's name: _____

My spouse's Social Security #: _____

Thank you.

Sincerely,

_____

[signature]

Form 10

LETTER REQUESTING INDIVIDUALIZATION OF CREDIT REPORT

_____ [your name and address]

_____

_____

_____ [name and address of
_____ creditor/collection agency]

_____

_____ [date]

Dear Sir or Madam:

I recently received a copy of my credit report and noticed that it contains information about my spouse, as well as about me. I would like my spouse's information removed from my report.

My Social Security #: _____

Number of my file or report number from your agency: _____

My spouse's name: _____

My spouse's Social Security #: _____

Thank you.

Sincerely,

_____

[signature]

Form 11

LETTER TO CREDITOR REGARDING BILLING ERROR

_____ [your name and address]
_____
_____

_____ [creditor's name and address]
_____
_____

_____ [date]

Dear Sir or Madam:

I recently received a bill from you that contains an error.

My account number is: _____

The item that is incorrect is _____ for
$_____, dated _____ .

This is incorrect because _____
and should be for _____ .

I would appreciate it if you could correct this item and send me a corrected statement.

Sincerely,

_____

[signature]

Form 12

COLLECTION AGENCY VALIDATION LETTER

_____ [your name and address]

_____

_____

_____ [creditor/collection agency

_____ name and address]

_____

_____ [date]

Dear Sir or Madam:

This letter is sent in response to the notice you sent me on _____ [date]. Be advised this is not a refusal to pay, but a notice pursuant to the Fair Debt Collection Practices Act, 15 USC 1692g Sect. 809(b) that your claim is disputed and validation is requested.

This is NOT a request for "verification" or proof of my mailing address, but a request for validation pursuant to the above named law. I request that you provide me with competent evidence that I have a legal obligation to you for the debt.

Please provide me with the following.

☐ An explanation of what the amount owed is for and how it was incurred.

☐ An explanation of how this amount was calculated.

☐ Copies of any documents that show I agreed to pay this amount.

☐ A verification or copy of any judgment, if applicable.

☐ An identification of the original creditor.

☐ Proof that the statute of limitations has not expired on the account.

☐ Proof that you are licensed to collect in my state.

☐ Your license numbers and registered agent documentation.

If your offices have reported invalidated information about me to any of the three major credit bureaus-Equifax, Experian, or TransUnion-this may constitute fraud under federal and state laws. If any negative mark is placed on any of my credit reports by your company or the company that you represent, I will not hesitate to bring legal action against you for violation of the Fair Credit Reporting Act, violation of the Fair Collection Practices Act, and defamation of character.

If your offices are able to provide the proper documentation I have requested, I require at least thirty days from the date of my receipt to investigate this information. During this time all collection activity by you must cease and desist. During this validation period, if any action is taken that could be considered detrimental to any of my credit reports, I will consult an attorney and consider legal action.

If your offices fail to respond to this request within thirty days from the date of your receipts, all references to this account must be deleted and completely removed from my credit file and a copy of such deletion must be sent to me immediately.

I formally request that you and your representatives do not contact me by telephone at my home or my place of employment. If your offices attempt telephone communication with me, including but not limited to computer-generated calls and calls or correspondence sent to or with any third parties, it will be considered harassment and I will instruct my attorney to proceed with legal action. All future communication with me must be in writing and sent to the address noted in this letter by USPS.

This letter is an attempt to correct your records and any information obtained shall be used for that purpose only.

Thank you.

Sincerely,

_____

[signature]

Form 13

LETTER TO CREDITOR DISPUTING CREDIT REPORT

_____ [your name and address]

_____

_____

_____ [credit reporting agency

_____ name and address]

_____

_____ [date]

Dear Sir or Madam:

I recently received my credit report from your agency. My file or report number is _____. In reviewing my report, I noticed the following error(s):

1. _____

   This item is incorrect because _____
   and should instead indicate _____

2. _____

   This item is incorrect because _____
   and should instead indicate _____

3. _____

   This item is incorrect because _____
   and should instead indicate _____

I would appreciate it if these errors could be corrected. I look forward to hearing from you within thirty days.

Thank you.

Sincerely,

_____

[signature]

Form 14

SECOND REQUEST FOR REINVESTIGATION

_____ [your name and address]

_____

_____

_____ [credit reporting agency

_____ name and address]

_____

_____ [date]

Dear Sir or Madam:

On_____ [date] I sent you a written request for reinvestigation (your file or report number_____) of the following errors on my credit report:

1. _____

2. _____

3. _____

I am enclosing a copy of the letter I sent you. Thirty days have passed and I have not received any response from you regarding this matter. I would appreciate it if you would please notify me of the status of this request as soon as possible.

Sincerely,

_____

[signature]

Form 15

LETTER REQUESTING CORRECTION OF REAPPEARING INCORRECT ITEM

_____ [your name and address]
_____
_____

_____ [credit reporting agency
_____ name and address]
_____

_____ [date]

Dear Sir or Madam:

I am writing to you in regard to my credit report, your file, or report number_____.

On _____ [date] you removed the following incorrect information from my report: _____
_____
_____
_____
at my request because _____
_____
_____
_____

On the latest copy of my credit report, dated _____
[date], this incorrect information has reappeared. I am requesting

that you immediately remove this incorrect information and replace it with the following correct information: _____

_____

_____

_____

Please advise me when the correction has been made and send me a corrected credit report.

Thank you.

Sincerely,

_____

[signature]

Form 16

LETTER TO CREDITOR REGARDING INCORRECT
CREDIT REPORT

_____ [your name and address]

_____

_____

_____ [name and address of creditor]

_____

_____

_____ [date]

Dear Sir or Madam:

I am writing to you in regard to my account, number _____. I recently received a copy of my credit report from the following credit reporting agency: _____. My account with you is incorrectly listed as _____ , when in fact it is _____. I have asked that the credit reporting agency verify this with you and was told you did not verify the correct information.

I am requesting that you immediately contact the credit reporting agency with the correct information regarding this account. Please provide me with a copy of your correspondence correcting this. I am prepared to enforce my rights under the Fair Credit Reporting Act if you do not report the correct information to this agency.

Thank you.

Sincerely,

_____

[signature]

Form 17

LETTER SHOWING CREDITOR ERROR

_____ [your name and address]
_____
_____

_____ [name and address of credit
_____ reporting agency]
_____

_____ [date]

Dear Sir or Madam:

I am writing to you in regard to my file or report number
_____. There is an error on this report.
_____ is listed incorrectly. I have
contacted the creditor directly and the creditor has made an error in
reporting this account to you. I am enclosing written proof of this
and am requesting that you change this listing on my report as soon
as possible and send me a correct copy of my report.

Thank you.

Sincerely,

_____
[signature]

Form 18

LETTER REQUESTING DISCHARGE

_____ [your name and address]

_____

_____

_____ [name and address of creditor]

_____

_____

_____ [date]

Dear Sir or Madam:

I am writing to you in regard to a judgment against account number _____, which resulted in a judgment in your company's favor dated _____ for $_____. This judgment has been paid in full and I am requesting that your company complete and file a formal discharge with the court immediately. Please send me a copy of the discharge and report it to all credit reporting agencies, as well.

Thank you.

Sincerely,

_____

[signature]

Form 19

LETTER REQUESTING INCLUSION OF ACCOUNTS

_____ [your name and address]
_____
_____

_____ [name and address of credit
_____ reporting agency]
_____

_____ [date]

Dear Sir or Madam:

I recently received my credit report (your file or report number) _____ from you. I noticed that some accounts of mine do not appear on the report. Since these reports demonstrate excellent payment histories, I would appreciate it if you could include them on my credit report. The name of the creditors, addresses, and account numbers are listed below. I am attaching the copies of my most recent statements from these accounts for verification purposes.

Name of Creditor	Address	Account Number

Please notify me when the information has been included.

Thank you.

Sincerely,

_____
[signature]

Form 20

LETTER REQUESTING ADDITION OF INFORMATION

_____ [your name and address]

_____

_____

_____ [name and address of credit
_____ reporting agency]

_____

_____ [date]

Dear Sir or Madam:

I recently received a copy of my credit report from your agency
[your file or report number] _____. I would like
you to include the information listed below on my report. This
information is not included on the current report and demonstrates
stability and would thus make my report more favorable. I would
appreciate your assistance with this.

_____

_____

_____

_____

_____

_____

_____

Thank you.

Sincerely,

_____

[signature]

LETTER REQUESTING REMOVAL OF INQUIRY

_____ [your name and address]
_____
_____

_____ [name and address of credit
_____ reporting agency]
_____

_____ [date]

Dear Sir or Madam:

I recently obtained my credit report and it contained a listing that you placed an inquiry about me that I did not authorize. Since I did not give you permission to make such an inquiry, I request that you remove it from my credit report immediately, since it is making it difficult for me to obtain credit.

Please send me documentation showing that you have removed this. If you believe I am incorrect, please send me the authorization you have.

Thank you.

Sincerely,

_____

[signature]

Form 22

LETTER WITH 100 WORD STATEMENT

_____ [your name and address]

_____

_____

_____ [name and address of credit

_____ reporting agency]

_____

_____ [date]

Dear Sir or Madam:

In accordance with Section 611b of the Fair Credit Reporting Act, I am including a 100 Word Statement to be included with my credit report.

This statement is in reference to account number _____ with _____ [creditor] _or_ this statement is in reference to my general credit situation, [delete the clause that does not apply.]

Please add this statement to my file:

_____

_____

_____

_____

_____

_____

_____

_____

Please notify me within thirty days once this has been added to my file.

Thank you.

Sincerely,

_____

[signature]

Form 23

CORRESPONDENCE LOG

Date	Business Name	Name of Contact	Account Number or Item	Type of Correspondence	Action	Steps to Take

1. _____

2. _____

3. _____

4. _____

5. _____

6. _____

7. _____

8. _____

9. _____

10. _____

11. _____

12. _____

DEBT PRIORITIZATION

Look at the debts on your **DEBT ASSESSMENT**. List them in order of importance below, so that you can pay or settle the most urgent first.

Priority	Item	Amount
1	_____	
2	_____	
3	_____	
4	_____	
5	_____	
6	_____	
7	_____	
8	_____	
9	_____	
10	_____	
11	_____	
12	_____	
13	_____	
14	_____	
15	_____	
16	_____	
17	_____	
18	_____	
19	_____	
20	_____	

Form 25

LETTER REQUESTING PAYMENT PLAN

_____ [your name and address]

_____

_____

_____ [name and address of creditor]

_____

_____

_____ [date]

Dear Sir or Madam:

I am the holder of account number _____ . I have been experiencing financial difficulties and have been having trouble paying on this account. I fully intend to pay you the full amount due, but I find that right now my finances are not able to pay for this account. I would like to arrange a payment plan as follows: _____

_____

_____

_____

_____

I would also propose that as part of this plan, you will report my account to credit reporting agencies as follows:

_____

_____

_____

_____

Please respond to this proposal in writing within fourteen days.

Thank you.

Sincerely,

_____
[signature]

Form 26

STUDENT LOAN LOG

Name of Loan: _____

Name of Lender: _____

Account Number: _____

Contact Information for Lender: _____

Date	Description of Activity

Form 27

Collection Information Statement for Wage Earners and Self-Employed Individuals   Form 433-A

Name_____   SSN_____

Section 5	**11. CHECKING ACCOUNTS.** List all checking accounts. (If you need additional space, attach a separate sheet.)

Section 5

Banking, Investment, Cash, Credit, and Life Insurance Information

*Complete all entry spaces with the most **current** data available.*

11. CHECKING ACCOUNTS. List all checking accounts. (If you need additional space, attach a separate sheet.)

	Type of Account	Full Name of Bank, Savings & Loan, Credit Union or Financial Institution	Bank Routing No.	Bank Account No.	Current Account Balance
11a. Checking		Name _____	_____	_____	$ _____
		Street Address _____			
		City/State/Zip _____			
11b. Checking		Name _____	_____	_____	$ _____
		Street Address _____			
		City/State/Zip _____	**11c. Total Checking Account Balances**		$

12. OTHER ACCOUNTS. List all acounts, including brokerage, savings, and money market, not listed on line 11.

	Type of Account	Full Name of Bank, Savings & Loan, Credit Union or Financial Institution	Bank Routing No.	Bank Account No.	Current Account Balance
12a. _____		Name _____	_____	_____	$ _____
		Street Address _____			
		City/State/Zip _____			
12b. _____		Name _____	_____	_____	$ _____
		Street Address _____			
		City/State/Zip _____	**12c. Total Other Account Balances**		$

ATTACHMENTS REQUIRED: Please include your current bank statements (checking, savings, money market, and brokerage accounts) for the past three months for all accounts.

13. INVESTMENTS. List all investment assets below. Include stocks, bonds, mutual funds, stock options, certificates of deposits, and retirement assets such as IRAs, Keogh, and 401(k) plans. (If you need additional space, attach a separate sheet.)

⤳ **Current Value:** Indicate the amount you could sell the asset for today.

	Name of Company	Number of Shares / Units	⤳Current Value	Loan Amount	Used as collateral on loan?
13a.	_____	_____	$ _____	$ _____	☐ No ☐ Yes
13b.	_____	_____	_____	_____	☐ No ☐ Yes
13c.	_____	_____	_____	_____	☐ No ☐ Yes
	13d. Total Investments		$		

14. CASH ON HAND. Include any money that you have that is not in the bank.

	14a. Total Cash on Hand	$

15. AVAILABLE CREDIT. List all lines of credit, including credit cards.

	Full Name of Credit Institution	Credit Limit	Amount Owed	Available Credit
15a. Name	_____	_____	_____	$ _____
	Street Address _____			
	City/State/Zip _____			
15b. Name	_____	_____	_____	$ _____
	Street Address _____			
	City/State/Zip _____	**15c. Total Credit Available**		$

Page 2 of 6

Section 5 continued on page 3 →
(Rev. 5-2001)

Collection Information Statement for Wage Earners and Self-Employed Individuals   Form 433-A

Name_____   SSN_____

Section 5 continued	**16. LIFE INSURANCE.** Do you have life insurance with a cash value? ☐ No ☐ Yes

(Term Life insurance does not have a cash value.)

If yes:

16a. Name of Insurance Company _____

16b. Policy Number(s) _____

16c. Owner of Policy _____

16d. Current Cash Value $_____   **16e.** Outstanding Loan Balance $_____

☐ Check this box when all spaces in Sect. 5 are filled in and attachments provided.

Subtract "Outstanding Loan Balance" line 16e from "Current Cash Value" line 16d = 16f $_____

ATTACHMENTS REQUIRED: Please include a statement from the life insurance companies that includes type and cash/loan value amounts. If currently borrowed against, include loan amount and date of loan.

Section 6
Other Information

17. OTHER INFORMATION. Respond to the following questions related to your financial condition: (Attach sheet if you need more space.)

17a. Are there any garnishments against your wages? ☐ No ☐ Yes
If yes, who is the creditor?_____ Date creditor obtained judgement _____ Amount of debt $_____

17b. Are there any judgments against you? ☐ No ☐ Yes
If yes, who is the creditor?_____ Date creditor obtained judgement _____ Amount of debt $_____

17c. Are you a party in a lawsuit? ☐ No ☐ Yes
If yes, amount of suit $_____ Possible completion date _____ Subject matter of suit _____

17d. Did you ever file bankruptcy? ☐ No ☐ Yes
If yes, date filed _____ Date discharged _____

17e. In the past 10 years did you transfer any assets out of your name for less than their actual value? ☐ No ☐ Yes
If yes, what asset? _____ Value of asset at time of transfer $_____
When was it transferred?_____ To whom was it transferred? _____

17f. Do you anticipate any increase in household income in the next two years? ☐ No ☐ Yes
If yes, why will the income increase? _____ (Attach sheet if you need more space.)
How much will it increase? $_____

17g. Are you a beneficiary of a trust or an estate? ☐ No ☐ Yes
If yes, name of the trust or estate_____ Anticipated amount to be received $_____
When will the amount be received? _____

☐ Check this box when all spaces in Sect. 6 are filled in.

17h. Are you a participant in a profit sharing plan? ☐ No ☐ Yes
If yes, name of plan _____ Value in plan $_____

Section 7
Assets and Liabilities

⨂ **Current Value:** Indicate the amount you could sell the asset for today.

18. PURCHASED AUTOMOBILES, TRUCKS AND OTHER LICENSED ASSETS. Include boats, RV's, motorcycles, trailers, etc. (If you need additional space, attach a separate sheet.)

Description (Year, Make, Model, Mileage)	⨂ Current Value	Current Loan Balance	Name of Lender	Purchase Date	Amount of Monthly Payment
18a. Year _____ Make/Model _____ Mileage _____	$	$	_____		$
18b. Year _____ Make/Model _____ Mileage _____	$	$	_____		$
18c. Year _____ Make/Model _____ Mileage _____	$	$	_____		$

Section 7 continued on page 4 →
(Rev. 5-2001)

Collection Information Statement for Wage Earners and Self-Employed Individuals   **Form 433-A**

Name_____   SSN_____

Section 7 continued	19.	**LEASED AUTOMOBILES, TRUCKS AND OTHER LICENSED ASSETS.** Include boats, RV's, motorcycles, trailers, etc. (If you need additional space, attach a separate sheet.)

		Description (Year, Make, Model)	Lease Balance	Name and Address of Lessor	Lease Date	Amount of Monthly Payment
	19a.	Year _____ Make/Model _____	$			$
	19b.	Year _____ Make/Model _____	$			$

ATTACHMENTS REQUIRED: Please include your current statement from lender with monthly car payment amount and current balance of the loan for each vehicle purchased or leased.

20. **REAL ESTATE.** List all real estate you own. (If you need additional space, attach a separate sheet.)

	Street Address, City, State, Zip, and County	Date Purchased	Purchase Price	⊐Current Value	Loan Balance	Name of Lender or Lien Holder	Amount of Monthly Payment	*Date of Final Payment
20a.			$	$	$		$	
20b.			$	$	$		$	

⊐ **Current Value:** Indicate the amount you could sell the asset for today.

✻ **Date of Final Payment:** Enter the date the loan or lease will be fully paid.

ATTACHMENTS REQUIRED: Please include your current statement from lender with monthly payment amount and current balance for each piece of real estate owned.

21. **PERSONAL ASSETS.** List all Personal assets below. (If you need additional space, attach separate sheet.) *Furniture/Personal Effects* includes the total current market value of your household such as furniture and appliances. *Other Personal Assets* includes all artwork, jewelry, collections (coin/gun, etc.), antiques or other assets.

	Description	⊐Current Value	Loan Balance	Name of Lender	Amount of Monthly Payment	✻Date of Final Payment
21a.	Furniture/Personal Effects	$	$		$	
	Other: (List below)					
21b.	Artwork	$	$		$	
21c.	Jewelry					
21d.						
21e.						

22. **BUSINESS ASSETS.** List all business assets and encumbrances below, include Uniform Commercial Code (UCC) filings. (If you need additional space, attach a separate sheet.) *Tools used in Trade or Business* includes the basic tools or books used to conduct your business, excluding automobiles. *Other Business Assets* includes any other machinery, equipment, inventory or other assets.

	Description	⊐Current Value	Loan Balance	Name of Lender	Amount of Monthly Payment	✻Date of Final Payment
22a.	Tools used in Trade/Business	$	$		$	
	Other: (List below)					
22b.	Machinery	$	$		$	
22c.	Equipment					
22d.						
22e.						

☐ Check this box when all spaces in Sect. 7 are filled in and attachments provided.

Page 4 of 6   Section 8 begins on page 5 →

Collection Information Statement for Wage Earners and Self-Employed Individuals   Form 433-A

Name_____   SSN_____

Section 8 Accounts/ Notes Receivable	**23. ACCOUNTS/NOTES RECEIVABLE.** List all accounts separately, including contracts awarded, but not started. (If you need additional space, attach a separate sheet.)

Use only if needed.

☐ *Check this box if Section 8 not needed.*

Description	Amount Due	Date Due	Age of Account
23a. Name _____ Street Address _____ City/State/Zip _____	$ _____	_____	☐ 0 - 30 days ☐ 30 - 60 days ☐ 60 - 90 days ☐ 90+ days
23b. Name _____ Street Address _____ City/State/Zip _____	$ _____	_____	☐ 0 - 30 days ☐ 30 - 60 days ☐ 60 - 90 days ☐ 90+ days
23c. Name _____ Street Address _____ City/State/Zip _____	$ _____	_____	☐ 0 - 30 days ☐ 30 - 60 days ☐ 60 - 90 days ☐ 90+ days
23d. Name _____ Street Address _____ City/State/Zip _____	$ _____	_____	☐ 0 - 30 days ☐ 30 - 60 days ☐ 60 - 90 days ☐ 90+ days
23e. Name _____ Street Address _____ City/State/Zip _____	$ _____	_____	☐ 0 - 30 days ☐ 30 - 60 days ☐ 60 - 90 days ☐ 90+ days
23f. Name _____ Street Address _____ City/State/Zip _____	$ _____	_____	☐ 0 - 30 days ☐ 30 - 60 days ☐ 60 - 90 days ☐ 90+ days
23g. Name _____ Street Address _____ City/State/Zip _____	$ _____	_____	☐ 0 - 30 days ☐ 30 - 60 days ☐ 60 - 90 days ☐ 90+ days
23h. Name _____ Street Address _____ City/State/Zip _____	$ _____	_____	☐ 0 - 30 days ☐ 30 - 60 days ☐ 60 - 90 days ☐ 90+ days
23i. Name _____ Street Address _____ City/State/Zip _____	$ _____	_____	☐ 0 - 30 days ☐ 30 - 60 days ☐ 60 - 90 days ☐ 90+ days
23j. Name _____ Street Address _____ City/State/Zip _____	$ _____	_____	☐ 0 - 30 days ☐ 30 - 60 days ☐ 60 - 90 days ☐ 90+ days
23k. Name _____ Street Address _____ City/State/Zip _____	$ _____	_____	☐ 0 - 30 days ☐ 30 - 60 days ☐ 60 - 90 days ☐ 90+ days
23l. Name _____ Street Address _____ City/State/Zip _____	$ _____	_____	☐ 0 - 30 days ☐ 30 - 60 days ☐ 60 - 90 days ☐ 90+ days

☐ Check this box when all spaces in Sect. 8 are filled in.

Add "Amount Due" from lines 23a through 23l = 23m $ _____

Collection Information Statement for Wage Earners and Self-Employed Individuals   Form 433-A

Name_____   SSN_____

Section 9					
Monthly Income and Expense Analysis	*Total Income*			*Total Living Expenses*	
	Source	Gross Monthly		Expense Items [4]	Actual Monthly
	24. Wages (Yourself)[1]	$		35. Food, Clothing and Misc.[5]	$
	25. Wages (Spouse)[1]			36. Housing and Utilities[6]	
	26. Interest - Dividends			37. Transportation[7]	
	27. Net Income from Business[2]			38. Health Care	
If only one spouse has a tax liability, but both have income, list the total household income and expenses.	28. Net Rental Income[3]			39. Taxes (Income and FICA)	
	29. Pension/Social Security (Yourself)			40. Court ordered payments	
	30. Pension/Social Security (Spouse)			41. Child/dependent care	
	31. Child Support			42. Life insurance	
	32. Alimony			43. Other secured debt	
	33. Other			44. Other expenses	
	34. Total Income	$		**45. Total Living Expenses**	$

[1] **Wages, salaries, pensions, and social security:** Enter your gross monthly wages and/or salaries. Do not deduct withholding or allotments you elect to take out of your pay, such as insurance payments, credit union deductions, car payments etc.
To calculate your gross monthly wages and/or salaries:
   If paid weekly - multiply weekly gross wages by 4.3. Example: $425.89 x 4.3 = $1,831.33
   If paid bi-weekly (every 2 weeks) - multiply bi-weekly gross wages by 2.17. Example: $972.45 x 2.17 = $2,110.22
   If paid semi-monthly (twice each month) - multiply semi-monthly gross wages by 2. Example: $856.23 x 2 = $1,712.46

[2] **Net Income from Business:** Enter your monthly net business income. This is the amount you earn after you pay ordinary and necessary monthly business expenses. This figure should relate to the yearly net profit from your Form 1040 Schedule C. If it is more or less than the previous year, you should attach an explanation. If your net business income is a loss, enter "0". Do not enter a negative number.

[3] **Net Rental Income:** Enter your monthly net rental income. This is the amount you earn after you pay ordinary and necessary monthly rental expenses. If your net rental income is a loss, enter "0". Do not enter a negative number.

[4] **Expenses not generally allowed:** We generally do not allow you to claim tuition for private schools, public or private college expenses, charitable contributions, voluntary retirement contributions, payments on unsecured debts such as credit card bills, cable television and other similar expenses. However, we may allow these expenses, if you can prove that they are necessary for the health and welfare of you or your family or for the production of income.

[5] **Food, Clothing and Misc.:** Total of clothing, food, housekeeping supplies and personal care products for one month.

[6] **Housing and Utilities:** For your principal residence: Total of rent or mortgage payment. Add the average monthly expenses for the following: property taxes, home owner's or renter's insurance, maintenance, dues, fees, and utilities. Utilities include gas, electricity, water, fuel, oil, other fuels, trash collection and telephone.

[7] **Transportation:** Total of lease or purchase payments, vehicle insurance, registration fees, normal maintenance, fuel, public transportation, parking and tolls for one month.

ATTACHMENTS REQUIRED: Please include:

- A copy of your last Form 1040 with all Schedules.

- Proof of all current expenses that you paid for the past 3 months, including utilities, rent, insurance, property taxes, etc.

- Proof of all non-business transportation expenses (e.g., car payments, lease payments, fuel, oil, insurance, parking, registration).

- Proof of payments for health care, including health insurance premiums, co-payments, and other out-of-pocket expenses, for the past 3 months.

- Copies of any court order requiring payment and proof of such payments (e.g., cancelled checks, money orders, earning statements showing such deductions) for the past 3 months.

☐ Check this box when all spaces in Sect. 9 are filled in and attachments provided.

☐ Check this box when all spaces in all sections are filled in and all attachments provided.

⚠ CAUTION *Failure to complete all entry spaces may result in rejection or significant delay in the resolution of your account.*

Certification: *Under penalties of perjury, I declare that to the best of my knowledge and belief this statement of assets, liabilities, and other information is true, correct and complete.*

_____   _____   _____
Your Signature   Spouse's Signature   Date

(Rev. 5-2001)

Form 27A

Worksheet to Calculate an Offer Amount

For use by Wage Earners and Self-Employed Individuals.

Keep this worksheet for your records.
Do not send to IRS.

Use this Worksheet to calculate an offer amount using information from Form 433-A.

1. Enter total checking accounts from Item 11c

A

2. Enter total other accounts from Item 12c

B

If less than 0 , enter 0

3. Enter total investments from Item 13d

C

4. Enter total cash on hand from Item 14a

D

5. Enter life insurance cash value from Item 16f

E

6. Enter total accounts/notes receivable from Item 23m

F

Subtotal: Add boxes A through F =

G

---

7. Purchased Automobiles, Trucks, and Other Licensed Assets

	Enter current value for each asset	Enter loan balance for each asset	Individual asset value (if less than 0 , enter 0)
From line 18a $	x .8 = $	— $	=
From line 18b $	x .8 = $	— $	=
From line 18c $	x .8 = $	— $	=

Subtotal = **H**

---

8. Real Estate

	Enter current value for each asset	Enter loan balance for each asset	Individual asset value (if less than 0 , enter 0)
From line 20a $	x .8 = $	— $	=
From line 20b $	x .8 = $	— $	=

Subtotal = **I**

---

9. Personal Assets

	Enter current value for each asset	Enter loan balance for each asset	Individual asset value (if less than 0 , enter 0)
From line 21b $	x .8 = $	— $	=
From line 21c $	x .8 = $	— $	=
From line 21d $	x .8 = $	— $	=
From line 21e $	x .8 = $	— $	=

Subtotal = **J**

| From line 21a $ | x .8 = $ | — $ | = |

Subtract   — $ 7040.00

Subtotal = **K**

---

10. Business Assets

	Enter current value for each asset	Enter loan balance for each asset	Individual asset value (if less than 0 , enter 0)
From line 22b $	x .8 = $	— $	=
From line 22c $	x .8 = $	— $	=
From line 22d $	x .8 = $	— $	=
From line 22e $	x .8 = $	— $	=

Subtotal = **L**

| From line 22a $ | x .8 = $ | — $ | = |

Subtract   — $ 3520.00

Subtotal = **M**

11. Add amounts in Boxes G through M to obtain your total equity and assets   = 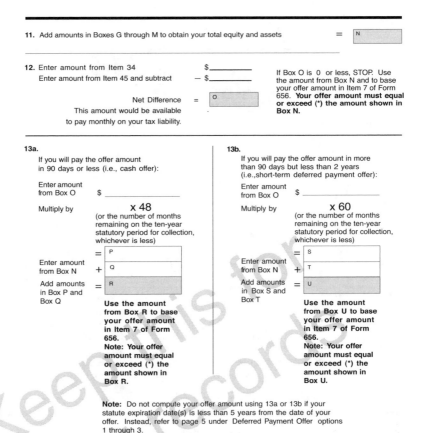 N

12. Enter amount from Item 34 $ _____

   Enter amount from Item 45 and subtract   − $ _____

   Net Difference = [O]

   This amount would be available to pay monthly on your tax liability.

If Box O is 0 or less, STOP. Use the amount from Box N and to base your offer amount in Item 7 of Form 656. **Your offer amount must equal or exceed (*) the amount shown in Box N.**

13a.

If you will pay the offer amount in 90 days or less (i.e., cash offer):

Enter amount from Box O $ _____

Multiply by   **x 48**
(or the number of months remaining on the ten-year statutory period for collection, whichever is less)

= [P]

Enter amount from Box N   + [Q]

Add amounts in Box P and Box Q   = [R]

Use the amount from Box R to base your offer amount in Item 7 of Form 656.
Note: Your offer amount must equal or exceed (*) the amount shown in Box R.

13b.

If you will pay the offer amount in more than 90 days but less than 2 years (i.e., short-term deferred payment offer):

Enter amount from Box O $ _____

Multiply by   **x 60**
(or the number of months remaining on the ten-year statutory period for collection, whichever is less)

= [S]

Enter amount from Box N   + [T]

Add amounts in Box S and Box T   = [U]

Use the amount from Box U to base your offer amount in Item 7 of Form 656.
Note: Your offer amount must equal or exceed (*) the amount shown in Box U.

Note: Do not compute your offer amount using 13a or 13b if your statute expiration date(s) is less than 5 years from the date of your offer. Instead, refer to page 5 under Deferred Payment Offer options 1 through 3.

* Unless you are submitting an offer under effective tax administration or doubt as to collectibility with special circumstances considerations, as described on page 4.

Form 28

Form **656** (February 2007)	Department of the Treasury — Internal Revenue Service ## Offer in Compromise

Attach Application Fee and Payment *(check or money order)* **here.**

IRS RECEIVED DATE

Section I   **Taxpayer Contact Information**

Taxpayer's First Name and Middle Initial   Last Name

If a joint offer, spouse's First Name and Middle Initial   Last Name

Business Name

Taxpayer's Address *(Home or Business) (number, street, and room or suite no., city, state, ZIP code)*

Mailing Address *(if different from above) (number, street, and room or suite no., city, state, ZIP code)*

DATE RETURNED

Social Security Number (SSN)
(Primary)   *(Secondary)*

Employer Identification Number (EIN)
(EIN included in offer)   *(EIN not included in offer)*

-     -   -   -   -   -

Section II   **To: Commissioner of Internal Revenue Service**

I/We *(includes all types of taxpayers)* submit this offer to compromise the tax liabilities plus any interest, penalties, additions to tax, and additional amounts required by law *(tax liability)* for the tax type and period marked below: *(Please mark an "X" in the box for the correct description and fill-in the correct tax period(s), adding additional periods if needed).*

☐ 1040/1120 Income Tax — Year(s) _____

☐ 941 Employer's Quarterly Federal Tax Return — Quarterly period(s) _____

☐ 940 Employer's Annual Federal Unemployment (FUTA) Tax Return — Year(s) _____

☐ Trust Fund Recovery Penalty as a responsible person of *(enter corporation name)*_____ ,

for failure to pay withholding and Federal Insurance Contributions Act taxes (Social Security taxes), for period(s) ending _____

☐ Other Federal Tax(es) [specify type(s) and period(s)]_____

Note: If you need more space, use a separate sheet of paper and title it "Attachment to Form 656 Dated _____." Sign and date the attachment following the listing of the tax periods.

Section III   **Reason for Offer in Compromise**

I/We submit this offer for the reason(s) checked below:

☐ Doubt as to Collectibility — "I have insufficient assets and income to pay the full amount." You must include a complete Collection Information Statement, Form 433-A and/or Form 433-B.

☐ Effective Tax Administration — "I owe this amount and have sufficient assets to pay the full amount, but due to my exceptional circumstances, requiring full payment would cause an economic hardship or would be unfair and inequitable." You must include a complete Collection Information Statement, Form 433-A and/or Form 433-B and complete Section VI.

Section IV   **Offer in Compromise Terms**

I/We offer to pay $_____ *(must be more than zero).* Complete Section VII to explain where you will obtain the funds to make this offer.

Check **only** one of the following:

☐ **Lump sum cash offer** – 20% of the amount of the offer $_____ must be sent with Form 656. Upon written acceptance of the offer, the balance must be paid in 5 or fewer installments.

$_____ payable within _____ months after acceptance
$_____ payable within _____ months after acceptance
$_____ payable within _____ months after acceptance
$_____ payable within _____ months after acceptance
$_____ payable within _____ months after acceptance

☐ **Short Term Periodic Payment Offer** – Offer amount is paid within 24 months from the date IRS received your offer. The first payment **must** be submitted with your Form 656. You **must** make regular payments during your offer investigation. Complete the following:

$_____ will be submitted with the Form 656. Beginning in the month after the offer is submitted *(insert month_____),* on the _____ day of each month, $_____ will be sent in for a total of _____ months. *(Cannot extend more than 24 months from the date the offer was submitted.)*

Catalog Number 16728N   www.irs.gov   Form **656** (Rev. 2-2007)

Section IV Cont.

☐ **Deferred Periodic Payment Offer** – Offer amount will be paid over the remaining life of the collection statute. The first payment **must** be submitted with your Form 656. You must make regular payments during your offer investigation. Complete the following:

$ _____ will be submitted with the Form 656. Beginning in the month after the offer is submitted *(insert month* _____ *)*, on the _____ day of each month, $_____ will be sent in for a total of _____ months.

Optional - Designation of Required Payment under IRC 7122(c)

You have the option to designate the required payment you made under Section IV above. If you chose not to designate your required payment, then the IRS will apply your payment in the best interest of the government. Please complete the following if you choose to designate your payment:

$_____ paid under IRC 7122 (c) is to be applied to my _____ Tax Year/Quarter*(s) (whichever is applicable)* for my/our tax form_____.

If you pay more than the required payment when you submit your offer and want any part of that additional payment treated as a deposit, check the box below and insert the amount. It is not required that you designate any portion of your payment as a deposit. **Note:** If the required payment is not paid, the offer will be returned even if you make a payment you designate as a deposit.

☐ I am making a deposit of $_____ with this offer.

Section V   By submitting this offer, I/we have read, understand and agree to the following conditions:

(a) I/We voluntarily submit all tax payments made on this offer, including the mandatory payments of tax required under section 7122(c). These tax payments are not refundable even if I/we withdraw the offer prior to acceptance or the IRS returns or rejects the offer. If the offer is accepted, the IRS will apply payments made after acceptance in the best interest of the government.

(b) Any payments made in connection with this offer will be applied to the tax liability unless I have specified that they be treated as a deposit. Only amounts that exceed the mandatory payments can be treated as a deposit. Such a deposit will be refundable if the offer is rejected or returned by the IRS or is withdrawn. I/we understand that the IRS will not pay interest on any deposit.

(c) The application fee for this offer will be kept by the IRS unless the offer was not accepted for processing.

(d) I/We will comply with all provisions of the Internal Revenue Code relating to filing my/our returns and paying my/our required taxes for 5 years or until the offered amount is paid in full, whichever is longer. In the case of a jointly submitted Offer in Compromise joint liabilities, I/we understand that default with respect to the compliance provisions described in this paragraph by one party to this agreement will not result in the default of the entire agreement. The default provisions described in Section V(i) of this agreement will be applied only to the party failing to comply with the requirements of this paragraph.

(e) I/We waive and agree to the suspension of any statutory periods of limitation (time limits provided by law) for the IRS assessment of the liability for the periods identified in Section II. I/We understand that I/we have the right not to waive these statutory periods or to limit the waiver to a certain length or to certain periods. I/We understand, however, that the IRS may not consider this offer if I/we refuse to waive the statutory periods for assessment or if we provide only a limited waiver. The amount of any Federal tax due for the periods described in Section II may be assessed at any time prior to the acceptance of this offer or within one year of the rejection of this offer. I/We understand that the statute of limitations for collection will be suspended during the period an offer is considered pending by the IRS (paragraph (k) of this section defines pending).

(f) The IRS will keep all payments and credits made, received or applied to the total original liability before submission of this offer and all payments required under section 7122(c). The IRS will also keep all payments in excess of those required by section 7122(c) that are received in connection with the offer and that are not designated as deposits in Section IV. The IRS may keep any proceeds from a levy served prior to submission of the offer, but not received at the time the offer is submitted. As additional consideration beyond the amount of my/our offer, the IRS will keep any refund, including interest, due to me/us because of overpayment of any tax or other liability, for tax periods extending through the calendar year in which the IRS accepts the offer. The date of acceptance is the date on the written notice of acceptance issued by the IRS to me/us or to my/our representative. I/We may not designate an overpayment ordinarily subject to refund, to which the IRS is entitled, to be applied to estimated tax payments for the following year.

(g) I/We will return to the IRS any refund identified in paragraph (f) received after submission of this offer.

(h) The IRS cannot collect more than the full amount of the liability under this offer.

(i) I/We understand that I/we remain responsible for the full amount of the liabilities, unless and until the IRS accepts the offer in writing and I/we have met all the terms and conditions of the offer. The IRS will not remove the original amount of the liabilities from its records until I/we have met all the terms and conditions of the offer. I/We understand that the liabilities I/we offer to compromise are and will remain liabilities until I/we meet all the terms and conditions of this offer. If I/we file for bankruptcy before the terms and conditions of this offer are completed, any claim the IRS files in the bankruptcy proceedings will be a tax claim

(j) Once the IRS accepts the offer in writing, I/we have no right to contest, in court or otherwise, the amount of the liability.

(k) The offer is pending starting with the date an authorized IRS official signs the form. The offer remains pending until an authorized IRS official accepts, rejects, returns or acknowledges withdrawal of the offer in writing. If I/we appeal an IRS rejection decision on the offer, IRS will continue to treat the offer as pending until the Appeals Office accepts or rejects the offer in writing.

If I/we don't file a protest within 30 days of the date the IRS notifies me/us of the right to protest the decision, I/we waive the right to a hearing before the Appeals Office about the Offer in Compromise.

(l) If I/we fail to meet any of the terms and conditions of the offer and the offer defaults, the IRS may:

- immediately file suit to collect the entire unpaid balance of the offer;

- immediately file suit to collect an amount equal to the original amount of the liability, minus any payment already received under the terms of this offer;

- disregard the amount of the offer and apply all amounts already paid under the offer against the original amount of the liability; and/or

- file suit or levy to collect the original amount of the liability, without further notice of any kind.

The IRS will continue to add interest, as section 6601 of the Internal Revenue Code requires, on the amount the IRS determines is due after default. The IRS will add interest from the date the offer is defaulted until I/we completely satisfy the amount owed.

(m) The IRS generally files a Notice of Federal Tax Lien to protect the Government's interest on offers with deferred payments. Also, the IRS may file a Notice of Federal Tax Lien during the offer investigation. This tax lien will be released when the payment terms of the offer agreement have been satisfied.

(n) I/We understand that IRS employees may contact third parties in order to respond to this request and I/we authorize the IRS to make such contacts. Further, by authorizing the IRS to contact third parties, I/we understand that I/we will not receive notice, pursuant to section 7602(c) of the Internal Revenue Code, of third parties contacted in connection with this request.

(o) I/We are offering to compromise all the liabilities assessed against me/us as of the date of this offer and under the taxpayer identification numbers listed in Section II above. I/We authorize the IRS to amend Section II, above, to include any assessed liabilities we failed to list on Form 656.

Section VI	Explanation of Circumstances

I am requesting an Offer in Compromise for the reason(s) listed below:

Note: *If you believe you have special circumstances affecting your ability to fully pay the amount due, explain your situation. You may attach additional sheets if necessary. Please include your name and SSN or EIN on all additional sheets or supporting documentation.*

Section VII	Source of Funds

I / We shall obtain the funds to make this offer from the following source(s):

Section VIII	Mandatory Signatures

	If I / We submit this offer on a substitute form, I/ we affirm that this form is a verbatim duplicate of the official Form 656, and I/we agree to be bound by all the terms and conditions set forth in the official Form 656.
Taxpayer Attestation	Under penalties of perjury, I declare that I have examined this offer, including accompanying schedules and statements, and to the best of my knowledge and belief, it is true, correct and complete.

Signature of Taxpayer	Date
Signature of Taxpayer	Date

Official Use Only

I accept the waiver of the statutory period of limitations on assessment for the Internal Revenue Service, as described in Section V(e).

Signature of Authorized Internal Revenue Service Official	Title	Date

Section IX	Application Prepared by Someone Other than the Taxpayer

If this application was prepared by someone other than the taxpayer, please fill in that person's name and address below.

Name

Address *(if known) (Street, City, State, ZIP code)*

Section X	Paid Preparer Use Only

Name of Preparer

Signature of Preparer	Date	Check if self-employed ☐	Preparer's CAF no. or PTIN

Firm's name (or yours if self-employed), address, and ZIP code	EIN
	Telephone number ( )

Section XI	Third Party Designee

Do you want to allow another person to discuss this offer with the IRS? ☐ Yes. Complete the information below. ☐ No

Designee's name	Telephone number ( )

Privacy Act Statement

We ask for the information on this form to carry out the internal revenue laws of the United States. Our authority to request this information is Section 7801 of the Internal Revenue Code.

Our purpose for requesting the information is to determine if it is in the best interests of the IRS to accept an Offer in Compromise. You are not required to make an Offer in Compromise; however, if you choose to do so, you must provide all of the taxpayer information requested. Failure to provide all of the information may prevent us from processing your request.

If you are a paid preparer and you prepared the Form 656 for the taxpayer submitting an offer, we request that you complete and sign Section X on Form 656, and provide identifying information. Providing this information is voluntary. This information will be used to administer and enforce the internal revenue laws of the United States and may be used to regulate practice before the Internal Revenue Service for those persons subject to Treasury Department Circular No. 230, Regulations Governing the Practice of Attorneys, Certified Public Accountants, Enrolled Agents, Enrolled Actuaries, and Appraisers before the Internal Revenue Service. Information on this form may be disclosed to the Department of Justice for civil and criminal litigation.

We may also disclose this information to cities, states and the District of Columbia for use in administering their tax laws and to combat terrorism. Providing false or fraudulent information on this form may subject you to criminal prosecution and penalties.

Catalog Number 16728N   www.irs.gov   Form **656** (Rev. 2-2007)

Form 28A

Offer in Compromise Application Fee and Payment Worksheet

If you answered YES to question one on Page 2, **then do not proceed any further.** You are not eligible to have your offer considered at this time.

If you answered NO to question one on Page 2 of this booklet, then you may be eligible to have your offer considered and you may proceed completing the worksheet. However, it is important that you use the current version Form 656 (Rev. 02-2007), *Offer in Compromise,* and the (Rev. 5-2001) versions of Forms 433-A, *Collection Information Statement for Wage Earners and Self-Employed Individuals,* and / or 433-B, *Collection Information Statement for Businesses* that are included in this package.

The application fee and payment does not apply to individuals whose income falls at or below levels based on IRS Offers in Compromise Monthly Low Income Guidelines. The exception for taxpayers with incomes below these levels only applies to individuals; it does not apply to other entities such as corporations or partnerships. If you are self employed, then you must first look at Section 9, Line 27 of the Form 433A. If you entered a net income from your business, then you may need to make an adjustment for this item. For the purposes of determining item 2, Total Household Monthly Income, you must deduct any depreciation of assets that you itemized on your Tax Form 1040 Schedule C, that was used to determine your net income from your business, line 27. Adjusting line 27 will affect the amount on line 34 of the Form 433A. Therefore line 34 must be adjusted and carried over to this worksheet item 2 for Total Household Monthly Income. If you had no depreciation of assets on Schedule C, then there is no adjustment to be made.

If you are an individual, follow the steps below to determine if you must remit the application fee along with your Form 656, Offer in Compromise.

1. **Family Unit Size_____.** Enter the total number of dependants (including yourself and your spouse) listed in Section 1 of Form 433-A, *Collection Information Statement for Wage Earners and Self-Employed individuals.*

2. **Total Household Monthly Income_____.** Enter the amount of your total household monthly income from Section 9, Line 34 of the Form 433-A, *Collection Information Statement for Wage Earners and Self-Employed Individuals.* Please see Page 4 under Step Two, item 5, for a definition of total household income.

3. Compare the information you entered in items 1 and 2, above, to the monthly IRS OIC Monthly Low Income Guidelines table below. Find the "Family Unit Size" equal to the number you entered in item 1. Next, find the column which represents where you reside (48 Contiguous states, DC …, Hawaii or Alaska). Compare the "Total Household Monthly Income" you entered in item 2 to the number in the row and column that corresponds to your family unit size and residence. *For example, if you reside in one of the 48 contiguous states, and your family unit size from item 1 above is 4, and your total household monthly income from item 2 above is $3000, then you are exempt from the fee and payment because your income is less than the $4,167 guideline amount.*

IRS OIC Monthly Low Income Guidelines

Size of Family Unit	48 Contiguous States and D.C.	Hawaii	Alaska
1	$2,042	$2,348	$2,552
2	$2,750	$3,163	$3,438
3	$3,458	$3,977	$4,323
4	$4,167	$4,792	$5,208
5	$4,875	$5,606	$6,094
6	$5,583	$6,421	$6,979
7	$6,292	$7,235	$7,865
8	$7,000	$8,050	$8,750
For each additional person, add	$708	$815	$885

4. If the total household monthly income you entered in item 2 is **more** than the amount shown for your family unit size and residence in the monthly IRS OIC Monthly Low Income Guidelines table above, **you must send the $150 application fee and any 20% payment or first initial installment with each OIC you submit.**

   Your check or money order should be made payable to the "**United States Treasury**" and attached to the front of your Form 656, *Offer In Compromise.* **Do Not Send Cash.** Send a separate application fee with each OIC; do not combine it with any other tax payments as this may delay processing of your OIC. Your OIC will be returned to you without further consideration if the application fee and the required payments are not properly remitted, or if your check is returned for insufficient funds.

5. If the total income you entered in item 2 is **equal to or less than** the amount shown for your family unit size and residence in the table above, do not send the application fee or the required payments. Sign and date Form 656-A, *Income Certification for Offer in Compromise Application Fee and Payment.* **Attach the certification and this worksheet to the front of your Form 656.**

Form **656-A** (February 2007)	Department of the Treasury — Internal Revenue Service **Income Certification for Offer in Compromise** **Application Fee and Payment** (For Individual Taxpayers Only)

If you are not required to submit the fee or payments based on your income level, you must complete this form and attach both it and the worksheet to the front of your Form 656.

Your Name *(Last, First, Middle initial) (Please Print)*	Social Security Number (SSN) or Taxpayer Identification Number (TIN)
Spouse's Name *(Last, First, Middle initial) (Please Print)*	Social Security Number (SSN) or Taxpayer Identification Number (TIN)

Certification: I/We certify under penalty of perjury that I am not required to submit an Offer in Compromise application fee and payment, based on my family unit size and income.

Your Signature	Date
Spouse's Signature *(if submitting a joint Offer in Compromise)*	Date

Note: If the Internal Revenue Service determines that you were required to pay a fee or payment, your Offer in Compromise will be returned without further consideration.

Form 29

LETTER OFFERING TO RETURN SECURED PROPERTY

_____ [your name and address]

_____

_____

_____ [name and address of creditor]

_____

_____

_____ [date]

Dear Sir or Madam:

I am the holder of account number_____ , which I used to purchase the following items on a secured basis:

_____

_____

_____

_____

As you may be aware, I have been experiencing financial difficulties lately. I wish to propose the following settlement offer for this account. I will return the secured property to you in exchange for cancellation of the debt and a neutral/positive rating for this account being reported to credit reporting agencies.

Please respond to this proposal in writing within fourteen days.

Thank you.

Sincerely,

_____

[signature]

Form 30

LETTER PROPOSING SETTLEMENT

_____ [your name and address]

_____

_____

_____ [name and address of creditor]

_____

_____

_____ [date]

Dear Sir or Madam:

With regard to account #_____ , which I do not acknowledge to be a debt I owe, I make the following settlement offer in order to conclude this matter as swiftly as possible. This is not a renewed promise to pay and it is not an agreement unless you sign it and return it or we mutually sign a written agreement document. I maintain my right to seek further proof of this debt.

I will pay you $_____ in full satisfaction of this debt. Upon receipt of the payment, your company will report this debt to all three major credit reporting agencies—Equifax, Experian, and TransUnion—as "paid as agreed" and you will remove all references to delinquency on this account. As the company reporting the status of this account, you have full authority to change the way it is listed with credit agencies.

This is a restricted offer. If you agree, sign and return this letter and I will send payment by certified mail. The terms of this offer are confidential. I will make no payment without a written agreement.

Thank you.

Sincerely,

_____

[signature]

Form 31

AGREEMENT TO SETTLE DEBT

_____ [Creditor], and
_____ [your name] (Debtor),
agree to compromise the indebtedness between them. CREDITOR
agrees to compromise the indebtedness due CREDITOR according
to the following terms and conditions:

The CREDITOR and the DEBTOR agree that the present debt due
is $ _____ . The parties agree that the CREDITOR shall
accept the sum of $ _____ as full payment on the debt.
The acceptance of the payment will serve as a complete discharge of
all monies due. The payment shall be made in cash or cash
equivalent.

In addition, upon acceptance of the $ _____ , the
CREDITOR will notify all Credit Reporting Agencies that account
is "PAID AS AGREED," and delete any entries showing this
account as ever being late.

This compromise is expressly conditioned upon the payment being
received by _____ [date]. If the DEBTOR fails to pay the
compromised amount by this date, the original amount owed by the
DEBTOR will be reinstated in full, and immediately due.

This Agreement shall be binding upon and inure to the benefit of the
parties, their successors and assigns.

_____   _____   _____   _____
[CREDITOR]   [DATE]   [DEBTOR]   [DATE]

Form 32

LETTER REQUESTING NO PAYMENT

_____ [your name and address]

_____

_____

_____ [name and address of creditor]

_____

_____

_____ [date]

Dear Sir or Madam:

I am writing in regard to my account number _____.
I am behind on my payments and am experiencing some temporary
financial difficulties. I fully intend to repay this account in full;
however, I am unable to make any payments at this time for a period
of _____. I am requesting that you allow me to miss
_____ payment(s) while I get back on my feet financially.

I would be very appreciative if you could help me in this way. Please
let me know in writing if this is possible.

Thank you.

Sincerely,

_____
[signature]

Form 33

LETTER EXPLAINING JUDGMENT PROOF STATUS

_____ [your name and address]

_____

_____

_____ [name and address of creditor]

_____

_____

_____ [date]

Dear Sir or Madam:

I am aware that I am behind on my payments to my account number _____ . I am unable to make payments because I am experiencing financial difficulties. I would like to notify you that I am without income or assets and have nothing for you to pursue. Since I am judgment proof, please do not waste your time and energy pursuing this matter. I will resume making payments as soon as possible.

Thank you.

Sincerely,

_____

[signature]

Form 34

LETTER EXPLAINING PLAN TO GO BANKRUPT

_____ [your name and address]

_____

_____

_____ [name and address of creditor]

_____

_____

_____ [date]

Dear Sir or Madam:

I am writing in regard to my account number _____ .
Please be advised that I am about to file for bankruptcy and that I
will be including this debt in the proceeding. Please contact my
attorney _____ at _____
about this matter in the future.

Thank you.

Sincerely,

_____
[signature]

Form 35

LETTER CLOSING ACCOUNT

_____ [your name and address]
_____
_____

_____ [name and address of creditor]
_____
_____

_____ [date]

Dear Sir or Madam:

Please close my account number _____ with you. I will no longer be using this account.

Thank you.

Sincerely,

_____
[signature]

Form 36

CREDIT CARD LIST

	Card	Name on Card	Account Number	Expiration Date	Phone Number	Credit Limit
1.						
2.						
3.						
4.						
5.						
6.						
7.						
8.						
9.						
10.						
11.						
12.						

Form 37

LETTER TO U.S. BANKRUPTCY TRUSTEE

_____ [your name and address]

_____

_____

_____ [name and address of

_____ bankruptcy trustee]

_____

_____ [date]

Dear Sir or Madam:

I am the victim of identity fraud. It has recently come to my attention that this fraud has been continued in bankruptcy court. Enclosed please find _____
_____ [whatever proof you have of the bankruptcy fraud] and a copy of my driver's license. I have not filed or had dealings with the bankruptcy court. Please advise me how you will handle this matter.

Thank you.

Sincerely,

_____

[signature]

Form 38

IDENTITY THEFT TRACKING SHEET

Credit Bureaus—Report Fraud

Bureau	Phone Number	Date Contacted	Contact Person	Comments
Equifax	800-525-6285			
Experian	888-397-3742			
TransUnion	800-680-7289			

Banks, Credit Card Issuers, and Other Creditors
(Contact each creditor promptly to protect your legal rights.)

Creditor	Address and Phone Number	Date Contacted	Contact Person	Comments

Law Enforcement Agencies—Report Identity Theft

Agency	Phone Number	Date Contacted	Contact Person	Report Number	Comments
Federal Trade Commission	877-IDTHEFT				
Local Police Department					

Form 39

ID THEFT AFFIDAVIT

Victim Information

(1) My full legal name is ——————————————————
          (First) (Middle) (Last) (Jr., Sr., III)

(2) (If different from above) When the events described in this affidavit took place, I was known as

——————————————————————————————
(First)   (Middle)   (Last)   (Jr., Sr., III)

(3) My date of birth is ———————————
        (day/month/year)

(4) My Social Security number is ————————————————

(5) My driver's license or identification card state and number are

——————————————————————————————

(6) My current address is ————————————————————

City ————————— State ————— Zip Code —————

(7) I have lived at this address since ———————————————
            (month/year)

(8) (If different from above) When the events described in this affidavit took place, my address was ————————————————————

——————————————————————————————

City ————————— State ————— Zip Code —————

(9) I lived at the address in Item 8 from ——————— until —————
            (month/year)   (month/year)

(10) My daytime telephone number is (___) ————————————
My evening telephone number is (___) ————————————

DO NOT SEND AFFIDAVIT TO THE FTC OR ANY OTHER
GOVERNMENT AGENCY

Name _____ *Phone number* _____ *Page 2*

How the Fraud Occurred

Check all that apply for items 11 – 17:

(11)　☐　I did not authorize anyone to use my name or personal information to seek the money, credit, loans, goods or services described in this report.

(12)　☐　I did not receive any benefit, money, goods or services as a result of the events described in this report.

(13)　☐　My identification documents (for example, credit cards; birth certificate; driver's license; Social Security card; etc.) were　☐ stolen ☐ lost　on or about _____ .
　　　　　　　　　　　(day/month/year)

(14)　☐　To the best of my knowledge and belief, the following person(s) used my information (for example, my name, address, date of birth, existing account numbers, Social Security number, mother's maiden name, etc.) or identification documents to get money, credit, loans, goods or services without my knowledge or authorization:

Name (if known)	Name (if known)
Address (if known)	Address (if known)
Phone number(s) (if known)	Phone number(s) (if known)
Additional information (if known)	Additional information (if known)

(15)　☐　I do NOT know who used my information or identification documents to get money, credit, loans, goods or services without my knowledge or authorization.

(16)　☐　Additional comments: (For example, description of the fraud, which documents or information were used or how the identity thief gained access to your information.)

_____

_____

_____

_____

_____

(Attach additional pages as necessary.)

DO NOT SEND AFFIDAVIT TO THE FTC OR ANY OTHER
GOVERNMENT AGENCY

*Name*_____ *Phone number* _____ *Page 3*

Victim's Law Enforcement Actions

(17) (check one) I ☐ am ☐ am not willing to assist in the prosecution of the person(s) who committed this fraud.

(18) (check one) I ☐ am ☐ am not authorizing the release of this information to law enforcement for the purpose of assisting them in the investigation and prosecution of the person(s) who committed this fraud.

(19) (check all that apply) I ☐ have ☐ have not reported the events described in this affidavit to the police or other law enforcement agency. The police ☐ did ☐ did not write a report. In the event you have contacted the police or other law enforcement agency, please complete the following:

_____	_____
(Agency # 1)	(Officer/Agency personnel taking report)
_____	_____
(Date of report)	(Report number, if any)
_____	_____
(Phone number)	(email address, if any)
_____	_____
(Agency # 2)	(Officer/Agency personnel taking report)
_____	_____
(Date of report)	(Report number, if any)
_____	_____
(Phone number)	(email address, if any)

Documentation Checklist

Please indicate the supporting documentation you are able to provide to the companies you plan to notify. Attach copies (NOT originals) to the affidavit before sending it to the companies.

(20) ☐ A copy of a valid government-issued photo-identification card (for example, your driver's license, state-issued ID card, or your passport). If you are under 16 and don't have a photo-ID, you may submit a copy of your birth certificate or a copy of your official school records showing your enrollment and place of residence.

(21) ☐ Proof of residency during the time the disputed bill occurred, the loan was made, or the other event took place (for example, a rental/lease agreement in your name, a copy of a utility bill or a copy of an insurance bill).

DO NOT SEND AFFIDAVIT TO THE FTC OR ANY OTHER
GOVERNMENT AGENCY

*Name*_____ *Phone number* _____ *Page 4*

(22) ☐ A copy of the report you filed with the police or sheriff's department. If you are unable to obtain a report or report number from the police, please indicate that in Item 19. Some companies only need the report number, not a copy of the report. You may want to check with each company.

Signature

I certify that, to the best of my knowledge and belief, all the information on and attached to this affidavit is true, correct, and complete and made in good faith. I also understand that this affidavit or the information it contains may be made available to federal, state, and/or local law enforcement agencies for such action within their jurisdiction as they deem appropriate. I understand that knowingly making any false or fraudulent statement or representation to the government may constitute a violation of 18 U.S.C. §1001 or other federal, state, or local criminal statutes, and may result in imposition of a fine or imprisonment or both.

_____   _____
(signature)   (date signed)

_____
(Notary)

[Check with each company. Creditors sometimes require notarization. If they do not, please have one witness (non-relative) sign below that you completed and signed this affidavit.]

Witness:

_____   _____
(signature)   (printed name)

_____   _____
(date)   (telephone number)

DO NOT SEND AFFIDAVIT TO THE FTC OR ANY OTHER
GOVERNMENT AGENCY

INSTRUCTIONS FOR COMPLETING THE ID THEFT AFFIDAVIT

To make certain that you do not become responsible for any debts incurred by an identity thief, you must prove to each of the companies where accounts were opened or used in your name that you didn't create the debt.

A group of credit grantors, consumer advocates, and attorneys at the Federal Trade Commission (FTC) developed an ID Theft Affidavit to make it easier for fraud victims to report information. While many companies accept this affidavit, others require that you submit more or different forms. Before you send the affidavit, contact each company to find out if they accept it.

It will be necessary to provide the information in this affidavit anywhere a **new** account was opened in your name. The information will enable the companies to investigate the fraud and decide the outcome of your claim. If someone made unauthorized charges to an **existing** account, call the company for instructions.

This affidavit has two parts:
- **Part One**—the ID Theft Affidavit—is where you report general information about yourself and the theft.
- **Part Two**—the Fraudulent Account Statement—is where you describe the fraudulent account(s) opened in your name. Use a separate Fraudulent Account Statement for each company you need to write to.

When you send the affidavit to the companies, attach copies (NOT originals) of any supporting documents (for example, driver's license or police report). Before submitting your affidavit, review the disputed account(s) with family members or friends who may have information about the account(s) or access to them.

Complete this affidavit as soon as possible. Many creditors ask that you send it within two weeks. Delays on your part could slow the investigation.

Be as accurate and complete as possible. You may choose not to provide some of the information requested. However, incorrect or incomplete information will slow the process of investigating your claim and absolving the debt. Print clearly.

When you have finished completing the affidavit, mail a copy to each creditor, bank, or company that provided the thief with the unauthorized credit, goods, or services you describe. Attach a copy of the Fraudulent Account Statement with information only on accounts opened at the institution to which you are sending the packet, as well as any other supporting documentation you are able to provide.

Send the appropriate documents to each company by certified mail, return receipt requested, so you can prove that it was received. The companies will review your claim and send you a written response telling you the outcome of their investigation. Keep a copy of everything you submit.

If you are unable to complete the affidavit, a legal guardian or someone with power of attorney may complete it for you. Except as noted, the information you provide will be used only by the company to process your affidavit, investigate the events you report, and help stop further fraud. If this affidavit is requested in a lawsuit, the company might have to provide it to the requesting party. Completing this affidavit does not guarantee that the identity thief will be prosecuted or that the debt will be cleared.

DO NOT SEND AFFIDAVIT TO THE FTC OR ANY OTHER
GOVERNMENT AGENCY

If you haven't already done so, report the fraud to the following organizations:

1. Any one of the nationwide consumer reporting companies to place a fraud alert on your credit report. Fraud alerts can help prevent an identity thief from opening any more accounts in your name. The company you call is required to contact the other two, which will place an alert on their versions of your report, too.

   - **Equifax:** 1-800-525-6285; www.equifax.com
   - **Experian:** 1-888-EXPERIAN (397-3742); www.experian.com
   - **TransUnion:** 1-800-680-7289; www.transunion.com

   In addition to placing the fraud alert, the three consumer reporting companies will send you free copies of your credit reports, and, if you ask, they will display only the last four digits of your Social Security number on your credit reports.

2. The security or fraud department of each company where you know, or believe, accounts have been tampered with or opened fraudulently. Close the accounts. Follow up in writing, and include copies (NOT originals) of supporting documents. *It's important to notify credit card companies and banks in writing.* Send your letters by certified mail, return receipt requested, so you can document what the company received and when. Keep a file of your correspondence and enclosures.

   When you open new accounts, use new Personal Identification Numbers (PINs) and passwords. Avoid using easily available information like your mother's maiden name, your birth date, the last four digits of your Social Security number or your phone number, or a series of consecutive numbers.

3. Your local police or the police in the community where the identity theft took place to file a report. Get a copy of the police report or, at the very least, the number of the report. It can help you deal with creditors who need proof of the crime. If the police are reluctant to take your report, ask to file a "Miscellaneous Incidents" report, or try another jurisdiction, like your state police. You also can check with your state Attorney General's office to find out if state law requires the police to take reports for identity theft. Check the Blue Pages of your telephone directory for the phone number or check www.naag.org for a list of state Attorneys General.

4. The Federal Trade Commission. By sharing your identity theft complaint with the FTC, you will provide important information that can help law enforcement officials across the nation track down identity thieves and stop them. The FTC also can refer victims' complaints to other government agencies and companies for further action, as well as investigate companies for violations of laws that the FTC enforces.

   You can file a complaint online at **www.consumer.gov/idtheft**. If you don't have Internet access, call the FTC's Identity Theft Hotline, toll-free: 1-877-IDTHEFT (438-4338); TTY: 1-866-653-4261; or write: Identity Theft Clearinghouse, Federal Trade Commission, 600 Pennsylvania Avenue, NW, Washington, DC 20580.

DO NOT SEND AFFIDAVIT TO THE FTC OR ANY OTHER GOVERNMENT AGENCY

*Name*_____ *Phone number*_____ *Page 5*

FRAUDULENT ACCOUNT STATEMENT

Completing this Statement
- Make as many copies of this page as you need. **Complete a separate page for each company you're notifying and only send it to that company.** Include a copy of your signed affidavit.
- List only the account(s) you're disputing with the company receiving this form. **See the example below.**
- If a collection agency sent you a statement, letter, or notice about the fraudulent account, attach a copy of that document (**NOT** the original).

I declare (check all that apply):

☐   As a result of the event(s) described in the ID Theft Affidavit, the following account(s) was/were opened at your company in my name without my knowledge, permission or authorization using my personal information or identifying documents:

Creditor Name/Address *(the company that opened the account or provided the goods or services)*	Account Number	Type of unauthorized credit/goods/services provided by creditor *(if known)*	Date issued or opened *(if known)*	Amount/Value provided *(the amount charged or the cost of the goods/services)*
Example Example National Bank 22 Main Street Columbus, Ohio 22722	01234567-89	Auto loan	01/05/2002	$25,500.00

☐   During the time of the accounts described above, I had the following account open with your company:

Billing name _____

Billing address _____

Account number _____

DO NOT SEND AFFIDAVIT TO THE FTC OR ANY OTHER
GOVERNMENT AGENCY

Form 40

STATEMENT OF CIRCUMSTANCES

_____ [your name and address]

_____

_____

_____ [name and address of
_____ potential creditor]

_____

_____ [date]

Dear Sir or Madam:

I am writing in reference to my application to you for credit. I have seen my credit report and realize that there may be items on it that concern you. Please allow me to explain. I have experienced the following circumstances: _____
_____
_____
_____,

which caused the problems you see on the credit report. My current circumstances are:
_____
_____
_____,

and I would ask you to understand that my situation has improved. I will be able to make all payments to you without any problem and hope that you will give my application consideration.

Thank you.

Sincerely,

_____

[signature]

Form 41

REQUEST TO OPT-OUT

_____ [your name and address]

_____

_____

_____ [name and address of credit
_____ reporting agency opt-out
_____ program]

_____ [date]

Dear Sir or Madam:

I do not wish to have any information released about me to companies seeking to send me promotional materials. Please do not release any such information about me. I do not wish to receive mailings or phone calls from companies soliciting their services.

Thank you.

Sincerely,

_____
[signature]

Form 42

BUDGET

For the month of _____

Enter in your estimated monthly expenses on this form. You should include everything you spend money on. Be sure you include expenses and incomes for your entire household.

HOUSEHOLD EXPENSES

Rent/Mortgage	_____
Home equity loan payment	_____
Real estate taxes (if not included in mortgage)	_____
Renter's/Homeowner's Insurance	_____
Electric	_____
Gas	_____
Water	_____
Telephone (local and long distance)	_____
Cell Phone	_____
Cable	_____
Internet access	_____
Home repairs	_____
Food	_____
Alcohol	_____
Bank fees	_____
Household supplies	_____
Household items	_____
Furniture purchases and maintenance	_____
Lawn/Yard expenses	_____
Other	_____

TOTAL HOUSEHOLD EXPENSES: _____

PERSONAL EXPENSES

Clothing	_____
Laundry/Dry Cleaning	_____

Haircuts and styling   _____
Other personal care (nails, salons)   _____
Gym membership   _____
Other clubs or memberships   _____
Life insurance   _____
Health insurance   _____
Prescription plan   _____
Co-pays   _____
Optical   _____
Dental   _____
Other medical   _____
Grooming/Personal care items   _____
Charity   _____
Baby-sitter   _____
Household help   _____
Hobbies   _____
Cigarettes   _____
Income taxes   _____
Children's allowances   _____
Pet expenses   _____
Other   _____

TOTAL PERSONAL EXPENSES: _____

AUTOMOTIVE EXPENSES
Car loan or lease payment   _____
Bus/Train/Taxi/Plane   _____
Gas   _____
Car wash   _____
Parking/tolls   _____
Other   _____

TOTAL AUTOMOTIVE EXPENSES:_____

ENTERTAINMENT EXPENSES
Restaurants/Take out   _____

Movies, theater, etc.   _____
Books, newspapers, magazines   _____
Video/DVD rentals   _____
Other   _____

TOTAL ENTERTAINMENT EXPENSES: _____

FRIENDS AND FAMILY
     Party Supplies   _____
     Birthday, anniversary, wedding gifts   _____
     Cards and wrapping paper   _____
     Payment on personal loan   _____
     Other   _____

TOTAL FRIENDS AND FAMILY: _____

CREDIT CARDS AND LOANS
(list each separately with monthly payment)

_____   _____

_____   _____

_____   _____

_____   _____

_____   _____

TOTAL CREDIT CARDS AND LOANS: _____

SAVINGS
     Investment   _____
     Savings account   _____
     College savings plan   _____
     Retirement plan   _____

TOTAL SAVINGS: _____

EDUCATION (for all household members)
     Tuition   _____

Student loan payment _____
School supplies and materials _____
Other _____

TOTAL EDUCATION COSTS: _____

YEARLY EXPENSES (divided by 12)
    Car repairs/maintenance _____
    Driver's license _____
    Car registration _____
    Car insurance _____
    Car inspection _____
    Vacation _____
    Holiday gifts _____

TOTAL YEARLY EXPENSES: _____

OTHER

_____   _____
_____   _____
_____   _____
_____   _____

TOTAL OTHER EXPENSES: _____

Add together all your **TOTAL MONTHLY EXPENSES:**
_____

MONTHLY INCOME
    Salary _____
    Child support/alimony _____
    Other income (nonreported, interest, etc.) _____

TOTAL INCOME: _____

Form 43

SPENDING LOG

For _____ [month and year]

Date	Item	Cost	Daily Total

INDEX

About the Author

Brette McWhorter Sember received her law degree from the State University of New York at Buffalo. She is a former New York state attorney and skilled mediator. She was on the Law Guardian panel in four counties and acted as a volunteer mediator for the Better Business Bureau.

Sember is experienced in helping seniors sort through options and evaluate choices that involve lifestyle, care facilities, finances, and estate and health planning. Her one-to-one experience with seniors gave her understanding about the deeply personal nature of senior planning and also developed her belief that senior planning is an issue for the entire family. Additionally, her own family experience with aging grandparents makes senior care a day-to-day issue.

Sember is an expert at explaining and simplifying business concepts. She has written more than thirty books, including *File for Divorce in New York*, *The Complete Credit Repair Kit*, and *Seniors' Rights*.

Her website is **www.BretteSember.com**.